Power Tools

Handyman Club Library™

Handyman Club of America
Minneapolis, Minnesota

Power Tools

Printed in 2004.

CREDITS

Tom Carpenter
Creative Director

Mark Johanson
Book Products Development Manager
Handyman Club of America

Dan Cary
Senior Book Production Assistant

James Barrett, Mark Johanson
Contributing Writers

Bill Nelson
Series Design, Art Direction and Production

Gina Seeling
Art Direction and Production

Mark Macemon
Photography

Robert Ginn
Technical Advisor & Builder

Larry Okrend
Technical Consultant

PHOTO CREDITS

Pages 77, 101
Delta International Machinery Corp.

ISBN 0-914-697-81-1
©1997 Handyman Club of America
7 8 9 10 11 / 07 06 05 04

Handyman Club of America
12301 Whitewater Drive
Minnetonka, Minnesota 55343
www.handymanclub.com

Table of Contents

Power Tools

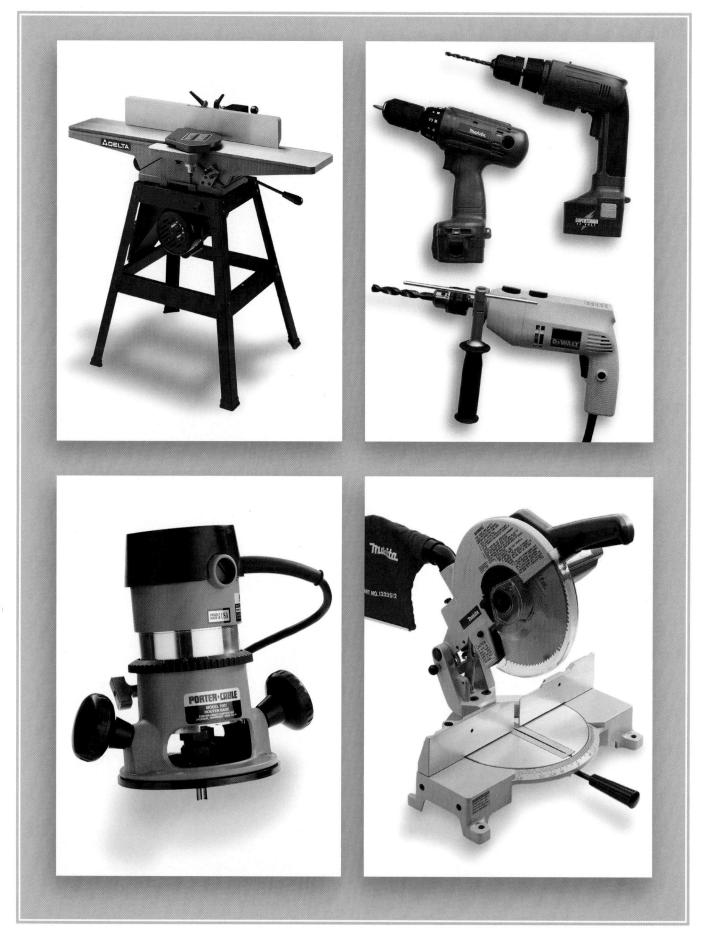

Power Tools

Handymen everywhere share one basic feeling: we love power tools. Whether you're a weekend dabbler or a professional tradesman, you understand the appeal: the familiar sound of your table saw building to peak power; the crisp, clean shoulders on a perfect dado that's cut with a finely tuned router; the satisfaction and pride you feel when you turn a time-consuming chore into a pleasure by finding just the right power tool for the job.

If you're like most handymen, you have one or two favorite power tools that you know and understand better than you know and understand most of your friends and relatives. You also have one or two power tools that you fire up fairly often for very specific jobs. And you probably have a handful of power tools that seemed like the solution to all your problems when you bought them, only to end up gathering dust in that special corner of your shop reserved for forgotten tools.

In this book, we take a hard look at more than two dozen of the most popular power tools. You can take a refresher course on your favorite machines—and maybe even pick up a few new pointers in the process. You can learn more about the tools you use less frequently—sometimes all it takes is one special jig or bit or blade to completely change the way you use a tool. And don't forget about your forgotten tools. It's amazing how quickly an underused space-gobbler can move from a dusty corner to a place of prominence once it gets an opportunity.

Power tools are major investments. In this book, we show you ways to maximize and protect that investment. You'll see clear, step-by-step photos that show how to tune up even the fussiest tools in your shop. We share information to help you choose the best blade or bit for the job at hand. If there's something you need to know to maintain your tool properly, you'll find it in this book. And of course, we wouldn't be doing our job if we didn't include all the important information you need to operate your power tools safely.

If you stop and think about it, most of us really only have two kinds of tools: the ones in our shops and the ones on our wish lists (and usually, we have a lot more of the second type). If you're hoping to add to your tool collection, you'll find plenty of tips and suggestions to help you make good tool-buying decisions.

This book was produced by the Handyman Club of America for our members only. You won't find it in book stores or in libraries. We chose the tools that are featured in this book because we know that they're the machines our members use the most. We hope that you enjoy reading this book as much as we enjoyed making it.

IMPORTANT NOTICE

For your safety, caution and good judgment should be used when following instructions described in this book. Take into consideration your level of skill and the safety precautions related to the tools and materials shown. Neither the publisher, North American Outdoor Group, nor any of its affiliates can assume responsibility for any damage to property or persons as a result of the misuse of the information provided. Consult your local building department for information on permits, codes, regulations and laws which may apply to your project.

About Power Tools

The amount of money you can spend on power tools and power tool accessories is virtually unlimited. With each new tool catalog that shows up in your mailbox, with every tool demonstration you catch at your favorite local hardware store, you find something new. It might be a clever twist on a traditional saw blade design, or maybe a new, special-purpose sharpening tool that impresses you with its ability to accomplish its purpose with lightning speed. The constantly changing and improving landscape of power tools is exciting. But before you get caught up too deeply, it's usually a good idea to step back and take another look at the tools you already own.

In this chapter of *Power Tools*, we'll discuss some of the most basic information that all or most power tools share. We'll also discuss some general points you should know about equipping your workshop, and about keeping all of your power tools in peak running condition.

Along with information on maintaining and understanding the tools you already own, you'll find some basic strategies for buying new tools and accessories, and few things to think about before you step up to the cash register with your new tool in hand.

Power tool basics

Most power tools consist of two essential parts: a motor and the thing the motor turns. Saws, drills, sanders, planers, routers, even biscuit joiners and air compressors fit into this group (yes, there are exceptions, like the portable jig saw and the orbital finishing sander). The main difference between power tools lies in what kind of blade, bit or cutter attaches to the spinning part, and in what kind of framework the tool has to support and align the workpiece.

Motors & power. Power tool motors range from the tiny 1/6 horsepower (hp) versions you'll find on detail sanders and other lightweight tools, up to around 3 hp on the largest stationary power tools. The vast majority, on both portable and stationary tools, fall in the 1/2- to 1 1/2-hp range. But ask any tool expert and he'll tell you that horsepower is not as reliable a measure of real working power as *amperage*. Horsepower ratings can be fudged pretty easily, usually by taking measure at *peak horsepower,* when the the tool is not under load (engaging materials). The number of amps a motor draws establishes precisely the upper limit of the tool's power.

But keep in mind that power is also affected by how well the tool is made, its general condition, and the condition of the blade or bit being used. It takes more energy to push a dull blade through a board than a sharp one, but you're not seeing any benefit from the added juice. So don't be surprised if a tool that costs twice as much as another one that does the same thing actually has a smaller motor. Likely, it simply doesn't need the bigger power plant.

There are two basic motor types found on power tools: *universal* and *induction*. Typically, lower-end tools have universal motors, which tend to be louder and are more prone to burnout. Induction motors are more expensive, but you'll appreciate the quieter, smoother performance.

Bearings. Because most power tools are designed to spin arbors or spindles at high velocity, the tool needs bearings to house the ends of the spindle. Better bearings usually include ball-bearing rollers, rather than simply a fixed metal sleeve.

Top Five Questions to Ask Before Buying a New Power Tool

1. Do I really need it? If the motor just burned out on your 20-year-old table saw (the one with the warped table and the rip fence that just won't stay in place) and you've got a few hundred board feet of rock maple to rip for the custom cabinets you said you'd finish in time for Thanksgiving, then the answer is pretty simple. But if you just read that your 9.6-volt cordless drill is now available in a 14.4-volt version, take a minute to think about it before you run down to the hardware store with your credit card flying out of your pocket. Has your old drill ever come up short on power in the past? If it did, were you using it for a job that could just as easily have been done with your corded drill? Think about the projects you've done in the last year or two. Would the tool you're considering have been helpful?

2. Where will I put it? If you're like most handymen, shop space is always at a premium. Does the new tool add enough capacity to your shop to justify the floor space or cabinet space it will command?

3. Do I have enough power to run it? Some tools, like a good single-stage or better dust collector, should have their own dedicated 20-amp circuit. And most top-of-the line stationary tools run on 230-volt service. Will that new cabinet table saw improve your shop enough to justify running a brand new 230-volt service line out from the basement? Have you considered that in the cost? Will you want to run the new tool at the same time as any other appliances or tools? Add up the total amperage draw on existing circuits, and see how the new tool fits in. A brand new 15-amp router may be a big step up in power, but if it trips your circuit breaker every time you turn it on you're better off with your trusty old 8-amp model.

4. Can parts and accessories be found easily? In tool-making, as in other industries, success breeds copycats. If the tool you're looking at has a nameplate you don't know well, check to make sure there's a ready supply of blades, bits, accessories and spare parts. And ask yourself if the supply is likely to be there next year as well.

5. Does it have dust-collection? These days, you can find a power tool of just about any variety that has at least an optional dust-collection function. Don't overlook this important detail. Is the dust collection feature compatible with your existing equipment? Is there an adapter you can buy to make it fit easily?

Make a master plan. Before investing a large amount of money in your tool collection, sit down and make a master-plan priority list. The fact is, most tools are purchased on an as-needed basis, without a lot of forethought. You're free to change the list as your needs change, but having a plan allows you to take the time to find the best tools at the best prices, when you can afford them.

Material. These days, it's hard to find any tool that doesn't have some high-impact plastic or light-gauge aluminum parts. That's because manufacturers try to reserve heavy cast-iron for those parts that truly need it. If you've noticed that your new circular saw feels lighter than the old clamshell saw you bought a few years back, you're not necessarily getting stronger in your advancing years. Tools are lighter today, with new magnesium alloys and other metallurgical advances.

Still, there are some tool parts that, on the best tools, remain cast-iron. Specifically, milled cast-iron tables will outperform and outlast their pressed aluminum counterparts, and there's nothing like a good, sturdy cast iron base to keep your lathe or drill press immobile while you work. But because cast iron can rust, you should make a practice of rubbing the iron and steel surfaces on your tools occasionally with a light coat of machine oil (*See photo, below*).

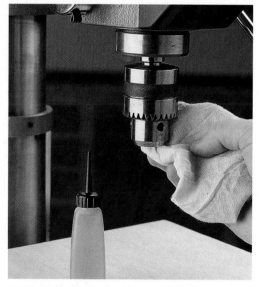

Treat steel and iron tool parts with a light coating of machine oil to preserve clean operation and to prevent rust.

Casings. Hand-held portable power tools are made almost exclusively with double-insulated high-impact plastic casings. The double-insulated casings are the main reason you seldom see three-prong grounded plugs on portable tools.

Knobs and adjustment devices. The precision and ease of movement of the adjustment devices, as well as the acces-sibility and holding power of knobs and levers, is a foremost consideration for many tool buyers. An ON/OFF switch that can be worked without taking your hands off the tool is an especially good feature to look for on portable power tools.

Cost. The price tag is one of the most important considerations for tool buyers. The conventional wisdom is "Buy the best tool you can afford." This is certainly a worthwhile guideline, but rules are made to be broken. If you only use a jig saw once or twice a year, for example, opt for a lower-end model and use the savings to upgrade a level on a tool that you use more frequently.

Building your tool collection

The most common power tools are purchased in a surprisingly similar order. A home handyman usually starts out with the very basics: a jig saw, circular saw, drill and sander. From there, he may add a router and perhaps a power miter saw. Then comes another sander (this time, probably a random-orbit sander). As interest increases, he starts to move into the stationary tools. First a table saw, then maybe a drill press. He'll add some accessories for the portable tools, like a router table or some fancier cutting guides. From there, the directions diverge a little bit.

If a person's interest is in more detailed work, a band saw is likely to follow, or perhaps a scroll saw. If his interest is more in basic carpentry skills and do-it-yourself tasks, an air compres-sor and a set of air tools makes sense. Meanwhile, he'll begin assembling a selection of tools designed to maintain the ones he already owns: a bench grinder or sharpening center is a good bet. And with all this activity going on, a dust-collection system becomes very important.

For developing woodworkers, a jointer and a power planer will take his capabili-ties to a new level. He may even look into a lathe for creating custom furniture parts or even decorative wood items. And meanwhile, the holes are filled in: an oscillating spindle sander, a reciprocating saw, a biscuit joiner, until the collection is quite large. Now, the process of replacing and upgrading begins in earnest.

Maintenance

The rules for power tool maintenance are brief: *keep it clean and keep it sharp.* Operating a power tool that's not well lubricated and free of impediments is dangerous, yields poor results, and shortens the lifespan of the tool. Here are some basic tool maintenance items:

Before each use:

• Test the drive belt tension (*See photo, right*).

• Check to make sure the blade or bit is secure, that all adjustment knobs and locking levers are tightened, and ventilation ports near the motor are clear.

After each use:

• Wipe off dust and debris from all tool parts. Blow out ventilation holes or slots if blocked.

• Return tool to proper storage area or case, with cord coiled and out of the way.

Ongoing maintenance:

• Clean pitch, tar and general buildup from blades, using oven cleaner or pitch removal compound (*See photo, right*).

• Inspect carbon brushes (*See photo, below*) for excessive wear and replace if needed. The brushes usually are accessed by removing part of the portable tool housing. In some cases, they can be removed for inspection without dismantling the tool casing. And with some tools, the casing cannot be opened for inspections (these are *disposable* tools).

• Observe maintenance procedures as specified by the tool manufacturer.

Use oven cleaner or pitch removing compound to clean gummy, pitchy blades. Dirty blades impede tool performance.

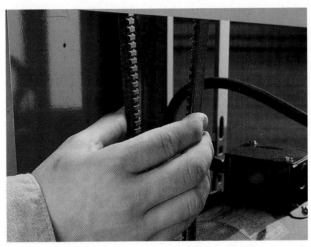

Test belt tension on drive belts by pulling the sides of the belt together with moderate pressure. The distance between belts should not decrease by more than ½" to 1".

Brush   **Brush holder**

Disassemble the tool casing and inspect the carbon brushes that contact the spinning commutator for wear. Replace as needed.

Lubricate the bearings on your tools with penetrating oil. Check you owner's manual—some tools are not meant to be opened for maintenance or servicing.

The recommended safety gear varies from tool to tool. The most important pieces of safety gear for the home shop are protective eyewear, ear protection, and dust protection. Consult and comply with your tool user's manual.

Power Tool Safety

Even if you're a veteran home handyman or tradesman with extensive tool knowledge, you should review this safety material, as well as the additional safety tips for specific tools in their respective chapters. Also review the information in your owner's manuals occasionally, and keep important safety requirements posted near stationary tools and in portable tool cases.

While many tool-related injuries occur as a result of inexperience or lack of familiarity with a particular power tool or machine, just as many happen when the user becomes overconfident, which can lead to carelessness. No matter how familiar you are with a tool or machine and its uses, you should still maintain a healthy respect for the potential dangers involved in operating it. But simply following basic safety rules is only half the picture—the other half is using plain common sense and sound judgement when operating your power tools.

It doesn't take more than a split second of inattentiveness to ruin a work piece, lose a finger, or worse. So, when working with any tool, the first and foremost rule is: *Pay full attention to what you're doing at all times!* Never work with tools when you're tired, or under the influence of drugs, alcohol, or prescription medicines—all of which can slow down your reaction time or cloud your judgement.

Protective gear

While the type of protective gear you should wear depends on the tool you're using, you can't be too safe in this respect.

Eye protection. Even if you're working with a relatively "harmless" tool, such as a portable drill or small electric sander, get in the habit of wearing eye protection. Look for safety glasses with shatterproof polycarbonate lenses and side shields that meet ANSI standards *(See photo, above right)*. Or you can buy prescription safety glasses with plastic lenses. When using some tools, such as a bench grinder or lathe, a full-face safety shield *(See photo, above left)* provides better protection than goggles alone.

Ear protection. Ear plugs or muffs should be worn with many stationary and portable power tools (*See photo, previous page middle*). Use your own judgement as to when it's necessary—most owner's manuals will tell you whether or not you need it for the tool you're using. Better hearing protection devices dampen constant machine noise, yet enable you to hear important intermittent noises.

Lung protection. Dust masks are a must when using tools that create airborne sawdust—saws, routers and sanders, for example. All sawdust you inhale will eventually take its toll on your lungs. The best dust masks are rubber respirator masks with replaceable cartridge filters (*See photo, previous page right*). The replaceable cartridges have different ratings—dust only, dust and mist, dust, mist and vapors, etc. Equipped with the right filter, such masks will also protect you against toxic fumes from solvent-based paints and varnishes, for example, as well as particulate matter.

Other safety gear. Depending on the job, you may also need to wear a *hard hat* to protect your head. *Steel-toed boots* are recommended for all types of heavy construction work. Even for small shop projects, invest in a pair of *heavy work boots* or shoes with non-slip rubber soles. While *work gloves* come in handy for handling various materials, they can interfere with the safe and efficient operation of many portable power tools, especially those with small or hard-to-access switches and controls. When working with any tool, don't wear loose clothing or jewelry that could get in the way.

Using tools safely

Following are a few common sense rules that apply to all power tools.

Owner's manuals. Read the owner's manual or instruction booklet that comes with the tool. Most include a list of general safety procedures, as well as rules that are specific to the tool. Also use the manual to learn correct operating, troubleshooting and maintenance procedures. If you don't have an owner's manual, you can usually get a replacement by writing or calling the tool maker's customer service department. Store your owner's manuals in a file cabinet so they can be found easily.

Good condition

Needs replacement

Drive belts undergo considerable stress, and wear out eventually. Check them regularly for signs of deterioration, and replace them when wear starts to show.

The spot where the cord and tool meet is a problem area for power cords. Frayed cords and exposed wires can cause electric shock. Inspect cords regularly.

Keep tools clean and tuned up.
Keep tools clean and properly adjusted for maximum performance. Inspect them regularly to catch problems before they happen. Pay special attention to power cords and drive belts when inspecting tools. Worn drive belts (*See photo, top right*) can snap unexpectedly, causing a loss of power that will ruin your cut and interrupt your rhythm. The broken belt also will fly off the pulleys at a high speed—a serious hazard if the motor and pulleys are unprotected. Frayed cords (*See photo, below right*) create a serious risk of electrical shock. For more information on keeping tools running safely and efficiently, read the preceding

SAFETY TIP:

Look for the red safety tip boxes that appear throughout this book to highlight safety concerns.

Keep blade guards in place whenever possible to minimize your risk of injury.

chapter, *About Power Tools*, and see the many individual maintenance and tuning tips throughout this book.

Keep tools sharp. Keeping bits, blades and cutters sharp not only produces better results, it also makes tools safer to use. Dull bits and cutters can cause the tool or workpiece to drag, requiring more operator pressure to complete the operation. This, in turn, can result in loss of control, or cause the work or tool to kick back, and place more stress on the motor.

Remove-to-lock keys fit into the ON/OFF switch on some stationary power tools. Remove them when the tool is not in use, so unauthorized users can't turn on the tool. Keep the key in a safe, accessible place—they're very easy to misplace.

Tool guards. Over the last few decades, tool companies have come a long way in equipping portable and stationary machines with safe, effective guarding. For example, most table saws come with clear acrylic blade guard assemblies, replete with splitters and anti-kickback pawls (*See photo, top left*). Even so, many woodworkers are tempted to remove such devices to "get a better view of the work", or "make it easier to run the work through the machine (or vice-versa)"—especially if the guard starts hanging up. Check guards frequently to make sure they're in good working order. Use a soft cloth and window cleaner to remove dirt and sawdust from clear acrylic safety shields on routers, bench grinders, table saws, and the like.

Guards are not only found on blades bits and cutters. Many stationary tools are equipped with covers that protect motors, drive belts, pulleys, and other moving parts that are not applied to the workpiece. Treat these guards with as much respect as you treat blade, bit or cutter guards. While guards lessen the chance of accidents, they don't completely eliminate them. You still need to keep an eye on both hands at all times, keeping them well away from the blade, bit, or cutter.

"Remove-to-lock" keys. Many stationary power tools are equipped inserts that fit into the ON/OFF switch. Called "remove-to-lock keys", these fittings must be in place for the tool to be turned on (*See photo, bottom left*) on stationary machines.

Other safety features. In addition to guards, you'll find other specific safety features on certain power tools. These include blade brakes on saws, and trigger-lock buttons on portable tools.

The workpiece. When using portable tools, provide solid support for the workpiece. Make sure it's supported at a comfortable working height. Clamp or tack small pieces firmly to the bench or in a vise. Never rely solely on your hands, feet, or any other part of your body alone to hold or secure the work. Also, don't attempt to use tools on workpieces that are too small to be held securely.

Hold-downs keep the workpiece from shifting as it's fed into a blade. They're usually attached to either the miter gauge (like the table saw version shown above) or to the rip fence.

Extension Cord Length	Gauge	Maximum Amps
25 ft.	18	10
25 ft.	16	13
25 ft.	14	15
50 ft.	18	5
50 ft.	16	10
50 ft.	14	15
75 ft.	18	5
75 ft.	16	10
75 ft.	14	15
100 ft.	16	5
100 ft.	12	15
125 ft.	16	5
125 ft.	12	15
150 ft.	16	5
150 ft.	12	13

When possible, use hold-down clamps (*See photo above*), featherboards, and similar devices to secure the workpiece flat against machine tables. Always inspect your workpiece carefully before applying a power tool. Look for nails, screws, dense knots and other obstructions that may interfere with the cut and cause the saw to jam or kick back. Remove obstructions or select new stock.

Additional safety tips

•**Don't over-reach.** Posture yourself comfortably so that you have full control over the tool at all times.

• **Don't force tools.** Let the tool do the work. If the motor bogs down, back off.

• **Use the right accessories** for the tool. Check maximum rpm ratings for blades, bits and cutters—these should not be exceeded by tool speed.

• **Use the right tool** for the job; for example don't use a portable circular saw to cut tree limbs or logs. Learn and fully understand the capabilities and limitations of each tool.

• **Always unplug the tool** before making any adjustments to the tool or changing blades, bits or cutters.

• **Ground your tools** by plugging all three-prong plugs into grounded receptacles. Never remove the round grounding pin from a three-prong plug.

• **Use the right extension cord.** Make sure that any extension cords used are compatible with both the tool and the electrical outlet (*See chart above*). Use only three-wire cords with three-prong

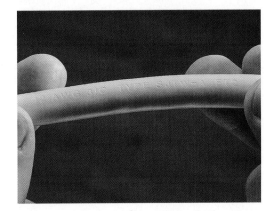

Make sure any extension cords you use are heavy-duty enough for the tool. Check the cord casing for markings that indicate the wire gauge, amperage capacity, and sometimes the cord jacket type (SJ for rubber cords, SJT for thermoplastic cords). The suffix W-A appearing after the jacket markings indicates the cord is exterior rated.

grounding plugs. Most power cords are imprinted with the wire gauge and sometimes the maximum amperage rating (*See photo, above*).

• **Keep an eye on the cord.** Before you start any job, make sure the power cord or extension cord won't get "hung up" on any obstacles in the work area or be in the way while you're working. If using an extension cord, tie a simple underhand knot between the extension and tool cord to prevent accidental disconnection.

• **Keep work area clean.** Make sure you have enough space to work comfortably, and don't allow chips, lumber scraps or sawdust to accumulate.

• **Provide adequate lighting.** In addition to good general shop lighting, you'll also need task lighting when working with certain machines or doing close work on the bench.

• **Store tools in locked cabinets,** out of the reach of children. Keep children and other bystanders away.

Portable Power Tools

The advantages of portable power tools over hand tools and stationary power tools can be summed up in two words: *versatility* and *convenience*. Compared to stationary tools, the term *portable* simply means that you can take the tool to the work, rather than taking the work to the tool. Aside from their obvious advantages for doing on-site building and repairs, portable power tools also have many uses in the workshop. You can use them to cut, drill, shape or sand workpieces and assemblies that are too large or bulky to run through a stationary machine. Granted, many portable power tools don't offer the speed, accuracy, capacity and control of their stationary counterparts. But with a good selection of portable power tools and accessories, you can build just about anything you could in a shop with a full complement of stationary tools.

TIP:

Cordless voltage ratings

Cordless tool makers frequently sell their products based largely on voltage ratings. The assumption being, the higher the voltage the better the tool. While there is certainly some truth to this, the fact is that once minimum voltage requirements for the tool type are met, additional volts do not add significantly to the performance of the tool (but they do hold a charge longer). In the case of cordless drills and drivers, for example, a good 12-volt model will handle just about any task you throw at it. In most cases, you're probably better off investing in non-power features, like a sturdy keyless chuck and a clutch.

Buying portable power tools

Within any given tool category, you'll find a good range of power, capacity, features and prices.

Light-duty tools are usually designed for occasional household use. When they burn out, as they eventually will in most cases, they're usually cheaper to replace than repair.

Professional tools have greater power, more features, more options, sturdier construction and increased accuracy. Tools from the professional lines are the most popular types with serious handymen and do-it-yourselfers.

Industrial tools are designed for continuous, everyday use. Their power ratings may be comparable to the professional lines, but generally they have sturdier construction that enables them to take an ongoing beating under stressful conditions.

As with any purchase, consider the types of tasks you expect the tools to perform for you, and make your tool-buying decision accordingly.

Cordless tools

Today, no discussion of portable tools would be complete without addressing cordless tools. Advancing technology has enabled manufacturers to produce cordless tools that rival the power of their corded counterparts. Improvements in the basic nickel-cadmium (NiCad) battery packs have boosted power and decreased recharge time down to less than an hour, making it possible to work continuously with some corded tools.

Circular Saws

Technically, a *circular saw* is any power saw equipped with a circular blade, including table saws, radial arm saws and power miter saws. But in recent years, the term has come to mean exclusively *portable circular saw* for most people. Today, anyone with even a passing interest in handyman skills likely owns at least one portable circular saw—and for good reason. You'd be hard-pressed to find any tool that matches the circular saw for portability, range, power, afford-ability and ease of use.

Think of the circular saw as a hand-held, upside-down table saw: the tool consists of a motor/blade assembly attached to an adjustable base (also called a *foot* or *shoe*) that supports the saw on the workpiece.

The base can be raised or lowered to control the depth of cut and can also be pivoted up to 45° or 50° for making bevel cuts. You turn the saw on and off with a trigger-style switch attached to the saw's D-shaped handle. A second auxiliary handle or knob is located at the top of the tool for sure-handed gripping with your other hand.

While you might associate circular saws with on-site building projects in your backyard or garage, they do have uses in the wood shop, as well. For example, you can use them to rough-cut sheet goods or long boards down to a safe, manageable size before running them through a stationary machine. And, armed with a good assortment of blades and a few basic accessories, you can do surprisingly smooth, accurate work with the tool.

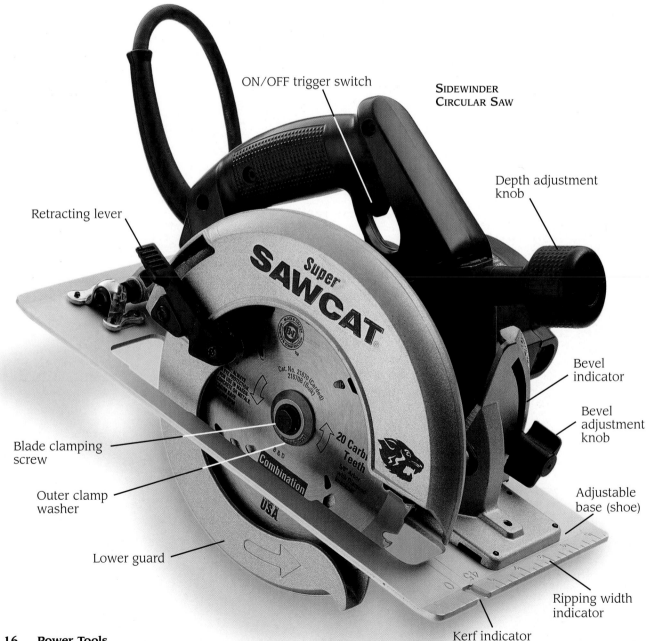

ON/OFF trigger switch

SIDEWINDER CIRCULAR SAW

Depth adjustment knob

Retracting lever

Blade clamping screw

Outer clamp washer

Lower guard

Bevel indicator

Bevel adjustment knob

Adjustable base (shoe)

Ripping width indicator

Kerf indicator

Circular Saw Fact Sheet		
Application	**Tool Recommendation**	**Accessories and Blades**
Light Use	Moderately priced 7¼" sidewinder drawing from 10 to 12 amps.	Rip guide and simple wood or metal straightedge with C-clamps. Set of three basic carbide or alloy steel blades—rip, crosscut, and finish.
Moderate Use	Top-end 7¼" sidewinder with electric brake. Consider adding a trim saw for finish work, or a worm-drive saw for heavy -duty use.	Protractor guide and manufactured eight-foot self-clamping aluminum straightedge. Add specialty blades as needed.
Heavy Use	Add 8¼" or larger cutoff saw. Keep your older or smaller circular saws for rough work or for cutting that will stress the saw or blade—like cutting into roof sheathing or subfloors.	Invest in top-of-the line carbide-tipped blades for all your most common cuts.

Circular saw types

By far the most common type of portable circular saw is the *sidewinder* like the one shown on the previous page. Saws of this type are available in many sizes, from small trim saws to large cutoff saws for timber framing. The *worm-drive* saw is also quite popular among carpenters who do a lot of framing or deck building.

Other than the type of drive mechanism, size is the most important variable among circular saws. Circular saws are "sized" by the largest blade diameter they will take. This, in turn, determines the saw's maximum depth of cut (*See chart, page 21*). Blade sizes range from 3⅜" on small, lightweight trim saws, up to 16¼" on large timber-framing saws and cutoff saws. Over the decades, the 7¼" saw has remained the most popular size, because it offers a good compromise between size, weight, and cutting capacity.

The sidewinder. These versatile tools are manufactured and sold by the hundreds of thousands every year. The term *sidewinder* refers to the fact that the motor shaft is mounted to the side of the blade, at a right angle to the direction of blade travel. All entry-level circular saws are sidewinders, usually with a 7¼" blade. Typical 7¼" sidewinders operate at 5,000 to 5,800 rpm utilizing a 2 to 3 hp motor that draws 10 to 13 amps. They weigh from 7½ to 12 pounds, making them light enough to handle easily.

Small trim saws, like the cordless model shown here, can be a convenient tool for making occasional cuts in thin stock. Corded trim saws, usually with a 4½"-dia. blade, are used frequently for cutting cabinet trim, countertops and finish moldings.

In recent years, some manufacturers have attempted to apply cordless technology to circular saws, particularly with smaller trim saws (*See photo above*). Some professional-line cordless trim saws can cut up to 130 feet of ½"-thick plywood in one charge. Most of these have blades either 3⅜" or 5⅜" in diameter. Consumer-line cordless trim saws are considerably less powerful, but also less expensive. They have some value for occasional light use.

The worm-drive circular saw is a favored tool of frame carpenters and deck builders because it can cut thick, dense wood without bogging down and it stands up to heavy, ongoing use.

The worm-drive. On worm-drive saws, the motor is mounted at a right angle to the blade arbor, making it parallel to the direction of cut. Worm-drive (hypoid) gears transmit power from the motor to the blade. This gearing arrangement provides worm-drive saws about 15% more torque than sidewinders with comparable motors, enabling them to plow easily through thick or dense materials without slowing down. However, they also run at lower blade speeds (3,500 to 4,000 rpm), so they won't cut lighter materials as quickly.

Also, worm-drive saws have a left-mounted blade for better visibility of the cutting line, while most 7¼" sidewinders have right-mounted blades.

The D-shaped handle on the worm-drive saw is located at the back of the tool. This gives you an extra boost when guiding the saw through heavier stock—but don't abuse the feature by trying to force the saw to cut too fast.

Overall, near bullet-proof construction and high torque have made worm-drive saws the tool of choice among many framing carpenters. However, they're also relatively expensive, heavy tools, weigh-

ing in between 14 and 16½ pounds. Recently, however, some manufacturers have begun using lightweight metal alloys, like magnesium, for some of the parts of the saw body. This design modification can reduce the weight of a worm-drive saw by more than two pounds.

Weight isn't the only factor working against the worm-drive when it comes to maneuverability. Their longer body length also makes them a little harder to control for precision cutting and trimming of smaller pieces.

Worm-drive saws are largely limited to 7¼" models, although several companies also offer smaller trim saws that employ this motor design.

Consumer vs. professional

The major saw manufacturers offer two distinct lines of circular saws: those intended for light-duty, occasional use, and those for heavy, daily use. However, different companies may apply different names to the lines. Heavy-use circular saws could be labeled "industrial rated," "professional," or "heavy duty" by their manufacturer. Lighter-duty "consumer" or "homeowner" circular saws seldom are listed as part of a particular tool line by the manufacturers. Though the names may differ, you'll have no trouble distinguishing between consumer and professional models when you visit your local tool store or read through a tool catalog.

In effect, "consumer" circular saws have smaller motors and less durable components, inside and out. Most have ball-and-sleeve bearings, as opposed to all-ball or roller bearing construction. The saw bases are usually made of thin-gauge stamped steel. The pivot points aren't as sturdy, and the knobs or wing nuts used for making base adjustments are quite small. While you can pay up to twice the price for the maker's top-of-the-line saw, it's usually worth the extra cost in terms of increased performance, durability, longevity and ease of use.

Consumer saws work fine if you only need to make an occasional cut in the shop or undertake a relatively small, simple building project. But, if you're planning to do a major remodeling project or two, a top-quality, heavy-duty saw is well worth the investment.

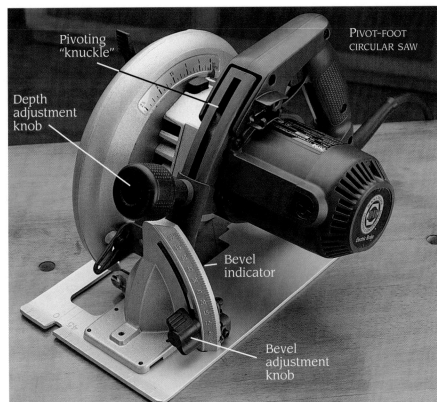

On most circular saws, the blade depth (here set at zero) is adjusted by pivoting the foot on a hinge or knuckle at the front of the foot. To make bevel cuts, the saw body is tilted on the foot and locked into place with a bevel adjustment knob.

Pivoting "knuckle"

PIVOT-FOOT CIRCULAR SAW

Depth adjustment knob

Bevel indicator

Bevel adjustment knob

Circular saw features

This discussion focuses primarily on the most popular circular saw, the 7¼" sidewinder. However, you can apply much of the same general advice to other sizes and types.

Power. As with other portable power tools, you can compare amperage ratings as a basic gauge of power, although many circular saws also list horsepower ratings. Most "professional" 7¼" saws have 12- to 13-amp motors, while lower-end "consumer" models have 10-to 11-amp motors. But motor amperage doesn't tell the whole story. Better saws usually have motors with heavier windings, more efficient gearing, and other beefed-up internal components to provide more power output per amp.

Gears and bearings. Lower-end circular saws generally have sleeve bearings or ball-and-sleeve bearings, while better saws use all-ball bearings or ball-and-roller/needle bearings. Better bearings reduce power loss between the motor and the blade, lessen blade wobble or runout, and increase tool life in general. Higher quality sidewinder models have precision-cut, hardened-metal helical (beveled) gears, as opposed to pressed-metal spur gears found on lower-end saws. Here too, the result is less power loss, smoother, quieter operation and increased longevity.

Cutting depth adjustment. The cutting depth of a circular saw is set by raising or lowering the saw foot relative to the bottom of the blade. To accomplish this, there are two basic types of saw foot: the *pivot-foot* and the *drop-foot*.

Most circular saws are of the pivot-foot variety, on which the base pivots on a hinge or knuckle at the front end of the saw. As you decrease the depth of cut, the handle position angles upward in relation to the work, making the saw a little more awkward to operate.

On drop-foot saws, the base attaches to a dovetailed slot at the front end of the saw body and moves straight up and down in relation to the saw body. When you raise or lower the base, the handle stays at the same angle, letting you keep the same hand and wrist position at different cutting depths. However, drop-foot models take a bit longer than pivot-foot models to adjust precisely and are generally more expensive.

SAFETY TIP:

Always wear gloves and a particle mask or respirator when cutting pressure-treated lumber—one of the most common uses for the circular saw. Most treated lumber contains dangerous chemicals, like copper chromium arsenate (CCA), which is a skin, eye and lung irritant and can be toxic if exposure is prolonged.

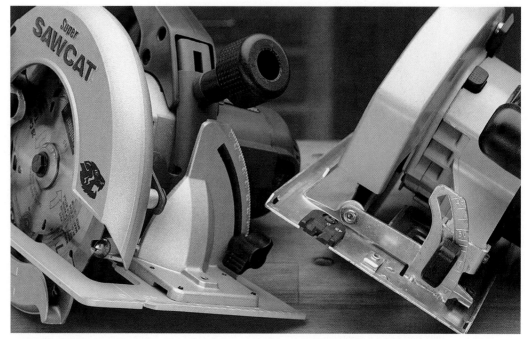

The thickness, scratch resistance, and rigidity of the saw base (sometimes called the shoe or foot) is a sure indicator of where the tool falls within the manufacturer's product line. Here, two saws from the same manufacturer have dramatically different feet. The consumer-line saw on the right has a thin, light-gauge stamped steel foot, and the professional-line saw on the left has a thick aluminum foot.

Saw base. To say that a building is only as good as its foundation also applies to circular saws. Lower-end consumer models typically have a base that is lightweight stamped steel and has flimsy depth and bevel adjustments. Better saws have heavier-gauge bases of nickel-plated steel, aluminum, nickel-plated aluminum or magnesium *(See photo above).*

Thicker aluminum saw bases have the advantages of added rigidity and light weight, but they scratch easily, eventually causing drag on the work surface. Nickel-plated bases in steel or aluminum are more durable. Bases on some cheaper saws have a slick, sprayed-on epoxy coating to reduce friction—however, this coating eventually wears off.

Magnesium bases combine the best of all worlds: they're durable, extremely lightweight, rigid, and scratch resistant. However, you'll pay a premium for models that employ this material.

No matter what type of metal the base is constructed from, look at the size and thickness. Saws with large, relatively thick bases provide better support and accuracy and follow a straightedge more easily. Alternately, saws with smaller, lightweight bases offer greater maneuver-

ability for framing, roofing, and other on-site applications that may require you to hold the saw vertically or at odd angles.

Handle. Circular saws have two basic handle styles: *top-handle,* like the side-winder saw shown on page 20, and *push-handle,* like the worm-drive saw on page 22. Top-handle saws center your weight over the top of the tool, providing better two-handed control when following a cut line on flat plywood panels or making precise cutoffs on trims and moldings. Push-handle versions let you apply more force behind the blade for plowing through thick or dense materials. Some models have a handle position that strikes a compromise between the two. As a rule, finish carpenters prefer top-handle designs, while rough-framing carpenters lean toward push-handle circular saws.

Safety features & other amenities. The primary safety features on a circular saw are the *blade guard* and the *blade brake.* On modern saws, the lower blade guards often have a molded lip on the front end to keep the guard from snagging on the workpiece—a particular problem when making angled cross-cuts. Many saws also have a retracting lever on the guard near the saw handle, so you can retract the guard safely before making plunge cuts. Because retracting the blade guard greatly increases the chance of accidents, keep the guard in place whenever possible.

Many high-end tools come equipped with an electric blade brake that stops the blade within about two seconds when the ON/OFF trigger is released. Though originally designed as an aid for repetitive cutting procedures, blade brakes are also a prime safety feature, because you don't have to wait 10 or 15 seconds for the blade to come to a complete stop before moving or laying down the tool.

Top-of-the-line saws also have a *slip-clutch mechanism* that allows the blade to "slip" on the arbor shaft should it bind or jam in the cut. Slip clutches help prevent saw kickback and motor damage when jams or bogging occur.

Cord length. Lower-end saws usually have short (6-ft.) cords with stiff thermo-plastic jackets, while better saws sport longer (9- to 10-ft.) flexible rubber cords. On tools with short cords, the extension cord connection is more likely to get hung up on the work. *(For more on cord safety, see page 13.)*

Circular saw blades

Like all other power saws, blades for circular saws are made in a wide array of styles, designed for specific cutting tasks *(See photo, right).*

When you buy a circular saw, it will usually come equipped with a standard combination blade for general ripping and crosscutting. Lower-end models usually have a cheap, stamped steel blade included, while many better saws come with a carbide-tipped blade. In most cases, you should replace the factory blade with a good quality, thin-kerf, carbide-tipped saw blade. These blades cut faster and stay sharp longer than conventional steel blades and cause less stress on the motor.

To get maximum performance from your circular saw, you should really invest in a whole set of blades for specific kinds of cutting. A set of three quality carbide blades may cost nearly as much as the saw, but the increase in performance and blade life is usually worth it—especially on cheaper, underpowered saws.

A good starter-set of 7¼" circular saw blades includes:

• A thin-kerf, carbide-tipped, 16-tooth rip blade for fast, rough cutting along the grain.
• A 36- or 40-tooth finish blade for super-smooth crosscuts, miters, and trim work.
• A 20-tooth ATB (alternate tooth bevel) combination blade for general-purpose use.

You'll also find a large selection of "specialty" blades and abrasive wheels designed for specific uses, such as for cutting plywood, iron and steel, soft metals, ceramics, masonry materials, plastics and composition materials, nail-embedded wood, and more.

While carbide blades generally outlast steel alloy blades many times over, the teeth are brittle, and can be easily damaged if abused or stored improperly. They're also much more expensive than their steel counterparts. If you need a specialty blade for a one-time task or for occasional use (such as a hollow-ground planer blade for making super-smooth miter cuts in molding, or a plywood blade

Saw Blade Depth Cutting Chart		
BLADE DIAMETER	**MAX. CUTTING DEPTH @ 90° (AVG.)**	**MAX. CUTTING DEPTH @ 45° (AVG.)**
3 3/8"	7/8"	NA
4 1/2"	1 5/16"	1 1/16"
5 1/2"	1 3/4"	1 3/16"
6"	1 15/16"	1 9/16"
6 1/2"	2 1/16"	1 5/8"
7 1/4"	2 3/8"	1 3/4"
8 1/4"	2 15/16"	2 1/4"
10 1/4"	3 3/4"	2 1/2"
16 1/4"	6 3/16"	4 3/16"

to prevent splintering of fine veneers) you can save money by picking up the steel alloy version. Avoid cheap "throwaway" steel blades, however—these wear out quickly and are not worth the cost of resharpening.

16-tooth combination blade

16-tooth, thin-kerf antikickback blade

14-tooth roofer's blade

24-tooth panel and trim-cutting blade

40-tooth, carbide-tipped cross-cutting blade

40-tooth, sharpened steel general-purpose blade

60-tooth plywood and smooth-cut blade

TIP:

Cut a piece of scrap wood the same width as the *setback distance* from the edge of the saw foot to the saw blade. Set the edge of the board on your cutting line, and use it to position your straightedge the right distance from the cutting line. If you switch blades, double-check the accuracy of the spacer before you use—a differing blade thickness will affect the saw blade setback.

Accessories

Some useful circular saw accessories include:

A rip guide that attaches to the foot of the saw and has a straight lip that follows the edge of the workpiece. Adjustable for making cuts of varying width, circular saw rip guides are very similar to router edge guides.

A protractor guide to use as a straight-edge for making miter-cuts *(See photo, below)*. With an on-board protractor, these guides can be locked into any cutting angle you need.

A long metal straightedge. Look for an aluminum model with built-in clamps *(See photo, right)*. A good straightedge will yield a straighter cut than a rip guide—be sure to leave enough space between the straightedge and your cutting line to allow for the width of the saw base (this distance is called the *setback*).

Dust bag. Many better circular saws can be fitted with an optional dust bag or connection for a standard shop vacuum hose. Dust bags offer greater mobility than the hose, but they quickly fill up with sawdust. Look for zippered bags that empty easily.

Carrying case. Some companies offer steel or plastic carrying cases for their higher-end saws. The case should provide ample room for the saw, a few extra blades, and smaller circular saw accessories.

Use a metal straightedge as a cutting guide. It provides a nice, clean edge for the saw foot to ride against, and it seldom warps or bows.

When making miter cuts, a protractor-type cutting guide ensures accurate, consistent cuts.

Changing blades

Circular saw blades are held in place by a nut at the end of the arbor. To change blades, simply loosen and remove the bolt *(See photo below)*. Your saw most likely came with a special

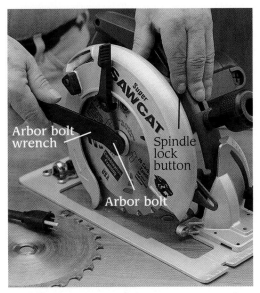

Arbor bolt wrench

Spindle lock button

Arbor bolt

To remove a circular saw blade, loosen the arbor bolt by turning it counterclockwise. If your saw has a spindle lock device (a button next to the blade guard on the saw shown above), use it to hold the blade still.

arbor bolt wrench—sometimes it's stored on-board the saw. If not, or if you've misplaced the wrench, use an open-end wrench. Better saws also have a spindle lock or blade changing lever that freezes the arbor when it's pushed forward—this keeps everything stationary while you loosen the bolt. If your saw doesn't have a spindle lock, set the blade securely in a block of wood to hold it. Remember that the arbor bolt is threaded against the rotation of the blade. When replacing the arbor bolt, be careful not to overtighten. Too much pressure can cause the blade to bind, and you'll also regret it next time you try to change the blade.

Using your circular saw

When compared to stationary power tools, a circular saw, like any portable power tool, is more prone to cause accidents and cutting errors. Be sure to follow all the standard safety practices outlined on pages 10 to 13. Providing stable support for the workpiece, clamping it in place if possible, and using a

straightedge guide are especially important when cutting with a circular saw.

Check your saw and blade. Before you operate your circular saw, run a quick safety check to make sure the blade is sharp and all controls and mechanisms are in good operating condition. Examine the lower blade guard to make sure it retracts smoothly and snaps firmly back in place; often, the mechanism gets clogged with sawdust, affecting performance. Weak return springs in the guard mechanism should be replaced.

Also check the condition of the saw cord; damaged or frayed cords should be replaced. If you notice excessive blade slippage while cutting, check the condition of the arbor bolt, washer and flanges; if they no longer secure the blade when tightened, clean or replace them. Saw blades should also be checked before each use. After a period of time, wood pitch and resin will build up on the blade, affecting performance. You can remove such deposits with a commercially available gum and pitch remover, or an all-purpose household cleaner. Also, it doesn't pay to use a dull blade; not only will it cut roughly and slowly, it also places more stress on the saw motor and bearings.

Very few woodworkers sharpen their own saw blades. Getting the angles correct can be quite tricky. Instead, take your blades to a sharpening center. The few dollars you spend will usually outweigh the aggravation you prevent.

Body position. When possible, keep a firm, two-handed grip on the saw. Maintain a firm stance and avoid situations that put you off balance (don't over reach to finish a cut). Never stand directly behind the saw when cutting; if the saw should kick back, you want to be out of the line of fire *(See photo, right)*.

Whenever possible, grip your saw with both hands as you work, and never stand directly behind the saw in case the saw kicks back.

Position the workpiece good-side-down when cutting with a circular saw. Tear-out generally occurs on the side facing up.

Setting up. When setting up a cut, make sure that most of the saw's weight is supported by the workpiece, and that the work itself is supported by a bench or sawhorses. Be sure to have the better face of the workpiece facing down—tearout and splintering occur on the side that is facing up with a circular saw *(See photo, left)*. Clamp smaller workpieces to the worksurface when possible. Set up the board so that the waste portion overhangs the end of the bench or sawhorse so the kerf won't close up from the weight of the cut-off piece.

Use a straightedge cutting guide whenever possible, but especially when making rip cuts. Always provide level support for the cut-off piece—the last thing you want is for it to break off before the cut is finished. Set the saw blade depth so it will cut about ¼" past the bottom of the workpiece.

Plunge cuts are a handy way to make interior cutouts in plywood or other types of sheet goods. If you're not comfortable with this technique, the alternative is to make a starter cut with a jig saw or hand saw (or to use these tools for the entire cut).

Making Plunge Cuts

Sometimes it's necessary to make a plunge cut (sometimes called a *pocket cut*) when you want to make an inside cutout in a panel. In this procedure, you must retract the lower blade manually to start the cut. Tilt the saw up on the front of the base, with the blade aligned with the cutting line (don't allow the

blade teeth to touch the workpiece). Fully retract the guard, keeping your hands well clear of the exposed blade. Allow the saw to reach full speed, then slowly lower it into the workpiece *(See photo above)*. Never stand directly behind the saw when making this cut. Above all, if you don't feel comfortable with this procedure, don't try it!

Making the cut. Position the front edge of the saw foot on the workpiece and turn the tool on. Allow the blade to build to full speed before feeding it into the workpiece. Keep an eye on the cord location at all times; when ripping long panels or boards, make sure the cord and extension are long enough to enable the saw to complete the cut. Also, position the cord so that the connection between the tool cord and extension cord won't get hung up on the edge of the bench or workpiece.

Feed the blade into the workpiece, and proceed at an even pace, listening to the motor. If you hear the saw starting to bog down, slow down your feed rate. When you've finished the cut, wait until the saw blade has come to a complete stop before you start the next cut or set the circular saw down.

BUYING TIPS:

When shopping for saws, heft the tool and notice the weight, balance, feel of the handle and trigger switch, and accessibility to various controls. Although tool companies have made significant ergonomic improvements in their saws, user comfort is still quite subjective; that is, not all saws fit all hands. Also, while you might think that a heavier saw would be more durable than a lightweight one, this isn't always the case. In recent years, tool companies have been able to reduce tool weight while retaining power and dura-bility. Overall, today's saws pack more punch in a lighter-weight package.

Replacing Brushes

One of the most common causes of power loss in small power tools is poor brush contact. The brushes are pieces of carbon that are pressed against the commutator of the motor by springs. As the commutator spins, the brushes gradually wear down. Eventually, they stop making clean contact with the commutator, resulting in a loss of power. To replace the brushes, simply remove the endpiece of the saw casing, then withdraw the plastic brush holders (there are two, on opposite sides of the commu-tator). There is usually a line near the base of each brush. If the line is no longer visible, you should replace the brushes.

Be sure to bring one of the old brushes (or what's left of it) with you to a tool service center so you know you're getting the correct size. Insert the new brushes into the holders, slip the holders back in place, then reassemble the casing. Before you use the saw, run it for about 10 minutes without a blade so the ends of the brushes become *seated,* forming a clean joint with the commutator. *Note:* Some newer saws simply have a brush inspection cap that can be unscrewed to allow access to the brushes.

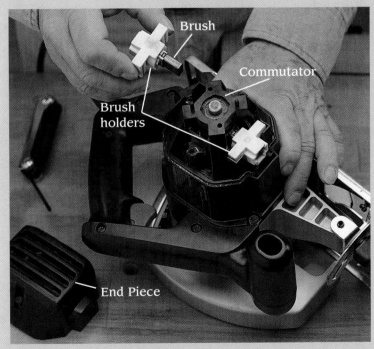

If your saw loses power, check the carbon brushes to see if they need replacement. The brush being examined in this photo is probably okay.

Jig Saws

Sometimes called a *saber saw* or *bayonet saw,* the portable jig saw ranks right up there with an electric drill and circular saw as a "must have" portable power tool for every home handyman. Because of its curve-cutting ability, you could call this tool a "poor man's band saw," although jig saws can make cuts that no stationary band saw or scroll saw can. Because jig saws are portable, and not limited by a throat depth as is a band saw or scroll saw, they enable you to cut curves or inside cutouts on panels or workpieces of any width or length—in the shop or on the job site.

Granted, a jig saw won't make the intricate, tight-radius cuts of a stationary scroll saw, nor does it provide the fast, smooth cutting action and resawing capability of a band saw. In fact, earlier versions (and some of the cheaper saws sold today) have earned jig saws the reputation of being slow, inaccurate, coarse-cutting tools for rough, hack-'em-up carpentry projects. However, advancing technology has brought such design improvements as aggressive orbital cutting action, better blade support systems, "smart" electronic speed control, and a host of other technological and ergonomic improvements that produce surprisingly smooth, accurate cuts in quick order. Armed with a healthy assortment of blades, you can cut patterns in a variety of materials, from styrene foam to steel, and just about anything in between.

It's safe to say that the differences in performance are more evident with jig saws than with most other portable power tools. If you've never used a top-of-the-line jig saw before, visit your local tool store and have them give you a demonstration. You'll hardly recognize it as a relative of the bargain-basement model you've been using all these years.

BARREL-GRIP JIG SAW

Blade guard

Blade plunger

Blade support

Base plate (foot)

Blade

Blade orbit selection lever

ON/OFF switch

Blade change knob

Lock-ON button

Bosch SDS

TOP-HANDLE JIG SAW

ON/OFF switch

BOSCH

1587VS

Blade plunger

Blade support

Base plate (foot)

Blade

Chip blower lever

Blade orbit selection lever

Jig Saw Fact Sheet		
Application	**Tool Recommendation**	**Accessories**
Light Use	A mid level top-handle or barrel grip saw with multiple speed settings, lower blade support, and minimum power of 3 to 5 amps.	Basic set of high-speed steel blades, edge-guide, straightedge cutting guide.
Moderate Use	A 5- to 7-amp saw with adjustable blade orbit setting, tilting foot for bevel-cuts, variable speed control, and lock-ON switch.	Complete set of bimetal blades, protective foot cover, circle cutting guide, carrying case.
Heavy Use	One D-handle saw, one barrel grip saw, a minimum of 7 amps power, "smart" electronic circuitry to adjust for load, dust collection port, quick-release blade change.	Dust collection bag, heavy-duty metal carrying case with blade storage area.

Jig saw types

Jig saws fall into two basic types, determined by body design: the *top-handle* saw and the *barrel-grip* saw.

Top-handle saws *(See photo below).* With a large, D-shaped handle centered over the motor housing, this style is by far the most popular among handymen, and it comes in the widest variety of motor sizes and price ranges. Designed for one-handed use, a top-handle jig saw enables you to place more downward pressure over the base of the tool, providing greater control when cutting thick or dense materials.

Also, the trigger-style ON/OFF switch mounted to the underside of the handle near the front of the saw is equally accessible to left- and right-handed users.

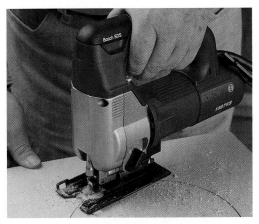

Top-handle jig saws can be operated with one hand. The location of the handle also lets you apply pressure directly over the blade.

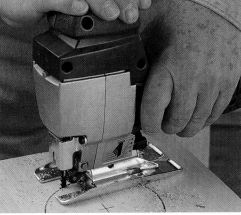

Barrel-grip jig saws are easier to maneuver in tight cuts than top-handle saws. But it takes two hands to operate them, and people with small hands may experience some difficulty managing the tool.

However, this design can often place your wrist, arm, or body in awkward positions when following intricate curved patterns.

Barrel-grip saws *(See photo above).* Some jig saws have a barrel-shaped body that serves as the handle for controlling the tool. A barrel-grip saw provides better maneuverability and control when you need to cut tight curves or cutouts in plywood or other relatively thin materials. Grasping the barrel with one hand and the top knob with the other, you can more easily guide the tool through twists and turns without contorting your wrists, arms, and body. On the downside, many barrel-grip saws have their sliding ON/OFF switch mounted on the left side of the motor housing—ideal for right-hand thumb operation, but an inconvenience for lefties. Also, if you have small hands, you may have trouble getting a firm grip on models with fatter barrels.

Cutting capacity

Most jig saws provide roughly the same cutting depth—between 2" and 2⅜" when equipped with a standard 4"-long blade. Although longer blades are available, installing one doesn't necessarily increase the cutting capacity of your saw. The maximum thickness the saw can handle depends upon the density of the material you're cutting, as well as the power of the motor. Like other portable tools, saws with higher amperage ratings usually have more guts. Motor amperage ranges from 2 to 6 amps; a 3.5- to 4.8-amp tool should breeze through most cutting chores without bogging down.

Cutting speed/stroke length

Other factors that influence saw performance include blade speed and stroke length; higher maximum blade speeds make for faster cutting, provided the motor has enough strength to maintain the cutting pace. Most saws operate at 3,000 to 3,200 strokes per minute (spm). A longer blade stroke also increases cutting speed because more teeth come into contact with the wood and each tooth takes a bigger bite. Stroke lengths range from ⅝" to 1".

Like electric drills and routers, most newer jig saws have *electronic variable speed control.* You'll normally be running the saw at or near top speed, but this feature comes in handy when you want to slow down the blade for cutting metals or other dense materials, or to make intricate cuts in thin sheet goods. On many top-handle units, you control the speed through the trigger switch—a small adjustable dial set into the trigger governs the top-end speed when the trigger is fully depressed. Some other top-handle units, as well as most barrel-grip saws, have separate calibrated speed control dials on the motor housing. Better saws incorporate "smart" electronic feedback circuits that maintain the selected speed setting under various load conditions (such as when sawing through a knot in wood) to produce smoother, more accurate cuts.

Choosing a cutting speed is mostly a matter of trial and error, but a few general rules apply:
• The denser and thicker the material, the slower the speed.
• The faster the blade speed, the faster the cut.
• The faster the blade is moving, the rougher the cut will be.

Blade action

Most newer, better-quality jig saws have an *orbital* blade action, as opposed to the straight up-and-down cutting action found on their predecessors. The orbital motion thrusts the blade slightly forward on the upstroke (the cutting stroke for most blades) then back on the downstroke to increase cutting speed. In addition to making faster cuts, the orbital action serves to clear sawdust and chips from the cut, which helps keep blades running cooler.

Most orbital-action saws have four-position switches that enable you to set the degree of orbit—from none (straight-line cutting) to maximum orbit for fastest cutting *(See photo, left).* Finding the right combination of degree of orbital action, blade speed and blade type gives you precise control over cutting speed. This translates into greater accuracy and smoothness, and less stress on your saw, in any cutting situation.

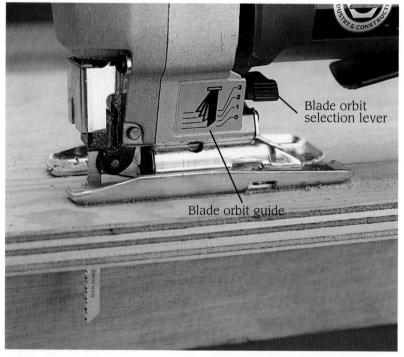

Blade orbit selection lever

Blade orbit guide

When sawing with orbital cutting action, the path of the saw blade actually makes an abbreviated arc that increases the cutting speed. Saws with a blade orbit selection lever let you adjust the amount of orbit to fit your cutting needs.

Blade support

Older-model jig saws (and some lower-end modern versions) provide no blade support between the saw's blade clamp and the workpiece. Without support, the thin blades break frequently and tend to deflect while cutting, either wandering off the cut line or skewing in the cut. Better saws have a lower blade support, which usually consists of a grooved rear roller just above the base plate of the saw. The roller helps prevent excessive side play and front-to-back blade movement. A few models also incorporate side blocks, like those used on a band saw, to further steady the blade. The lower guides not only keep the blade on a straighter path, they also help reduce metal fatigue at the blade's weakest point—just below the blade clamp—and they lower stress on the clamp and plunger assembly.

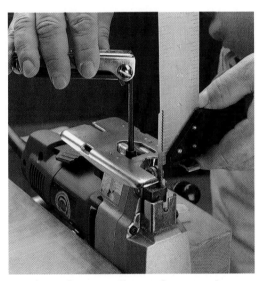

Saw base plates can slip out of square quite easily. Test the base regularly with a square and adjust it back to position as needed.

Base plates

With few exceptions, jig saws have a base plate (also called a *foot*) that tilts 45° to the left or the right for making bevel-cuts. On most saws, the plates are stamped or cast-steel; a few models have cast-aluminum bases with replaceable steel or plastic shoes. The base plate plays an important role in cutting accuracy. A good, sturdy base plate should tilt smoothly and lock firmly in place at any angle. Even good saws with positive

stops at 90° and 45° aren't terribly accurate. If you need to set a precise angle, you're better off using a protractor to set the base in relation to the blade. Also, if you do most of your cutting at 90°, you should check the base periodically with a reliable square *(See photo, left)*. Simply dropping the tool or jostling it around can knock the base out of alignment.

Scrolling action

You'll find this feature on some lower-end "consumer" models. Scrolling jig saws have a twist knob attached to the top of the plunge mechanism that enables you to rotate the blade during operation to follow tight curves and intricate cutouts *(See photo, below)*. The idea is to minimize or eliminate the need to twist and turn the saw body itself to follow a pattern. The mechanism can also be locked to keep the blade stable and square when making straight cuts.

While a scrolling mechanism makes some degree of sense, it's employed mostly on low-amp saws with lightweight straight-line plunge mechanisms. Applying scrolling features to orbital saws and saws with lower blade guides presents some technological difficulties, and many of the tradesmen who purchase higher-end saws have questioned the usefulness of the feature.

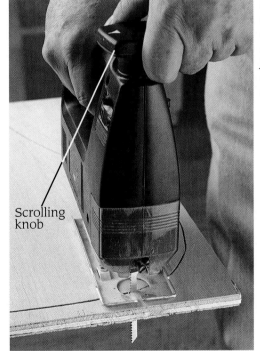

Scrolling knob

Scrolling jig saws feature a blade-angle adjustment knob at the top of the handle. By turning the knob, you change the blade direction—without turning the body of the saw.

Jig saw blades

Most major tool companies offer a dizzying assortment of jig saw blades for cutting a variety of materials: steel, copper, aluminum, fiberglass, PVC plastic, plywood, particleboard, pressure-treated woods, and so on. The best way to get a good feel for the types of blades you need is to read the blade selection charts in power tool catalogs. Some companies also include blade selection information in the saw owner's manual. Blade packages usually do a fair job of explaining the blade specs and uses as well.

To select the appropriate jig saw blade for any given job, you'll need to consider four things: the shank style required for your jig saw, the type and thickness of material to be cut, the desired smoothness of the cut, and how fast you'd like the cut or cuts to be made.

Shank style. The shank is the portion of the blade that clamps into the plunger of the saw. Different saws accept shanks with different shapes. The three most

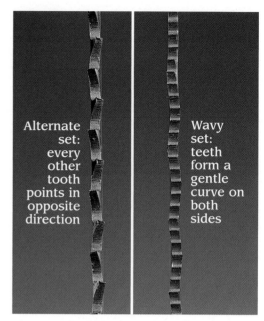

The set of the teeth refers to their relationship to the spine of the blade. The most common jig saw blades are alternate set and wavy set.

Tooth set. Blades are also categorized by tooth type: *wavy set, alternate (saw) set,* and *taper ground (See photo above).* On alternate-set blades, every other tooth points away from the spine of the blade in an opposite direction. On wavy-set blades, the set of the teeth forms a gentle curve. And on taper-ground blades, the teeth form a straight line, and the back of the blade spine tapers back away from the teeth to decrease cutting resistance.

Most of the saw blades made today are either wavy set or alternate set. Wavy-set and alternate-set blades produce a wider kerf than taper-ground blades, enabling them to navigate tighter curves; however, they don't cut as cleanly. Wavy-set blades usually have more tpi than alternate-set blades, and are often used to make relatively smooth, tight cuts in plywood, hardboard, and pressed materials.

Material. The metals commonly used in jig saw blades include: carbon steel, high-speed steel (HSS), bimetal, and carbide. Carbon steel blades are used for general wood cutting, while HSS blades can be used for wood, metal, and other materials. Bimetal blades have a flexible spring-steel body that bends without breaking and super-hard HSS teeth that stay sharper longer than conventional carbon or HSS blades; carbide-tipped bimetal blades last longer yet.

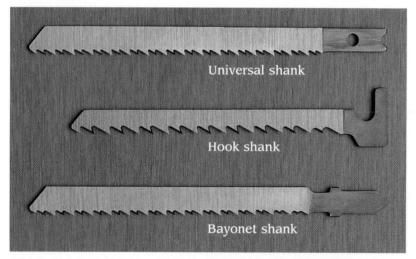

The shank (also called the tang) is the part of the saw blade that fits into the blade plunger. Shank styles vary between manufacturers. The three main types are the hook shank, the bayonet shank, and the universal shank.

common shank styles are the *universal,* the *bayonet* and the *hook (See photo above).* When you buy jig saw blades, double-check that they'll fit—buying the wrong type is an easy mistake to make.

TPI. The number of teeth per inch *(tpi)* determines cutting speed and the smoothness of the cut; tpi numbers range from 6 tpi for fast, rough cutting in wood, up to 36 tpi for extremely smooth cuts in thin metals and composites.

Flush-cutting blades are extra wide so the teeth will be even with the front of the saw, allowing you to cut all the way up to a vertical surface.

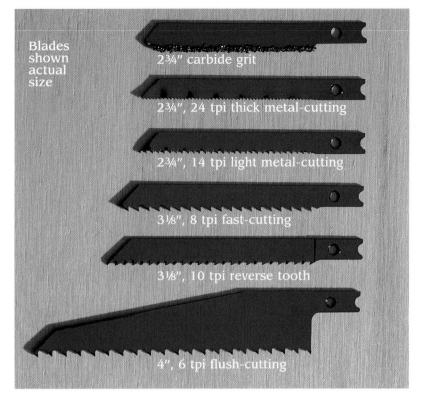

Blades shown actual size

2¾" carbide grit

2¾", 24 tpi thick metal-cutting

2¾", 14 tpi light metal-cutting

3⅛", 8 tpi fast-cutting

3⅛", 10 tpi reverse tooth

4", 6 tpi flush-cutting

A basic set of jig saw blades should include a variety of rough and smooth blades for cutting both wood and metal. Add specialty blades, like a flush-cutting blade, as the need arises.

Blade types. The photo to the right shows a small sampling of the many types of blades available today. These include several "specialty" blades that you may find useful: *Flush-cutting blades* have a wide body that sets the teeth forward so they're flush with the front of the saw base. This makes it possible to cut flush to a vertical surface *(See photo above)*. *Reverse-tooth* blades cut on the downstroke to prevent splintering in veneers and delicate surfaces like countertops. *Carbide grit* blades produce smooth cuts in hardwoods, steel, high-pressure laminates, ceramic tile and other dense or abrasive materials. Toothless *knife-ground* blades are used to cut rubber and vinyl, styrene foam, leather and fabrics. Some companies make files and rasps to fit their saws.

Changing blades

On most jig saws the blade is held in the blade clamp on the plunger by means of a set screw that you loosen with an allen wrench *(See photo, right)* or a flat-head screwdriver. The same wrench used for changing the blade usually fits the set-screw that's adjusting the base angle. Some jig saws have the convenient feature of on-board wrench storage. People whose work requires changing blades frequently can make good use of a

Traditionally, blades are secured in the jig saw plunger with a set-screw that you loosen, then tighten to change blades. Some newer saws, like the top-handle jig saw shown on the bottom of page 34, have a quick-release mechanism that lets you change blades without the need for tools.

saw with a quick-release blade changing mechanism. This feature enables you to release and remove the blade and snap another back in place with the turn of a knob or the flip of a lever *(See photo, page 34, bottom)*.

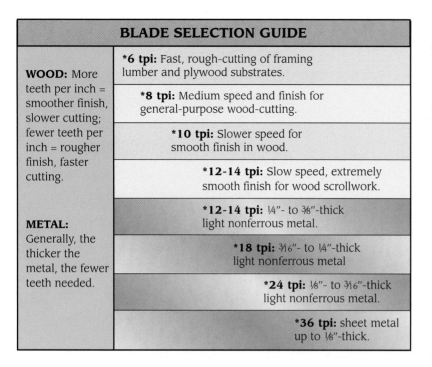

BLADE SELECTION GUIDE

WOOD: More teeth per inch = smoother finish, slower cutting; fewer teeth per inch = rougher finish, faster cutting.	***6 tpi:** Fast, rough-cutting of framing lumber and plywood substrates.
	***8 tpi:** Medium speed and finish for general-purpose wood-cutting.
	***10 tpi:** Slower speed for smooth finish in wood.
	***12-14 tpi:** Slow speed, extremely smooth finish for wood scrollwork.
METAL: Generally, the thicker the metal, the fewer teeth needed.	***12-14 tpi:** ¼"- to ⅜"-thick light nonferrous metal.
	***18 tpi:** 3⁄16"- to ¼"-thick light nonferrous metal
	***24 tpi:** ⅛"- to 3⁄16"-thick light nonferrous metal.
	***36 tpi:** sheet metal up to ⅛"-thick.

Jig saw accessories

Beyond the plethora of blades available for jig saws, you'll find several useful accessories to increase the tool's versatility and performance.

Carrying case. Obtain a sturdy plastic or metal carrying case, if your saw doesn't have one. The case not only protects the saw from dust and physical damage but also provides convenient storage for all the small blades you'll be collecting.

Circle-cutting/edge-following guide. An inexpensive combination circle-cutting/edge-following guide comes in handy when you need to make straight line cuts or circular cutouts. The guide attaches to the saw's base plate, enabling you to make straight rip cuts parallel to the edge of the workpiece. Most edge guides have a hole in one end that enables you to drive a nail or pin into the workpiece to serve as a pivot point for making circular cutouts.

Straightedge. A metal or wood straightedge clamped to the stock will enable you to make straight-line cuts with a jig saw on larger panels and sheet materials. You can make your own straightedge from a true board (a piece of 1 × 4 hardwood is a good choice). Or, use a self-clamping aluminum version that lets you make straight cuts up to 8 feet long *(See photo, page 22 top)*.

Stands. Bench-mounted stands enable you to use the saw much as you would a stationary scroll saw. In addition to dedicated jig saw stands, some router tables and extension wings on table saws can be fitted to accept a jig saw in the same manner.

Dust collection. Most jig saws are designed so the motor fan channels a stream of air behind the blade to remove dust from the cutting line. A few better models have a provision for dust collection—usually a port that accepts a standard shop vacuum hose.

Using your jig saw

Because jig saws cut on the upstroke, it helps to place the workpiece "good side down", when possible, and make the cut from the back side. This is especially critical when cutting expensive veneered panels and high-pressure laminates, to reduce splintering or chipping on the delicate surface. Also, the reciprocal action of the blade may cause the saw to vibrate or "chatter" in the cut, especially when working with small pieces or thin stock. To reduce this problem, firmly clamp or otherwise secure the stock to your bench or worksurface, and maintain a firm grip on the tool while cutting. Alternately, sandwich the workpiece between scrap boards.

When cutting extremely thin materials, provide firm support or backing as close to the cut line as possible. As with any tool, pace of the cut is very important. The saw should be running at full speed when you contact the workpiece.

TIP:

Remove the saw blade when your jig saw is not in use. A protruding jig saw blade is quite vulnerable to breakage if it's accidentally bumped or if the tool is dropped. In addition, the sharp jig saw blade teeth can cause damage to people and to walls and floors if accidental contact is made.

Plunge cuts are made by firmly resting the front of the base plate on the workpiece, then lowering the blade against the workpiece. Grip the saw with both hands to help keep it from skating as the blade impact pierces the wood.

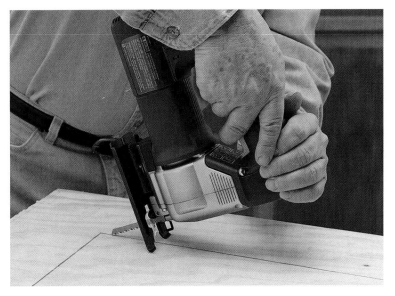

SAFETY TIP
If you use your jig saw to cut completely through a wall, floor, ceiling, or roof, you'll need to pay special attention to what's hidden behind the surface (electrical wires, pipes, duct-work...). Take a few minutes to plan out your cuts before making them. If you have blueprints of your mechanical system, always check them before cutting into a wall. And as an added precaution, shut off electrical power to the area, before making the initial cut.

Making a plunge cut

Unlike other curve-cutting saws, a jig saw can make plunge cuts or pocket cuts, eliminating the need for a starter hole. You do this by tilting the saw on its nose so the blade just clears the workpiece, then slowly lowering the moving blade into the material with the blade running *(See photo above)*. Usually, it's best to run the saw at or near top speed when making a plunge cut. In all cases, practice making a few cuts on scrap material.

Jig saw maintenance

Follow the same basic maintenance procedures as for other portable power tools *(See pages 6 to 9)*. After each use, blow or vacuum sawdust out of the motor. Periodically inspect the brushes, cords, and moving parts for wear or damage. Clean the saw body with a household cleaner, and clean the blades with a penetrating lubricant to remove pitch, resin and other compounds. Because jig saw blades are so inexpensive, they're seldom worth sharpening.

TIP:

Choose the best orbital setting for the cutting task you're performing. Most jig saws with orbital cutting capabilities have four different cutting path settings. Usually, a straight up-and-down cut with no orbital action is listed as "0" on the orbit selector. From there, the higher the number, the greater the amount of orbital action in the cutting path. Here are some suggested orbit settings by cutting task:

Blade orbit options (0 to IV) are shown on most orbital jig saws.

Orbit setting	Tasks
0	• Cutting metal, composites, and other hard, dense materials; cutting with a knife-ground or carbide grit blade; using a rasp accessory.
I	• Scrollwork, smooth-as-possible finish cuts in most woods.
II	• Faster cutting of hardwoods, particle-board, and other medium-density materials.
III	• Fastest cuts in softer woods and materials. Avoid using this setting for dense hardwoods.

Power Miter Saws

In the shop or on the jobsite, power miter saws excel at making clean, precise cuts at various angles. They're known by tool users generally as "chop saws," although this name refers most accurately to simple power miter boxes with a fixed arbor, like the model shown below. But whatever name you know them by, these versatile tools have taken the carpentry and woodworking worlds by storm in recent years. Advancing technology has improved the range, power and accuracy of these saws.

The power miter saw combines the convenience of a portable power tool with the accuracy and power of a stationary tool. But even though it's technically a portable tool, many people use their power miter saw as a stationary tool, setting it into a bench or table with the base flush to the work surface to support long stock. At the same time, many trim carpenters and frame carpenters have come to depend on the power miter saw because it can be set up so easily at the job site. In fact, in the carpentry trade the power miter saw has mounted a strong challenge to the circular saw for top honors as the most important power tool.

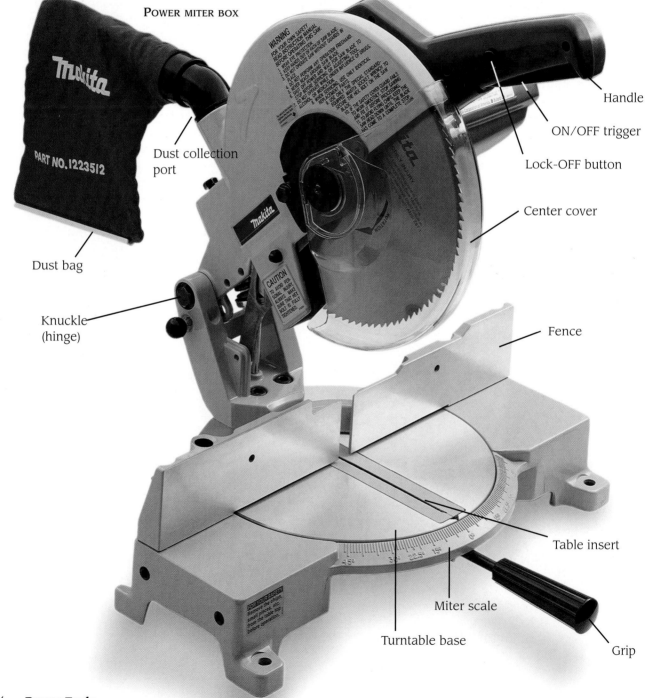

POWER MITER BOX

Dust collection port

Dust bag

Knuckle (hinge)

Handle

ON/OFF trigger

Lock-OFF button

Center cover

Fence

Table insert

Miter scale

Turntable base

Grip

Power Miter Saw Fact Sheet		
Application	**Tool Recommendation**	**Accessories**
Light Use	Low- to mid-priced conventional 10" power miter box (most woodworking and home improvement projects do not require compound miter cuts).	Carbide-tipped combination blade, work supports, hold-down clamps, replaceable table inserts.
Moderate Use	Midpriced to high-end 8¼" or 10" compound miter saw.	Extension rails, selection of carbide-toothed cross-cutting and non-wood-cutting blades.
Heavy Use	Sliding compound miter saw (8½" to 12"), 10" or larger chop saw for cutoff work.	Shop-built workstation or after-market work stand for on-site use, dust collection system.

Power miter saw types

These saws fall into three distinct categories: conventional power miter saws (also called chop saws or power miter boxes), compound miter saws, and sliding compound miter saws.

The power miter box. This first-generation design earned the name "chop saw," due to the downward chopping motion used to make cuts with it. On this saw, the motor/blade assembly pivots up and down on a large knuckle attached to a turntable set into the saw base. By rotating the turntable, you can make vertical miter cuts from 0° to 45° or more. A large scale on the front of the turntable base enables you to accurately set the miter angle within 1°, or even a fraction

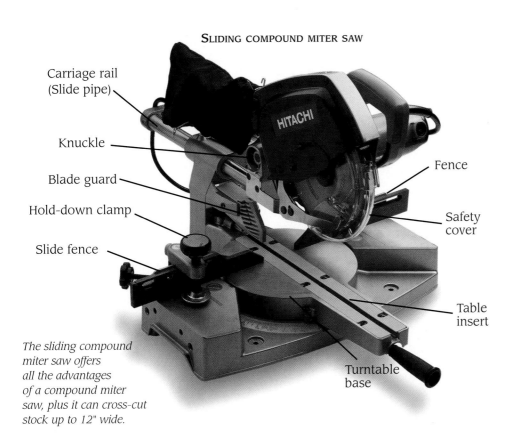

SLIDING COMPOUND MITER SAW

Carriage rail (Slide pipe)

Knuckle

Blade guard

Hold-down clamp

Slide fence

Fence

Safety cover

Table insert

Turntable base

The sliding compound miter saw offers all the advantages of a compound miter saw, plus it can cross-cut stock up to 12" wide.

SAFETY TIP:
Watch the position of your free hand when making cuts with a power miter saw, especially on short or small pieces. Even with a good blade guard, a portion of the blade will be exposed when you chop down on the work. When possible, use hold-down clamps *(See photo, page 37)* to secure the stock tightly against the fence and on the base so you can keep your hand well clear of the blade. This will also result in more accurate cuts.

of a degree on some models. A twist knob or handle located on the front of the turntable is loosened and tightened to move the turntable and lock it into position. Some of the better saws have positive stops at common angles: 0°, 22.5°, and 45°.

Most power miter boxes are fitted with a 10"-dia. blades, although a few oversize models will take blades up to 12" or even 15" in diameter. Called *cutoff saws,* these are popular for timber cutting and you'll find them frequently in lumber yards. A typical 10" saw will cut a 2 × 6 at both 90° and 45°; some will also cut a 4 × 4 at 90°.

Although not practical for making compound cuts, a power miter box has an advantage over compound miter saws if you do mostly straight vertical cutting. Because the blade is fixed in the vertical position, it's much less likely to fall out of alignment, so the power miter box requires less tuning up and set-up time. Also, as an entry level tool they normally have a lower cost than the compound saws—although the price gap is narrowing as compound miter saws increase in popularity.

The compound miter saw. This second generation design works like a conventional miter saw with the added feature of a tilting motor/blade assembly that enables you to make bevel cuts. All models tilt to the left only (although some sliding compound miter saws also tilt to the right). By combining the bevel angle with the miter angle, you can make compound miter cuts—hence the tool's name.

Typical blade sizes include 8¼", 10" and 12". Cutting capacities are roughly equivalent to power miter boxes with the same-size blade. Like some power miter boxes, compound saws have positive stops at commonly used miter angles, as well as common bevel angles. Most also have positive stops for cutting standard crown moldings.

A compound miter saw is the saw of choice if you frequently find yourself cutting decorative moldings, trims, and baseboards that require compound cuts. Carpenters also find them useful when cutting rafters and other framing components for complex roof structures, such as hip-and-valley roofs.

Sliding compound miter saws. Known affectionately as *sliders* in the trades, these saws are threatening to make the traditional radial arm saw obsolete. As with compound miter saws, a slider has a motor/blade assembly that rotates left or right for mitering and tilts for bevel cuts. In addition, the assembly slides back and forth on a carriage to increase cutting capacity to up to 12" on many models.

Blade sizes for sliders range from 8¼" to 12"; all sizes have a cross-cutting capacity from 11½" to 12" at 90°. You can increase any saw's cutting performance by equipping it with a thin-kerf blade. Thinner kerfs reduce stress on the motor, waste less material, and cut more quickly by maintaining higher blade speeds.

While a sliding compound miter saw provides greater versatility and cutting capacity than a power miter box or a compound miter saw, it's also the most expensive tool of the lot, with entry level sliders costing up to twice the price of a compound miter saw.

Power miter saw basics

Power. Motors on these saws range from 9 amps to 15 amps, which provides adequate power to handle the saw's maximum cutting capacity and blade size. But, if you routinely cut thick or dense woods and other materials, you'll be better off with a higher-amperage saw in any given size.

Cutting capacity. Even among saws of the same type and with the same blade diameter, cutting capacity varies greatly among different models. It's important to look at the actual cutting capacity of each individual tool, usually listed in the manufacturer's catalog specs. Then, if you're considering buying the saw, determine if the maximum width and thickness capacities will handle the type of work you do. For example, if you plan to use the saw mainly for house framing or garden building, one that cuts completely though a nominal 4 × 4 or 2 × 12 in one pass is preferable over one that "almost" does it, requiring you to use a handsaw to complete the cut.

Also be aware that while larger blade sizes usually mean greater cutting capacity, the cost increases accordingly. Generally, the price difference between 8½" and 10" blades isn't that significant. But if you step up to a 12" or larger blade, you'll pay a premium for it, and local sources will be more limited.

Adjustments. A good power miter saw should have accessible, smoothly operating adjustments; clear, easy-to-read miter and bevel scales; and positive locking knobs. It should be easy to set the saw to any given angle, then quickly return it to the 0° setting for making square crosscuts. When setting common miter and bevel angles, positive stops should snap firmly in place, with no slop.

Fence. On all power miter saws, you'll find a two-piece fence with a gap where the blade passes through. Compound saws require a wider gap than conventional miter saws, in order to accommodate angled blades for bevel-cutting. Consequently, the fence gap on some saws may be too wide to support short workpieces. Better saws have a sliding fence design that enables you to adjust the gap as needed. Others have optional fence inserts for additional support.

Blades

The blade-type options for a power miter saw are similar to those for any circular saw *(See page 21)*.

Manufacturers offer blades in various sizes (8¼", 10", 12" and up) designed especially for use with power miter saws and radial arm saws. Most of these typically have a lower hook or "rake" angle than blades used on table saws, to provide smoother cross-cuts. The angle of the cutting edge of each tooth is nearly perpendicular (-5° to 7°) to a line drawn from the hub of the blade. Blades with

greater hook angles (in excess of 10°) can cause the workpiece to lift or vibrate during the cut.

Cabinetmakers and trim carpenters usually fit power miter saws with a *fine-tooth finish blade* for making smooth miter cuts in trim, molding, and picture frames. Finish blades, usually with 80 to 100 teeth on a 10" blade, make glass-smooth, splinter-free cuts in hardwood moldings and trim work. Framing carpenters prefer a *general purpose blade* for fast, repetitive crosscutting of studs,

rafters, and other framing members. These blades (the best are carbide tipped) have 24 to 36 teeth on a 10" blade, and a more aggressive hook angle. Between the finish blade and the crosscutting blade, you can manage almost all of your cutting tasks. But if you'd rather not spend a lot of time switching from blade to blade, select a crosscutting blade with 40 to 60 teeth on a 10" blade and a hook angle of around 5°. It won't be as fast with framing lumber or as smooth with finish work, but it can still do a reasonably good job with either task.

Power miter saw accessories

Many of the more popular accessories for power miter saws are either included with the saw or are optional accessories that you can special-order.

Hold-down clamps. These clamps attach either to the fence or the base to secure workpieces for more accurate cuts *(See photo, above)*. Vertical fence-attached clamps apply downward pressure against

Hold-down clamps keep the workpiece secure while you cut it. If your saw is not equipped with a hold-down, you can likely find one that will fit your saw at your local woodworking store or in a tool catalog.

TIP:

Build your own benchtop work supports. If you frequently use your power miter saw on a workbench or other worksurface, build yourself a pair of easy workpiece supports. All you need is a chunk of 2 × 4 and a 12 × 12" scrap of plywood for each support. Measure the distance from the top of the saw base (the cutting table) to the worksurface, subtract the thickness of the plywood, then rip the 2 × 4 to that width. Attach the 2 × 4 to the plywood with a couple of countersunk screws, and you've got a very handy and stable power miter saw accessory. Build as many supports as you need to support longer workpieces.

A pair of homemade work supports can give you all the support you need for cutting long boards on your power miter saw. For reasons of accuracy and safety, always make sure your workpiece is stable before cutting.

the table, for cutting stock "on the flat." Table-mounted clamps secure narrow stock against the fence when cutting thinner moldings or stock on-edge.

Extension rails and stops. For extra workpiece support, most power miter saws are ready-made to accept U-shaped extension rails that fit into each end of the base. Extension rails usually include an adjustable flip-up stop for repetitive cutting to a specific length. If you're setting the saw into a permanent workstation, you won't need these.

Work stands and supports. If your saw will reside primarily in the shop, you can easily build a permanent work stand

or bench for the saw. Build a recess into the center of the worksurface, deep enough so the top of the saw base is flush with the worksurface when the saw is set into the recess. If you plan on using the saw outside the shop or are simply strapped for space, consider an after-market portable stand or extension tables for the tool. These support the saw at a comfortable height for safe, efficient cutting on larger jobs. A few models fold up like a TV tray for easy storage and transport.

For extra-long pieces, pick up a set of roller stands—you'll also find the stands handy when cutting long boards on a table saw, band saw, or any other stationary woodworking machine. Or, make your own simple supports for extra stability when using the saw on a worksurface *(See Tip, left).*

Adjusting the saw

If your power miter saw blade, fence and base are not adjusted properly, you won't get an accurate cut. The fence must be positioned exactly 90° to the blade travel, and the blade must be 90° to the base on the "0" bevel setting (except on power miter boxes, which don't bevel). Check these adjustments frequently with a reliable square *(See photo below).* Most miter saws have adjustments to compensate for out-of-square blade conditions (see the owner's manual that comes with the tool).

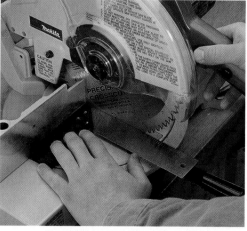

Check your saw blade with a square to make sure its line of travel is exactly perpendicular to the fence (on a compound saw, set the bevel setting to 0°). If the blade isn't perpendicular, the adjustment is usually made on the fence.

To cut with a sliding compound miter saw, pull the saw forward over the workpiece, then lower it into the front edge. Make the cut by pushing the blade carriage toward the back of the saw.

Using your power miter saw

To cut with a power miter box or a compound miter box, simply press or clamp the workpiece against the fence, then lower the blade (spinning at full speed) into the workpiece. To use a sliding compound miter saw, pull the raised blade toward you, chop down into the front edge of the workpiece, then push it back toward the fence to complete the cut *(See photo above)*. This chop and push action, the reverse of a radial arm saw, with which you pull the blade through the work, is considered a much safer procedure, with less chance of kickback, "climbing" or binding when cutting wide stock. On all saws, you can lock the head assembly at any position along the carriage to provide a straight chopping action and to keep the head from shifting when you move the saw.

Maintenance

Generally, power miter saws require the same basic maintenance as other portable power tools *(See pages 6 to 9)*. On sliding compound saws, however, watch for accumulations of sawdust and dirt on the carriage rails, which can hinder smooth sailing. Check and clean the rails on a regular basis. For slick operation, use a dry graphite or spray silicone lubricant *(See photo, right)*, rather than a petroleum-based oil or grease, which tends to attract even more sawdust and other gritty contaminants.

Cutting crown molding. For centuries, miter-cutting crown molding has been regarded as one of the most challenging cuts to be made in trim carpentry and woodworking. The profile simply does not lend itself to accurate crosscutting, and the cutting angles required are very precise. The power miter saw has greatly simplified this task. To make a miter cut with a power miter box, all you need is one simple jig. Attach a straight board about 3" wide (the fence) to a piece of plywood about 6" wide (the table). Insert the crown molding (either 45° or 38°) into the inside of the "L" formed by the table and fence, then adjust it until one beveled side is flush against the fence, and the other is flush against the table. Mark the position of the lower side onto the table, then install a thin stop at that position. The stop will hold the molding at the proper angle while you cut to your desired miter angle.

Note: Cutting crown molding can be done without the use of a jig on a compound miter saw. Some saws even come with positive stops at the required angles. Check your owner's manual for a listing of the necessary bevel and miter for each type of cut.

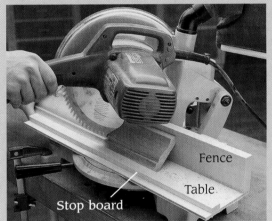

Fence

Table

Stop board

The crown molding jig shown here "re-creates" the relationship of the wall and ceiling. By positioning a piece of crown molding so the back beveled edges are flush against the surfaces of the jig, you can make a straight, accurate miter cut.

Use dry graphite or spray silicone lubricant to clean and lubricate the carriage rails on your sliding compound miter saw.

Reciprocating Saws

The reciprocating saw resides on more wish lists than it does in actual workshops. Everyone seems to want a reciprocating saw, but for some reason not too many people actually own one. If you're planning to take on a major home remodeling or renovation project, however, you'll find plenty of uses for this versatile cutting tool.

Many tradesmen know this tool as a *Sawzall* (a trademark of the Milwaukee Electric Tool Corp., which invented the tool). Called *recip saws* by most handymen, they are designed chiefly for rough-cutting when doing remodeling work. But because they are very powerful handheld saws with the potential to make cuts up to 12" deep, they can handle a number of other cutting chores no other portable power saw can manage, including cutting cast iron pipe and pruning trees. Remodeling contractors frequently rely on these tools for flush-cutting sills and framing members, which would otherwise have to be laboriously done with a handsaw. The saw also comes in handy for cutting or notching framing members, or even cutting completely through a wall, floor, ceiling, or roof.

The recip saw is also a popular tool among plumbers, electricians and heating/ventilating/air-conditioning contractors. They use it to cut pipes, conduit and duct work—and to notch framing members to accommodate them. Recip saws can also be used to make cutouts for vents, electrical boxes, and so-on. Wood turners often use these tools for roughing out large bowl blanks from green wood.

Hand grip

Blade

Blade plunger

Adjustable shoe

Trigger switch

Rear handle

Blade
cutting
direction
reversed

Frame carpentry provides many opportunities to use the recip saw. No other power saw has the ability to make quick, accurate flush cuts in framing members, like the cut being made here. To make flush cuts, many remodelers will reverse the position of the blade so the teeth are flush with the top of the saw base.

Recip saw basics

A reciprocating saw drives a saber-style blade in a back-and-forth (reciprocating) motion, much like a jig saw, except the blade motion is parallel to the tool body, rather than perpendicular to it. A recip saw is also a heavier-duty tool than a jig saw, with the capacity and power to accept longer, tougher blades. Most recip saws have a D-style handle at the back of the tool, which houses a trigger switch. On most models, the front end of the tool body is tapered down and contoured to provide a comfortable hand grip just behind the blade. In almost all cutting operations, you'll need both hands to control the tool.

The small shoe (foot plate) on the saw doesn't provide as much support as those on jig saws, but it enables you to cut in close quarters. A few low-end models have fixed shoes mounted perpendicular to the blade, but on most saws the shoe pivots up to 45° to facilitate plunge cuts and provide full support on the workpiece when you need to hold the saw at an angle. On better models, you can also move the shoe in or out to control cutting depth (adjusting the shoe inward or outward occasionally also helps distribute blade wear evenly).

As a rule, even the lowest-priced recip saws are designed for heavy contractor use—you probably won't find any "consumer" models, as you will with most portable power tools.

Cutting rough openings in walls is a very common use for the reciprocating saw. Be sure that the saw base is contacting the wall surface, and always check to make sure there are no pipes, wires or other obstructions in the cutting area.

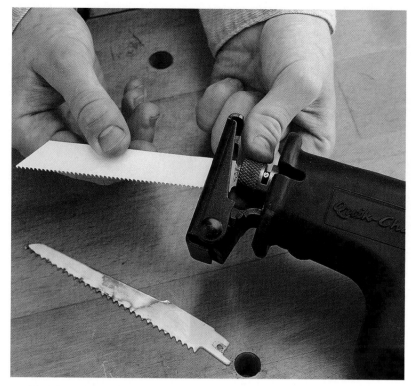

Quick-release blade change mechanisms are becoming increasingly popular on all sorts of portable power tools. On the saw shown above, the blade is secured with a tension knob mounted at the end of the blade plunger.

Power & features

The basic size and structure of reciprocating saws varies little from tool line to tool line. The greatest differences are in the amount of power and the number and types of features.

Power and speed. Because a recip saw normally uses a larger blade than a jig saw, it needs a more powerful motor. Amperages range from 4 to 8 amps. Top-end speeds average 2,400 strokes per minute (SPM). The blade stroke length also helps determine how fast the saw will cut with any given blade. Stroke lengths range from ⅝" to 1½", with 1" being the average. The longer the stroke length, the faster the cut.

With recip saws, there are two types of speed control: variable speed, and dual-range variable speed. A dual-range variable speed saw has a separate gear setting for lower and higher speeds, and the actual speed is still fully adjustable within each setting. A better saw will have electric feedback circuitry that enables the saw to maintain constant speed under load. On all types, you control the speed through the trigger switch, just like a drill or jig saw, although some models also sport a separate speed control dial to limit the top-end speed. Variable speed comes in

handy when you need to slow down the blade for cutting metals and other dense materials, or when starting a cut.

Gears and bearings. As with other portable tools, reciprocating saws with all ball-and-roller or ball-and-needle bearings will outlast those with cheaper ball-and-sleeve bearings. On most saws, the gearbox has precision-cut helical/bevel gears that include dual counterweights to reduce vibration—a problem with some earlier models.

Adjustable blade clamps. These mechanisms enable you to mount the blade upside down or sideways, or even offset it, in relation to centerline of the saw body. By doing this, you can make flush cuts in situations where the saw body would otherwise be in the way *(See photo, page 41, top).*

Adjustable orbit. A few models have an adjustable orbital feature, much like those found on many jig saws. The degree of orbit can be adjusted from "0" (straight line) to "3" (maximum orbit) for faster cutting.

Quick-release blade change. A few newer saws have a "tool-less" blade changing system that allows you to switch blades without using an allen wrench *(See photo, left).*

Recip saw blades

You'll find a variety of recip saw blades for cutting different materials—wood, nail-embedded wood, metal, stucco and plaster, fiberglass, composites, and just about any sawable material *(See photo, next page, bottom).* Tooth numbers range from 6 teeth per inch (tpi) for fast, coarse cutting of wood, up to 24 tpi for smooth cuts in hard metals. The saber-type blades come in various lengths and tooth configurations for making cuts up to 12" deep. Because they resemble jig saw blades in many ways, reading the section on jig saw blades *(pages 30 to 32)* is helpful. Generally, the cheapest general-purpose blades are made of high-alloy steel, although spring-steel and long-lasting bimetal types are also available, as well as tungsten carbide grit blades for smooth cuts in tough or abrasive materials. While jig saw blades are sold in a variety of shank styles, all recip saws sold today accept a ½"-shank universal blade.

Using a recip saw

Due to recip saw design, you'll need to keep a firm, two-handed grip at all times and keep the base or shoe planted firmly against the worksurface. Bear in mind that you're using the motorized equivalent of a hand saw or hack saw for on-site work; there is no guard protecting the moving blade, so be careful not to engage the trigger switch accidentally when you pick up the saw.

When recip saws are used to cut into weight-bearing framing members, the blade may bind partway through the cut. In such cases, you should make a start cut from one side, then complete the cut from the opposite side (much like you'd do when cutting a tree branch). When possible, use braces, props, or a temporary "wall" to release bearing pressure on framing members you're cutting.

Cutting metal and masonry. When using the saw to cut metal pipes, masonry, or other dense materials *(See photo, right)*, start slowly and bring the saw up to a speed where the blade is cutting at an appropriate pace. Excessive speeds or heavy operator pressure can easily overheat the blade, ruining it. In other words, don't force the cut. Use a blade designed for cutting these materials: in both cases, a sturdy blade with at least 18 tpi (you'll appreciate the stay-sharp capability of bimetal blades).

Fitted with an 18 tpi metal-cutting blade, recip saws make quick work of cutting pipes, tubing, conduit and even light-gauge sheet metal.

Plunge cuts. As with jig saws, you can make a plunge cut (also called a *pocket cut*) with a recip saw. The secrets are to use the shortest blade you can, to work slowly and to keep the base pressed firmly against the workpiece *(See the section on plunge cutting with a jig saw, page 33).*

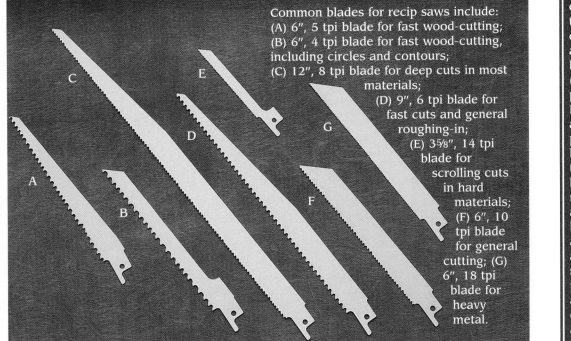

Common blades for recip saws include:
(A) 6", 5 tpi blade for fast wood-cutting;
(B) 6", 4 tpi blade for fast wood-cutting, including circles and contours;
(C) 12", 8 tpi blade for deep cuts in most materials;
(D) 9", 6 tpi blade for fast cuts and general roughing-in;
(E) 3⅝", 14 tpi blade for scrolling cuts in hard materials;
(F) 6", 10 tpi blade for general cutting; (G) 6", 18 tpi blade for heavy metal.

SAFETY TIP
Because recip saws can cut completely through a wall, floor, ceiling, or roof, pay special attention to what's on the other side of the structure you're cutting into, as well as what may be hidden inside it (electrical wires, pipes, or ductwork). In other words, take a few minutes to plan out your cuts before making them. If you have blueprints of your mechanical system, always check them before cutting into a wall. And as an added precaution, shut off electrical power in your work area and run an extension cord from a nearby circuit.

Portable Drills

In the world of power tools, the portable electric drill falls squarely at the top of the essential category. The first portable power tool to gain widespread home use, the electric drill enjoyed status as the focal point of most home workshops in the years surrounding World War II. Its popularity was boosted by a flood of attachments that, in theory anyway, could be used to convert the drill into just about any imaginable shop tool: it was used as a lathe, circular saw, drill press, sander—it even served as the power source for homemade sump pumps! Although most of these innovations never really fulfilled their promise (many were melted down for scrap metal), a few survive today in some form.

Although the drill is not the workhorse it once was, it's still one of the most versatile power tools, with applications far beyond simply drilling holes. With suitable bits, guides or jigs, you can use the drill for many specific drilling procedures, such as precise angle drilling, cabinet hardware installation, doweling, drilling pocket holes, and driving screws. Also, you can still find dozens of attachments, jigs, and fixtures for sanding, grinding, carving, shaping, buffing and polishing, routing and more.

The principal categories of electric drills are: *conventional drills, drill drivers,* and *hammer drills.* All of these are available both corded and cordless, and in a variety of sizes and body styles. There are also a number of specialty drills, like right-angle drills, that have applications mostly in the building trades.

Cordless 12-volt, pistol-grip, 3/8" variable speed drill-driver with clutch and keyless chuck.

Cordless, T-handle, 3/8" variable speed drill-driver with clutch and keyless chuck.

Corded, pistol-grip, 1/2" variable speed hammer drill with conventional chuck.

Corded, pistol-grip, 3/8" variable speed drill with keyless chuck.

Portable Drill Fact Sheet

Application	Tool Recommendation	Accessories and Bits
Light Use	Mid-priced ⅜" VSR (variable speed-reversible) corded drill (3.5 amp or higher) with conventional or keyless chuck. Cordless ⅜" VSR drill-driver (7.2 volts, 9.6 volts or higher) with adjustable clutch.	Good quality, complete set of high-speed steel (HSS) twist bits and spade bits with indexing cases. Assortment of hex-shank screwdriver bits (buy several extras in each size and type).
Moderate Use	Higher-power (4 to 6 amps) ⅜" or ½" VSR corded drill. 12-volt ⅜" VSR cordless drill.	Coated drill bit sets. Special-purpose driver bits and drill bits. Right-angle drilling guide and/or bench-mounted drill-press stand. Hole saw set.
Heavy Use	⅜" or ½" hammer drill. Right-angle drill for plumbing and electrical rough-ins. 12-volt or higher cordless drill with fast charger and extra battery pack.	Pocket-hole jig and bit. Plug cutters and full set of countersink/counterbore bits. Rasp and grinder attachments.

Drill size

Drills are sized by chuck capacity, which determines the largest diameter bit shank you can mount in the tool. Typical sizes are ¼", ⅜" and ½". Once a popular "entry-level drill," ¼" models have been dropped by most tool companies in favor of ⅜" tools that accept a wider range of bit sizes. Today, ⅜" drills represent the bulk of any toolmaker's drill offerings, having the widest range of power, features, options, and available accessories. At the top end of the scale, ½" drills are powerful, heavy-duty tools designed for drilling large holes in a variety of materials. Most are engineered for continuous daily use. Typically, ½" drills run at lower speeds but provide considerably more torque than ⅜" drills. Because of their hefty size and weight, most ½" drills are too bulky and awkward for many general drilling chores, especially when using smaller bits or working in confined spaces. The added weight can also fatigue your arms. Even so, most serious handymen eventually add a ½" drill to their portable power tool stable.

Drill types

More than any other portable power tool, drills have evolved into distinct groups for accomplishing various specialized tasks.

Conventional drills are designed primarily for drilling but can be used successfully for other procedures. With few exceptions, most have a variable speed trigger with a reversing switch—called VSR drills in many tool catalogs.

Drill-drivers operate the same way as conventional drills, with the added feature of an adjustable clutch for driving screws. Most models feature four or five clutch settings plus a lock-off setting for "drill mode." Generally, you set the clutch by means of an adjustable ring located behind the chuck. The clutch stops bit rotation at a specified torque level, which prevents the drill from "over driving" the screw or bolt, stripping the screw slot, or damaging the screwdriver bit.

Hammer drills (also called *impact drills*) combine a percussive hammering action with standard rotary motion. This combined action enables the tool to whiz through concrete and other masonry materials. A selector switch lets you switch between *hammering mode* and *straight rotary mode* for conventional drilling. Some models also feature a "hammer only" mode in which the chuck doesn't rotate, enabling you to fit the tool with chisel bits for chipping masonry, carving wood, and similar chiseling operations. Typically, hammer drills have an auxiliary handle for better control of the tool, as well as an adjustable depth stop.

TIP:

Most ⅜" drills have either single reduction or double reduction gearing: single reduction gearing offers top-end speeds at 2,000 to 2,400 rpm, while double reduction models operate at about half that speed but at a higher torque. Heavy-duty ½" drills operate at even lower speeds (450 to 900 rpm) but provide plenty of torque for driving screws, lag bolts, and the like. High-speed drills work best when you want to drill a lot of small holes in a hurry but they may bog down when you use larger diameter bits and cutters.

Miscellaneous types. There are a number of lesser-known members of the portable electric drill family, including: *right-angle drills*, used frequently by plumbers and electricians doing retrofit work; *power screwdrivers* for light-duty household use; *impact wrenches,* used mostly to loosen nuts, particularly in automotive work; and *drywall/deck drivers* that are easily set to drive and countersink drywall or deck screws to an exact depth. Investigate and acquire these tools as your needs demand it, keeping in mind that several of these specialty drills are available in air-tool version for use with your air compressor.

Portable drill basics
Speed and power.
As with other portable power tools, motor amperage is a good indication of how much power you can expect from a drill. Amperages range from 3 amps or less on low-end ¼" and ⅜" consumer models, up to about 7 amps on the most powerful ½" drills and drivers. When comparing two drills of roughly the same amperage, consider that higher-rated speed usually translates to lower torque.

Variable speed. All but the cheapest drills have variable speed triggers; on some, you can limit the top-end speed by adjusting a small dial inset into the trigger. Better drills have a dual-range variable speed feature. In effect, the tool has a two-speed transmission, operated by a separate switch: in high range, the drill has a higher top-end speed, but less torque; in low range, the gearing is reduced to provide higher torque and a lower top-end speed.

Reversibility. Practically all drills have a reversing switch to change the rotation direction of the chuck. You'll definitely need this feature for freeing jammed bits and backing out or removing screws.

Gears and bearings. As with other portable tools, drills with 100% ball-and-roller or ball-and-needle bearings will

Pistol Grip

T-Handle

outlast those with cheaper ball-and-sleeve bearings. Better drills have precision-cut, hardened alloy steel gears, rather than stamped steel gears. Most heavy-duty drills also have die-cast aluminum or steel gear housings, combined with a thick, impact-resistant plastic motor housing, while cheaper models have thinner-gauge, all-plastic bodies.

Handles. With ⅜" drills, you have two basic choices—*pistol grip* or *T-handle (See photos, left).* Traditional pistol-grip drills tend to be nose-heavy, making it harder to accurately position the bit when drilling into vertical surfaces. However, this design enables you to grip the tool higher up on the handle to apply more overhead pressure in-line with the bit.

T-handle drills have centered handles to provide better balance when starting holes (especially in cordless versions), plus a more compact design.

Larger ½" drills come in pistol-grip and D-handle versions (sometimes called *spade handles*). On D-handle models, the main handle is mounted at the back end of the drill, and a second center-mounted handle houses the trigger switch. Both styles usually come with an auxiliary removable side handle for better two-handed control.

Chucks. Most manufacturers offer both conventional (keyed) and keyless chuck versions of their most popular models. While keyless chucks offer convenience (no chuck key to keep track of), they generally don't provide the gripping power of a keyed chuck, especially when using large-diameter bits with small shanks (such as old-style spade bits). Nor is a keyless chuck a wise idea on large ½" drills or hammer drills, which are subject to excessive stress and vibration. However, the gripping power and durability of many modern keyless chucks has improved considerably over earlier versions.

POWER TOOLS BY THE NUMBERS

Cordless drill-drivers are rated by how many holes they can drill or how many screws they can drive in a specific material on a single battery charge (for example, a decent 12-volt drill-driver should be able to bore 250 ⅜"-dia. holes or drive 180 #6 × ½" wood screws in pine on one charge). Other specs may include the maximum hole size the drill can bore in wood and in steel.

Cordless drills

More than any other tool, the drill-driver can be credited for the cordless power tool revolution. Compared to other portable power tools, drills have relatively low power requirements and a basic ergonomic design that enables tool designers to stuff batteries or battery packs up into the handle (or attach them to the bottom), without sacrificing tool balance.

There is a vast selection of cordless drills and drivers on the market, from lightweight consumer models to heavy-duty ½" industrial-rated versions that nearly rival the power of their corded counterparts. Power ratings range from 3.6 to 18 volts; a 7.6- or 9.2-volt model will handle most general drilling and screwdriving operations, although you'll need at least a 12-volt tool if you expect to use the drill over extended periods of time. An extra battery pack and a 10- to 15-minute fast-charger will enable you to use the tool on a nearly continuous basis. Charging times and other instructions vary between manufacturers, so be sure to read the instructions thoroughly before charging up for the first time.

Drill bits & accessories

Although you'll find hundreds of different drill bits and accessories on the market, most fall into a few basic categories *(See photo below)*. Following are some of the more popular types:

Twist bits. These include a broad category of bits that you'll use most frequently for drilling smaller holes in a variety of materials (although they were originally designed for drilling metal exclusively). Twist bits range from ⅟64" all the way up to 1" in diameter. Typically, the hole diameter is the same as the shaft diameter. However, you can also buy "reduced shank" twist bits that enable you to drill holes larger than the drill's chuck capacity. Also, you can buy extension bits up to 28" long for special applications, such as drilling a cord hole in a wooden lamp base.

Spade bits. These are flat, relatively inexpensive general-purpose bits used for boring large holes in wood. Typical sizes range from ¼" to 1½", increasing in size in ⅟16" increments. The bits have a long point to start holes accurately, especially when you need to drill at an angle. Most of these drill fairly rough holes and often

TIP:

Most drill bits are made from high-speed steel (HSS). But their performance and longevity differ greatly, depending on the type of material used to coat and tip the bit. Most inexpensive HSS bits are coated with black oxide or chrome vanadium, but more expensive bits have a titanium nitride coating that lasts up to seven times longer. Cobalt-coated bits are used for frequent drilling of cast iron, stainless steel and other extremely hard or abrasive materials. A carbide tip will yield cleaner cuts than a plain, HSS coated bit, and will extend by as much as 50 times the useful life of the bit.

Drill bits used commonly with portable drills include: (A) twist bit, (B) brad-point bit, (C) spade bit, (D) vix bit, and (E) masonry bit.

Common bits and accessories for drill-drivers include: (A) Standard phillips-head driver (available in sizes from #2 to #8), (B) standard slotted-head driver, (C) magnetic tip holder (a useful item if you change tips frequently), (D) hooded slotted-head driver (the hood keeps the driver from slipping out of the slot), (E) socket driver with socket set, (F) hex driver (also called nut driver), (G) nail spinner.

TIP:

Most large spade bits, hole cutters, and other large drilling accessories won't operate efficiently or safely at high speeds. Generally, the larger the hole being bored, the slower the drill should run.

create splinters or leave chips on the bottom face of the wood. Better spade bits have tiny spurs at each end of the cutting edge to minimize tearout. As with twist bits, extension spade bits are available (up to 16" long) for drilling extra-deep holes or for extended reach.

Brad-point bits. These drill exceptionally clean, perfectly round holes in

A vix bit has a tapered steel tube surrounding a twist bit so you can get your screw pilot holes centered exactly inside the hardware guide holes.

wood. A small spur or brad point provides accurate hole-starting without need of a punch or awl. Common sizes range from ⅛" to ⅝", in 1/16" increments. Designed for furnituremaking, brad-point bits are often fitted with stop collars to drill holes of a precise depth for wood dowels or plugs.

Masonry bits. These bits are specially designed for drilling concrete, brick, slate, stucco, and other masonry materials. Better ones have carbide tips. Sizes range from ⅛" up to 1" in diameter for ⅜" drills, and up to 1½" in diameter for ½" drills.

Vix bits. These two-part specialty bits consist of a twist bit housed in a tapered steel tube. Used for installing hardware, the tube acts as a centerfinder for the twist bit so you can drill screw pilot holes that are perfectly aligned with the hardware you're installing *(See photo, left).*

Driver bits. An ever-increasing assortment of driver bits is becoming available as the popularity of the cordless driver grows *(See photo above).* You can find bits that will drive just about every type of fastener, including bits for phillips-head, slotted-head, square-drive, hex-head and torx screws; and socket drivers for nuts, bolts and lag screws. A special holder for finish nails, called a *nail spinner,* allows you to use brads and finish nails to drill pilot holes for small screws or nails.

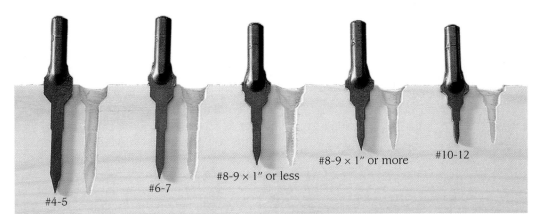

#4-5 #6-7 #8-9 × 1" or less #8-9 × 1" or more #10-12

Flat countersink/counterbore bits usually come in kits representing the most common screw sizes. The top portion of all bits bores a ⅜" hole to accept a ⅜"-dia. wood plug if you're counterboring. Always drill a pilot hole before using this type of bit—they're not designed for boring directly into the stock.

Countersink/counterbore bits.

When you need to recess screw heads or make holes for wood plugs, use a countersink/counterbore bit to cut the screw profile into your pilot hole. These bits come in many styles, including adjustable bits and bits that are designed to cut the pilot hole and the counterbore/shank hole at the same time. The most common countersink/counterbore bits are flat, shaped steel bits that usually come in sets *(See photo above)*. To use these bits, drill your pilot hole first, then go back with the countersink/counterbore bit and ream out the shank hole and counterbore hole. Standard countersink/counterbore bits are designed to drill counterbores for a ⅜"-dia. × ⅜"-deep wood plug.

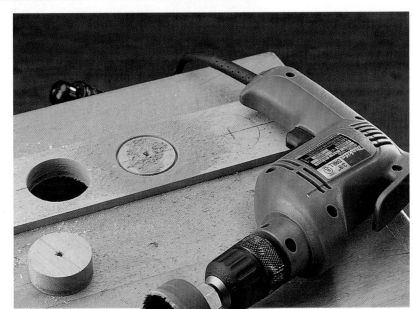

Hole saws.

Used mainly by plumbers and electricians, hole saws *(See photo above)* are installed in your drill for cutting larger-diameter holes that are too big to be handled with a spade bit. They range in size from ⅝"-dia. up to 2½"-dia. in most hole saw sets. Some industrial kits contain cutters up to 4¾" in diameter. If, like most handymen, you use hole cutters only for installing an occasional lockset or cutting holes for plumbing pipe in a 2 × 4, the lower-end sets will suit. But if you expect to use them a lot, go ahead and invest in carbide-tipped bimetal hole saws with a cutting depth of 1½".

Hole saws are used to cut large-diameter holes for such purposes as installing locksets and door handles, and running pipe or conduit through framing members. Find the centerpoint of the hole you want to cut, and use the drill bit inside the saw to drill a starter hole. Maintaining light, even pressure and keeping the drill square to the workpiece are critical to this technique.

Grinders, brushes and rasps.

You can fit portable drills with a variety of abrasive "chuck in" accessories, such as wire brushes and wheels, grinding wheels and profiled rasps *(See photo, left)*. You can also buy sanding disks and drums, flap-sanders, and polishing pads.

Grinding wheel

Wire brush

Wire wheel

Rasps

Wire wheels and brushes, grinding wheels, and rasps are a few of the abrasive accessories you can use with your portable drill. Wire wheels are used for cleaning metal or concrete, the grinding wheel can be used for tasks such as sharpening a lawn mower blade, and the rasps are available in a wide array of shapes and sizes to smooth out holes and contours.

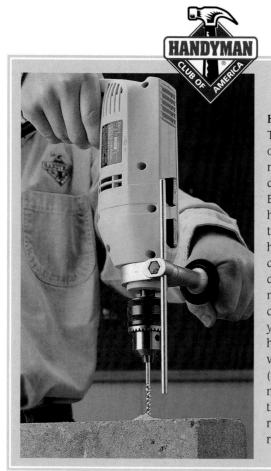

Hammer Drills:
The hammer function on a hammer drill helps makes quick work of drilling into concrete. But if you're using the hammer mode, be sure to equip the drill with a hardened tungsten-carbide masonry bit—do not use the hammer mode if you're using a conventional drill bit. If you use conventional high-speed steel bits with the hammer mode (regardless of the material you're drilling), the result will be a ragged hole and a ruined bit.

Specialty bits and cutters. Because drills perform such a simple and versatile action—spinning a spindle and chuck at high speeds—they're easily adapted to a variety of workshop chores. Here are a few of the more useful bits or jigs:

- *Reverse-thread screw extractor bits* for removing screws with stripped heads.
- *A depth-rod* for drilling holes to a precise depth *(See photo, left)*.
- *A doweling jig* for making perfectly aligned guide holes for dowel pins.
- *A pocket-hole jig (See photo below)* for making pocket joints.
- *A plug cutter* for cutting your own wood plugs (if you own a drill press, use it for plug-cutting instead).

There are also a number of noncutting drill attachments you may be able to use, including paint-mixing augers, earth augers, and flexible shaft attachments that let you use your drill as a rotary carving or grinding tool.

POWER TOOLS BY THE NUMBERS

Aside from the usual amp, speed and torque ratings, hammer drills are also rated in blows per minute (bpm). Most hammer drills will put out at least 10,000 to 20,000 bpm, which is adequate for typical concrete-drilling situations. Some drills can achieve up to 50,000 bpm for faster work. As with rpm, bpm is rated with no load.

Pocket-hole jigs allow you to drill pocket holes quickly and accurately for making pocket joints in wood. For best results, use the special drill bit, driver and screws that are usually sold along with the pocket hole jig. Pocket joints are especially handy when making face frames for cabinetry and furniture.

Bench-mounted accessories

Tool companies and after-market manufacturers offer a variety of bench-mounted stands to transform a portable drill into such items as a drill press *(See photo below)*, a disc sander, a drum sander, a mini-lathe, a bench grinder, and more. In effect, the drill serves as a motor to power these fixtures.

While such items, either manufactured or shop-made, promise increased capabilities for the tool, you shouldn't view them as perfect substitutes for the machines they imitate. Portable electric drills, with their lightweight, brush-type universal motors, aren't designed for continuous operation. For example, if you mount the drill in a bench stand, attach a sanding drum or disc, and lock the trigger in ON position, the motor will start to overheat within several minutes, possibly damaging the windings, brushes, and bearings. Also, while most of these accessories do work after a fashion, they simply don't offer the precision, power, and durability of the benchtop machines they're meant to replace.

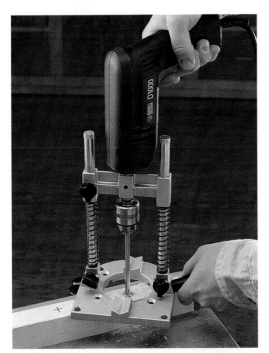

A bench-mounted drill guide converts your drill into a portable drill press. Guides can be set to bore perfectly perpendicular holes, as well as angled holes. On some models, such as the one shown above, you need to remove the drill chuck, slip the spindle through the guide, then reattach the chuck.

Using portable drills

The most important points to keep in mind when using a portable drill are to make sure the tool is square to the drilling line, and to avoid leaning in too hard as you drill—the added pressure only causes the tool to bog down or the bit to break. If your cut is going slower than you think it should, the chances are pretty good that you've got a dull bit—don't take it out on the drill.

Here are a few more tips:
• Don't use lighter-weight drills for heavy drilling tasks, like boring ½" holes in thick plate steel or concrete.
• Avoid accessories and uses that require you to keep the drill locked in the ON position for an extended time.
• If the drill becomes hot to the touch while working, give it a rest and allow the motor to cool off.
• Avoid overtightening the chuck. Keyless chucks should be hand-tightened only—don't use pliers.

Maintaining portable drills

Maintaining your drills is fairly simple, as it is with most portable power tools *(See pages 6 to 9)*. The most important point is frequently to blow out the motor to remove sawdust. Check the condition of the brushes, cord, and chuck regularly. When the chuck wears out and your bits start slipping, you can usually buy either a factory replacement from the manufacturer, or an after-market universal chuck at a hardware store or home center.

TIP:

If you need to remove your drill chuck, either to replace it or to install a drilling accessory, use penetrating lubricant to loosen the set screw that holds the drill chuck to the spindle. Open the jaws of the chuck as wide as they'll go, then insert a screwdriver with the correct head shape into the chuck and loosen the set screw.

Routers

A router is, in essence, a high-speed motor that spins sharp cutters with varying shaping profiles. For the beginning woodworker, the router can be a little intimidating at first because of its furious, high-pitched whine and aggressive cutting action. But once you get accustomed to this versatile tool, you'll become dependent on it for a multitude of tasks that no other power tool can perform as well.

Not only can routers create a variety of edge treatments, they can also be used to make many common woodworking joints, including the dovetail, mortise-and-tenon, tongue-and-groove, dado, rabbet, spline joint, and finger joint. Cutting freehand or following a template, you can use a router to shape or decorate the face of a workpiece. In addition, many woodworkers prefer to make interior cutouts or trim cuts with a router and straight bit, rather than a jig saw or circular saw, because a router can produce extremely smooth, splinter-free edges that require little or no sanding.

Dozens of jigs and fixtures are available to expand the tool's capabilities: auxiliary base plates, circle compasses, and jigs for creating or following templates are just a few of the many possibilities. And when mounted in a router table, a router can do many of the jobs of a stationary shaper, enabling you to create your own moldings and raised panels, among other things.

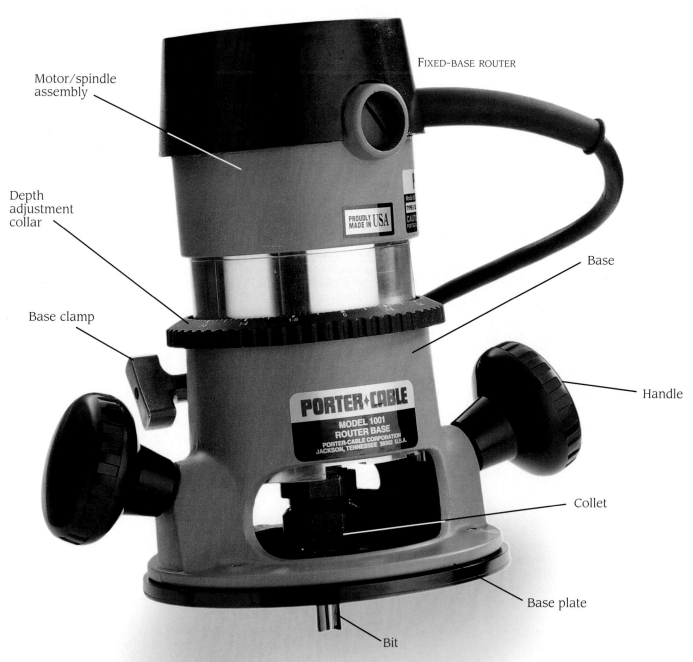

FIXED-BASE ROUTER

Motor/spindle assembly

Depth adjustment collar

Base clamp

Base

Handle

Collet

Base plate

Bit

PROUDLY MADE IN USA

PORTER·CABLE
MODEL 1001
ROUTER BASE
PORTER-CABLE CORPORATION
JACKSON, TENNESSEE 38302 U.S.A.

Router Fact Sheet		
Application	**Tool Recommendation**	**Accessories and Bits**
Light Use	Small, relatively inexpensive ¼"-collet fixed-base router with ¾ to 1 hp motor.	Edge guide. Basic assortment of high-speed steel bits. Inexpensive bench-top router table.
Moderate Use	Mid-priced ¼"- or ½"-collet, fixed-base or plunge router with variable speed control and a 1½ to 2 hp motor.	Auxiliary base plates, specialty bits, jigs and accessories as needed, guide bushings for pattern cutting.
Heavy Use	Add a ½"-collet router or plunge router with a 2½ to 3 hp motor that draws from 13 to 15 amps. Dust extraction is a useful feature on plunge routers.	Additional specialty bits, jigs and accessories as needed, floor-standing, heavy-duty router table with dedicated router.

Router types

Routers fall into two basic categories: *fixed-base routers (See photo, previous page)* and *plunge routers (See photo, right)*. Each category is further subdivided by size into ¼" and ½"-collet routers. These figures refer to the maximum bit shank diameter the tool will accept.

Fixed-base routers. This design consists of a motor/spindle assembly with a collet at one end. The assembly is secured vertically in a round base with knobs or handles for two-handed gripping. The motor/spindle assembly adjusts up or down in the base to control the depth of cut. With fixed-base routers, you adjust the cutting depth of the bit before you turn on the machine. While this poses no problems for most routing operations, it does make it harder to start cuts inside the workpiece, because you must tilt the base of the router and pivot the spinning bit down into the workpiece.

Plunge routers. On these tools, the motor/spindle assembly moves freely, straight up and down, on two metal columns. This enables you to lower and raise the bit as you cut so you can start interior cuts (such as stopped dadoes, mortises, and sign letters) with the base resting on the workpiece—a safer, more accurate way to rout. Because many router cuts are made by making a series of cuts of increasing depth, most plunge routers feature a three-to-six position revolving depth stop. You set the points on the revolving depth stop to staggered

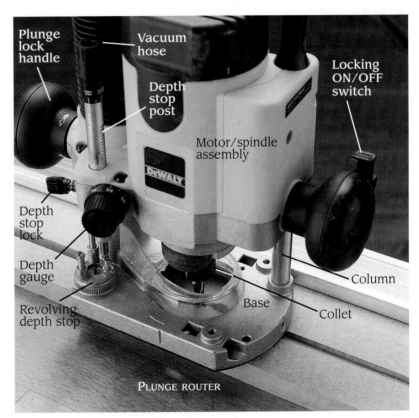

PLUNGE ROUTER

The cutting depth can be adjusted on the fly with a plunge router. This is a very useful capability when making stopped cuts and when cutting in multiple passes of increasing depth. On the model shown here, you rotate one of the handles to lock or unlock the router when making depth adjustments.

cutting depths to make a deep cut: for example, by setting the points to ¼", ½" and ¾", you can make a ¾"-deep cut in three equal passes. In addition, you can lock the motor/spindle assembly at any point on the columns to enable you to use the tool like a conventional fixed-base machine.

Router ratings

Bit capacity (collet size). A primary difference between routers is the shaft diameter of the largest bit the tool's collet will accept: either ¼" or ½" (much like the *chuck* on a drill, the collet is the locking jaw that secures the router bit). Generally, ¼" routers are smaller, more maneuverable tools, but are limited to bits with ¼" shanks. Most of the common cutting bits are available with a ¼" shank, but many of the more elaborate shaping and profiling bits are made only with a ½" shank (mostly because typical ¼" routers are not powerful enough to drive these cutters effectively). Conversely, ½" routers are larger, heavier, machines with the guts to drive larger ½" shank bits. Practically all of these come standard with collet inserts that accept ¼" bits, as well. Or in some cases, the ½" collet can be removed and replaced on the spindle with a ¼" collet *(See photo below)*. Some companies also offer collet reducers for ⅜" shank bits, although these are becoming increasingly rare on the market.

The ½" collet on bigger routers can usually be removed from the spindle and replaced with a ¼" collet if you need to use a smaller bit.

Power & size. While amperage is still considered a more meaningful measure of motor power, horsepower ratings do provide a good relative yardstick for comparing routers. The smallest routers range from ⅞ hp to 1 hp, have ¼" collets and weigh from 5 to 7 pounds, with amp ratings from 5 to 8 amps. These are good for light-duty edge routing, and provide good control for template routing and use with dovetail and other jigs. Midsized routers, from 1½ to 2 hp usually accept ¼", ⅜" and ½" collets, weigh from 7 to 10 pounds, and have 8- to 12-amp motors.

The largest routers (2½ to 3½ hp) can weigh up to 17 pounds with powerful 13 to 15-amp motors. Some of these take ½" dia. bits only. Generally, these behemoths are too horsey for intricate detail work, such as template routing or for use with many after-market jigs and fixtures. But they do come in handy if you routinely use large profile bits (such as raised panel cutters) in a router table, or need to make quite a few cuts in thick, dense materials.

Larger, high-power routers should come equipped with variable speed control. The large shaping bits they're designed to drive require cutting speeds as slow as 12,000 rpm.

Speed. Practically all routers, from the smallest to the largest, operate at high speeds—from 20,000 to 30,000 rpm. These high speeds are necessary to provide smooth, splinter-free cuts. As you might guess, those with more powerful motors are better able to maintain their top-end speed when the going gets tough. In most operations, you'll want to run the tool full tilt to achieve the smoothest cutting results. But, as with other portable power tools, variable speed is a feature that comes in handy when you need to slow things down a bit to allow better control. While not essential on smaller routers, variable speed is a must on bigger routers *(See photo above)*.

Router parts and features

The base. The base of the router is the lower housing into which the motor/spindle assembly is fitted. On fixed-base routers, it's a round collar that's secured to the motor housing with a locking knob. On plunge routers, the base is a two-piece assembly joined by a pair of steel columns. The halves of the base assembly slide apart on the columns to make cutting-depth adjustments. While most routers have a round base, some come equipped with a base that has a "flat" on one or two sides. The flat sides can ride against the edge of a straight-edge without wandering slightly, as round bases may.

The base plate. All routers have a replaceable phenolic plastic base plate (sometimes called a *subbase*), which is attached to the base with three or four flathead screws. The bit-opening holes in the base plate vary in size among different models, and are usually a good indicator of the largest bit the tool can handle. Larger openings provide better view of the cutting action, which is useful in following templates or patterns. Smaller holes provide better support when edge-routing board ends or narrow stock; some models come with base-plate inserts to reduce the hole size for such operations. On most routers, the base plates are designed to fit around template guide bushings *(See photo, page 62).*

Soft start. Better routers also have a "soft start" feature in which the motor takes a few seconds to wind up to top speed. Routers without this feature (especially more powerful models) will immediately jump to full speed with a twisting jerk, resulting in loss of control unless you have a firm grip on the tool.

Dust collection. Routers don't lend themselves to efficient dust collection, so you won't see many on the market with dust bags. However, a few plunge routers have a dust-collection port that can be hooked up to a shop vacuum hose. On these models, a clear plastic shroud around the opening in the base plate contains sawdust at the source, where it's drawn up into the vacuum hose through a hollow column *(See photo, page 53).* The collection port is attached to the top of the hollow column.

Router accessories

Any avid tool catalog reader knows that there is a never-ending parade of new router accessories offered for sale. Among the countless accessories on the market at any time (some of which are quite useful), there is a handful of well-established accessories that just about anyone can use effectively.

Edge guide. Edge guides are handy accessories for cutting grooves or dadoes without a lot of set-up time. They are basically adjustable metal mini-fences that are attached directly to the router base with steel rods. Provided the edge of the workpiece is straight, they can be used for making fairly accurate cuts *(See photo below).*

Auxiliary base plates. The base plate on your router is designed to be removed and replaced if your project demands it. Auxiliary base plates can be purchased in many sizes and shapes, or you can make your own. Most manufactured auxiliary

The tried-and-true router edge guide slides back and forth on a pair of parallel rods to set the distance of the bit from the edge of your workpiece. As long as the edge of the board is straight, they're reasonably accurate.

bases are made of ¼" or thicker clear acrylic or polycarbonate plastic to afford a clear view of the work. They often include separate handles for greater control. In many cases, the purpose of the auxiliary base is to provide additional support for the router for certain routing operations.

If you use a straightedge frequently, make your own extension base plate from a phenolic plastic, acrylic, or polycarbonate sheet. Find the center of the sheet, then trace the screw holes from your original base plate. Use a hole saw to cut an opening for the collet in the center. Use a V-bit to countersink the guide holes you drill for the screws that hold the base plate to the base.

The teardrop offset base plate increases the amount of wood surface supporting the router. These auxiliary base plates are especially useful when using piloted bits to shape the edge of your workpiece.

The circle compass is actually an auxiliary base plate that you attach directly to the router base. When using a fixed-base router, you'll need to drill a starter hole for the bit at the perimeter of the circle.

One of the most useful auxiliary bases is a *teardrop-shaped offset base plate (See photo, top right),* which helps distribute the router's weight over the workpiece when doing edge routing. The *extension base* is another type of offset base that provides additional support on two sides of the router base. Either square or triangular in shape, they come in handy for interior routing jobs, such as hollowing

out large areas where the standard base plate isn't large enough to span across the supporting edges of the stock. Square or rectangular bases make it easier to follow a straightedge. These, and other auxiliary base variations, can be purchased or made from phenolic plastic, acrylic, or polycarbonate sheets you can buy at most woodworking stores. Simply cut the sheet to the desired size, then draw diagonals to find the centerpoint. Use the original base plate as a template for marking the location for the screws that secure the base plate to the base *(See photo, top left).* Cut a hole for the collet at the center, using a hole saw. Then drill countersunk guide holes for the screws, so the screw heads can be recessed. You may need to replace the original screws with longer ones.

Circle compass. Circle compasses and trammels are similar to teardrop-shaped offset bases. Mounted to the router base, the compass is secured at the centerpoint of the circle being cut. Then the router, fitted with a straight bit, is plunged into the stock (or inserted into a starter hole) then rotated around the centerpoint, making a perfect circular cut *(See photo, below left).* In most cases, a ¼" straight bit is a good choice for circle cutting—thicker bits must remove more material.

Router pad. Many people are skeptical the first time they see a router pad in use. These pads use friction to hold a workpiece stable while it is machined (you can see one in use on the photo on page 61). Generally, thicker, solid pads that resemble carpet padding are more effective than thinner rubber mesh pads.

Pantograph. A pantograph is a carving accessory that uses a series of hinged arms to mechanically follow a pattern *(See photo, right)*. Simply place a full-size pattern (decorative or script) on a flat surface next to the workpiece. Assemble the pantograph according to the manufacturers directions. Fit the router with a thin, groove-forming bit. Lower the router into the workpiece (or into a starter hole if using a fixed-base router). Use the writing tool at the end of the pantograph arm to trace the pattern, and the router will automatically duplicate the movement of the writing tool. If you're trying this for the first time, practice on pieces of scrap wood until you get the hang of it.

The pantograph is a fairly well-known router accessory used mostly to carve words, numbers or decorative patterns. The hinged arms move the router to duplicate the movement of the writing tool as you trace a pattern.

Guide bushings. These thin metal sleeves attach to the router base plate, forming a sheath around the router bit so it can follow a template without cutting into it *(See Template routing, page 62)*.

Depth gauge. Because many router bits are beveled on the bottom edges of the cutters, precisely setting the cutting depth can be tricky. A handy solution to this problem is a depth gauge that's profiled like the bottom of a straight router bit *(See photo, left)*. Locate the proper depth setting on the gauge, press the top of the gauge up against the underside of the base plate, then lower the bit until it meets the gauge.

Other accessories. You'll find a slew of special-purpose accessories on the market. *Dovetail jigs* are perhaps the most popular of the lot. Most of these are benchtop units that align and clamp the mating boards to a dovetail template, which you use in conjunction with a template guide bushing and dovetail bit. You'll find models that make blind dovetails, through dovetails, finger joints, or all three. Jigs and accessories are available for cutting mortises, tenons, dadoes, and other joints, and even planing boards. Specialized fixtures include wood-threaders, biscuit-joiner attachments, and lathe attachments.

A depth gauge does away with the problem of trying to establish accurate cutting depth for bits that don't have a square bottom.

Router Bits

Chances are, you can find a router bit to make just about any profile you want. The vast array of router bits can be divided into two general categories: *edge-forming bits* and *groove-forming bits.* There is also a wide selection of profile-shaping and joint-cutting bits designed to be used only in a router table with a heavy-duty ½"-collet router.

Round over bit

Roman ogee bit

Edge-forming bits. As the name suggests, edge-forming bits are used to create profiles along the edge of a board. Popular styles include chamfer, rabbeting, ogee, Roman ogee, beading, slotting, cove, and panel-raising (there are many more). All edge-cutting bits require a pilot beneath (or occasionally above) the cutter that rides against the board edge to keep the bit on track. The pilot may be a simple solid extension of the bit itself, or a free-wheeling ball bearing, which significantly reduces friction that can burn the wood. Both types are available individually, or in "arbor sets," which include a single shaft or arbor, a pilot, and an assortment of interchangeable cutters.

Chamfering bit

Rabbeting bit

Groove-forming bits are nonpiloted bits used for routing the surface of a board or workpiece. Common styles include straight bits, V-groove bits, veining (core box) bits, and dovetail bits. Groove-forming bits usually work best with a plunge router.

Common router-bit materials are high-speed steel (HSS), HSS with carbide-tipped edges and solid carbide. Carbide tipped and solid carbide bits stay sharp longer than plain steel bits, and are the obvious choice for routing dense or abrasive materials, such as plastic laminates. However, they're more expensive and to sharpen them you need a diamond wheel or stone. Straight bits may be *single fluted* (one cutting edge), *double fluted* (two cutting edges), or even *triple fluted.* Multi-fluted bits produce smoother edges because they make at least twice as many cuts per revolution.

Flush-cutting bit

V-groove bit

Core box bit

Straight bit

Dovetail bit

Lightweight and inexpensive, an entry-level router table can perform many useful functions in your workshop.

Router Tables

A router table is probably the most versatile accessory you can buy or make for your router. In effect, it transforms the router into a stationary tool: sort of a mini-shaper that can be used for performing a variety of operations much more accurately and safely than doing the same work "freehand." Another advantage to router tables is that they're easy to fit with a dust collection hose to keep your shop as clean as possible.

If you're just learning to use a router table, look for one that's a good match for your current router. If you own a ¼"-collet, fixed-base router, a lightweight consumer-line router table will do fine for starters. But if you're serious about putting your router table to work, it's worth investing in a heavy-duty fixed-base router with a ½" collet, and a sturdy table with a precision fence and miter gauge. And if you're like a lot of woodworkers, you'll probably end up keeping the router permanently mounted in the router table.

If you lock the motor/spindle assembly in place on the column, you can install a plunge router in a router table, but you'll be neutralizing its best feature.

Cutting T-slots with your router

T-slots are just one of the special-purpose, but very useful, cuts your router gives you the ability to make. The bottom of a T-slot forms a wide track that accepts the head of a sliding T-bolt. When the T-bolt is installed, you can bolt the workpiece securely to just about anything—without marring the opposite face. One excellent application of this joinery method is for bolting an auxiliary fence to your table saw fence. To cut a T-slot with your router, first cut

a ⅜"-wide by ½"-deep groove in the workpiece with a ⅜" straight bit. Then, fit your router with the T-slot bit and make the "T" part of the slot that accepts the head of a T-bolt. When you're ready to fasten the workpiece to its mating part, thread the T-bolt through the mating part and attach a washer and nut.

Manufactured router tables.
Benchtop and freestanding router tables are sold at most building centers and tool stores in a wide range of quality levels and features. At the lower end are the lightweight benchtop router tables *(See photo above, left)*. Fitted with a suitable router, they can perform a number of basic operations, like cutting rabbets and dadoes. Higher-end router tables are usually floorstanding, featuring heavier construction, and enhanced accuracy *(for more information on buying router tables, see Tip, page 62).*

Cutting finger joints with a router

Anyone who's done much woodworking knows that if you need a wide part, you edge-glue two or more boards together. If you need a thick part, you face-glue boards together. But what do you do if you need a part that is longer than the stock you have on hand? The answer can be found on your router table.

Finger-joint cutters are multi-blade router/shaper bits that can be found in most woodworking catalogs and woodworking stores. Mount a finger-joint cutter into your router table router (it must be a powerful ½"-collet router). Then run the end of one board through the bit, using a pushblock pressed up against the router table fence. Be careful as you pass the throat opening in the fence—it can easily catch the front tip of the workpiece. Keep your hands well away from the cutter. Turn off the router. Set the machined board next to the cutter, then lower the cutter until the individual blades line up with the pins on the board. Lock the cutter at that height, then run the mating end of the other workpiece through the blades. The result will be a perfectly aligned finger joint. Practice this technique on some scrap before you cut any of your good stock.

Finger-joint cutter

Pushblock

Pins

End-to-end finger joints are a snap when you're using a finger-joint cutter and your trusty router table.

Homemade router tables. Custom-made router tables are among the most popular workshop building projects. Some ambitious woodworkers choose to make the entire project from scratch or by following a measured plan—you'll find plenty of router table plans in woodworking magazines and plan books.

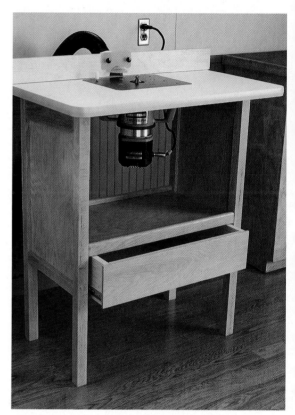

This homemade router table was built by a Handyman Club of America member, using a kit purchased from a woodworking catalog. The drawer is just the right size to store all of his router accessories.

But if you're not interested in building yourself a router table completely from scratch, and you're unable to find one to your liking in stores or catalogs, you've got one more option. A good compromise is to build a router table from a kit. Sold through the mail or at woodworking stores, router table kits usually include the table, mounting plate, fence, and leg set. Or you can buy the parts piecemeal. For example, you may want to buy the tabletop and mounting plate, then make the leg set, base, and fence to your own specifications *(See photo above)*. The table should be roughly the same height as other stationary tools.

Using your router

It would probably take the better part of a lifetime to learn and master all of the various router techniques, especially when you add in all the many jigs and accessories. Here are some basics you should know before you turn on the router for the first time:

Safety. *See Safety Tip, right.*

Setup. Before applying a router to a workpiece, first make sure that the workpiece is secure. You can use either clamps or a router pad to accomplish this (router pads have an advantage because they will not block the path of the router like a clamp will, but they can be used only with smaller workpieces). Make certain the workpiece is large and stable enough to support the router base. When using piloted bits, it's usually a good idea to position scrap boards the same thickness as the workpiece flush with each end. Otherwise, the bit will follow the corners of the workpiece.

Stance. Keep clear of the cutting path as much as you can while still maintaining firm control of the tool. Maintain an unobscured sight line to the router bit (this is why better router base plates are usually made of clear material). Always use both hands to guide the router. Draw the router toward yourself as you work. Don't ever push it forward.

Feed direction. As a general rule, you always move or "feed" the router against the bit rotation. Since the bit rotates clockwise, you should move the router from left to right as you face the front edge of the board, or counterclockwise around the perimeter of the workpiece.

Feed rate. The optimum feed rate depends on several factors: bit size and sharpness, material density, grain direction of the wood, and router speed. Moving or feeding the router too fast will result in a rougher, splintery cut; feeding it too slow will result in overheating, which can burn the bit and the stock, especially when using bits with solid pilots *(See photo, right)*.

Engaging the tool. The bit should be spinning at full speed before contacting the workpiece. If you're using a straight-edge guide, make sure the base is contacting the guide cleanly before you feed the bit into the workpiece.

When using a router, always wear ear and eye protection, and stand as far out of the line of the tool as you can, while still maintaining a clear sight line to the bit. Make sure the workpiece is secure and the router is set up correctly.

Feed rate has a great effect on the quality of a router cut. Above are example of boards cut at various feed rates.

Edge forming. This procedure can be tricky because less than half the base will be supported by the stock (the rest is hanging out over thin air); at corners, less than a quarter of the base will be supported. To compensate, you need to apply more downward pressure on the inboard side of the tool to keep it balanced. However, avoid sideways pressure against the workpiece, as this can cause overheating. Even if you're using a relatively small bit, it's best to make at least two passes; one at partial depth to remove most of the stock, then a light, final pass at full depth to "clean up" the profile.

Measure the router-bit setback every time you change bits or base plates. First, clamp a straightedge to a piece of scrap. Make a test cut with the bit and base you'll be using. Make sure the same spot on the base maintains contact with the straightedge. Remove the router, and measure from the near edge of the cut to the straightedge to find the setback.

Template routing

Template routing is the art of using patterns, or *templates,* to make decorative cuts on the face of your workpiece. If you want to attempt this craft, the first order of business will be to pick up a set of template guide bushings *(See photo below).* The bushings are used in combination with matching groove-cutting bits to follow patterns or templates. The thin-walled metal bushings form a sleeve around the router bit to keep it from cutting the template. The flat, flared end of the bushing is mounted between the base and the base plate so the cylinder extends past the base plate in an amount equal to the thickness of the workpiece.

Most router manufacturers sell template bushing kits for their tools, or you can pick up an after-market "universal" set that fits most routers. Most sets of universal bushings come with a large washer with guide holes for screws. The flat portion of the bushing is held in place between the washer and base plate.

When following any template, be aware that the actual routed surface will be slightly smaller on inside cutouts and slightly larger on outside cutouts, due to the thickness of the guide bushing. While this usually isn't critical for decorative work, it can be when using templates for hinge mortising, dovetails, or other joints. In the latter case, use only bushings supplied with the template.

Universal guide bushings are secured to the base plate with screws driven through the base plate and into guide holes in a large washer that comes with the set of bushings.

BUYING TIPS:

Shopping for a router table. Most *benchtop router tables* are designed for smaller routers. They have unitized construction, which includes the table/base assembly with universal mounting holes and plastic table inserts, adjustable fence, miter gauge, clear plastic cutter guard and separate ON/OFF switch. Better models have tilting fences that enable you to achieve a variety of profiles from one bit. Independently adjustable fence halves enable you to recess the outfeed fence to support the stock when taking "full" edge cuts. *Freestanding router tables* offer the same features, but are designed a bit differently. These usually consist of a plastic laminated MDF (medium-density fiberboard) tabletop with a cutout that accepts a removable acrylic, phenolic or polycarbonate (Lexan) mounting plate for the router, and are mounted to a leg set or base cabinet.

Interior straight cuts. To make these cuts, you'll either need a factory-supplied edge guide, or a straightedge clamped or tacked to the work to guide the router. Attaching a square or rectangular auxiliary base will further improve accuracy. To save time, use a pencil and reliable square or triangle to mark or lay out the locations of the cuts and the straightedge positions. Feed the router against the bit rotation and cut in several passes.

When routing with a straightedge guide, you'll need to know your router *setback.* The setback is the distance from the edge of the router bit to the edge of the router base that will contact the straightedge. Knowing the setback lets you position the straightedge the correct distance from your cutting line. Because the setback changes with every bit and with every auxiliary base, learn an easy measuring technique *(See photo, above).*

Using a router table. As with freehand routing, you'll be feeding against bit rotation; but this time, from right to left, because the router is upside down with the bit rotating counterclockwise. One advantage of a router table is that you can use nonpiloted (straight or groove-forming) bits in conjunction with the fence for edge routing. Also, instead of incrementally raising the bit for successive cuts, it's much easier to relocate the fence on each pass. Miter gauges provide support when routing the ends of boards.

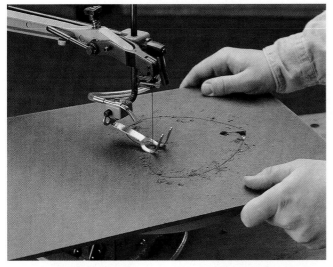
To make a template, draw your pattern onto hardboard, then cut it out with a scroll saw, jig saw or router and straight bit.

Install a bushing that's the same depth as the thickness of the template. Clamp or attach the template to the workpiece.

Cut through the workpiece until the bushing contacts the template. Then simply follow along the edge of the template.

How to make & use a router template

Step one: Make your template or pattern. For decorative work, ¼"-thick tempered hardboard is an inexpensive material to use for templates. But if you plan to use the template to produce a high volume of cuts, you're better off spending a little more and using clear acrylic—hardboard will degrade after repeated use. Draw the pattern onto the hardboard, then cut it out with a scroll saw, jig saw or router and straight bit. Remember to include the thickness of the guide bushing in your design, since the actual cutout will be smaller than the pattern by that amount.

Step two: Select the guide bushing that matches the thickness of the template—when using a ¼"-thick template, choose a bushing that will extend ¼" past the bottom of the base plate. Install a groove-cutting bit (a ¼"- to ½"-dia. straight bit is suitable for most template routing projects). Remove the router base and insert the flat end of the bushing between the base plate and the base. Reattach the base.

Step three: Clamp the template to the workpiece and secure the assembly to the worksurface. Position the template in the correct position over the workpiece, and clamp them together. You can also use spray adhesive or counterbored screws driven into the waste area of the workpiece. Clamp the assembly to your worksurface (in some cases you can use the same clamp to hold everything together).

Step four: Lower the bit so it extends past the end of the bushing. The amount will depend on the thickness and hardness of the material you're cutting—in some cases, you'll need to make multiple passes to get a clean, smooth cut. But if you're using a softwood like pine, you can usually get a good cut in a single pass—set the bit so that the distance from the bottom of the bushing to the tip of the bit is greater than the thickness of the workpiece.

Step five: Make the cutout. Start by plunging the spinning router bit into the workpiece (if you're using a fixed-base router, either plunge the router into the waste area, or drill a starter hole). Cut through the workpiece until the bushing contacts the template. Then, simply follow along the template, using the same techniques as you would when making any interior cut. If you've done careful work, you may not even need to sand the edges when you're done.

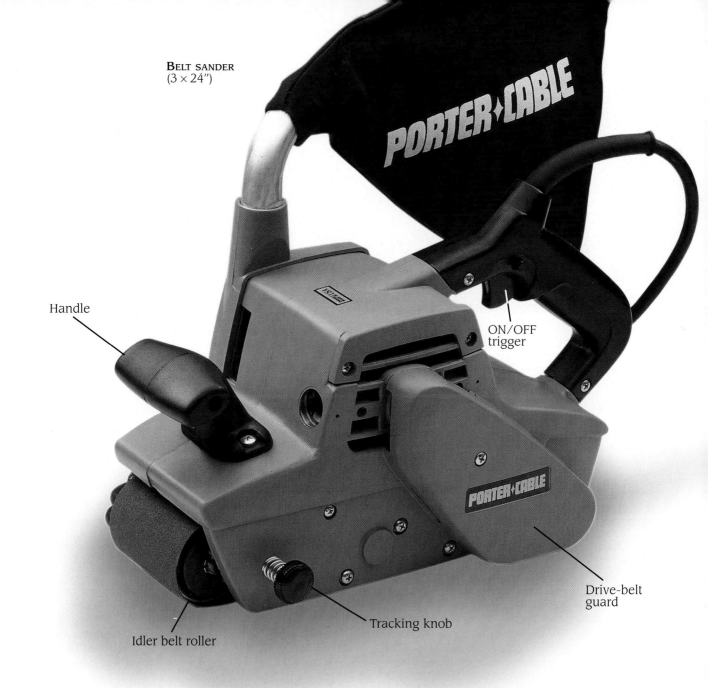

BELT SANDER
(3 × 24″)

Handle

ON/OFF trigger

Drive-belt guard

Tracking knob

Idler belt roller

Portable Sanders

It's a rare home shop that doesn't include at least one portable power sander. From belt sanders to detail sanders, these valuable tools do everything from removing multiple layers of paint, to preparing furniture to accept a finish, to shaping intricate parts so they fit together just right.

There's really no such thing as a "general purpose" sander (although the random-orbit sander comes closest). Each type of sander has one or two primary tasks that it can complete better than the rest. Typically, most do-it-yourselfers start out with just one power sander (usually a ½- or ⅓-sheet finishing

sander), and purchase additional sanders as they're faced with new tasks that demand specific power, maneuverability or sanding patterns. For example, a belt sander is the perfect tool for fast resurfacing, but it's too powerful and heavy for final finish sanding. A finishing sander, on the other hand, is designed for putting a glass-smooth surface on wood prior to applying a wood finish, but it doesn't have enough sanding area for efficient resurfacing.

Despite the many different types of power sanders available, don't expect to abandon hand-sanding entirely. Although it's viewed by many as a disagreeable chore, hand-sanding with a piece of fine sandpaper and the correct sanding block is still the most controllable form of sanding.

Sander Fact Sheet		
Application	Tool Recommendation	Accessories
Light Use	3 × 18″ or 3 × 24″ belt sander, inexpensive palm-grip finishing sander or random-orbit sander.	Coarse, medium and fine belts and papers for all sanders, sanding belt cleaning stick.
Moderate Use	Random-orbit finishing sander, detail sander (corded or cordless).	Bench-mounted stand for belt sander, wider range of papers, especially in finer grits. Buffing and polishing bonnets.
Heavy Use	4 × 24″ belt sander, high-end in-line or right-angle random orbit sander, high-end palm-grip random orbit sander or finishing sander, specialty sanders as needs dictate.	Dust collection system.

Portable sander types

Portable electric sanders fall into five basic categories: *belt sanders, random-orbit sanders, disc sanders, orbital finishing sanders* (also called *pad sanders*) and *detail sanders.* Although there may be some overlap in function, each is made to do a specific job, and do it well. All but the disc sanders are designed to sand wood; disc sanders are used primarily in automotive body work and metal fabrication applications—the cross-grain swirls left by these machines generally make them unsuitable for most woodworking and home remodeling work (for more information on air-driven disc sanders, see pages 148 to 153).

Some benchtop sanders, like the oscillating spindle sander (page 141), are light and portable enough that many people consider them portable sanders. But to be truly considered "portable," a tool needs to be designed to be applied to the workpiece (not *vice versa*).

ON/OFF switch

Sanding pad

DETAIL SANDER

Dust bag port

ON/OFF switch

RANDOM-ORBIT
FINISHING
SANDER

Dust collection box

Sanding pad

Belt Sanders

These aggressive sanding machines have a variety of uses on the jobsite, from sanding floors and rough countertops to smoothing and flattening rough, splintery boards for outdoor building projects. They also come in handy in the workshop, primarily for flattening glued-up panels that are too large to run through a surface planer or stationary belt sander.

Belt sanders basics

All belt sanders employ a continuous abrasive belt, held by the tension between two rollers (also called *drums*, *pulleys*, or *spools*). The stationary rear roller, or *drive roller,* connects to the motor with a pulley belt. The front roller, or *idler roller,* spins freely.

On the bottom of the machine, you'll find a flat metal *platen* between the two rollers. The platen provides flat-surfaced support for the sanding belt. The platen is covered with a replaceable shoe (either cork-backed stainless steel or a graphite-impregnated pad) to reduce friction.

Most belt sanders have a side-mounted knob that adjusts the *tracking* of the belt so the belt maintains correct position, centered on the rollers, as you sand *(See photo, above right).* The belt should overhang the outside ends of the rollers about 1/16". Some smaller machines have automatic tracking mechanisms.

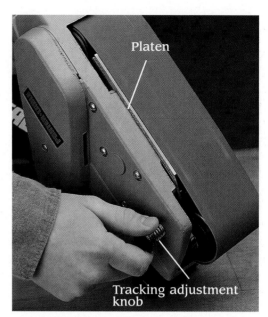

A tracking adjustment knob is used to keep the sanding belt centered on the rollers.

Size and weight. Belt sanders are "sized" by the width and overall length of the sanding belt. Common sizes include 3 × 18", 3 × 21", 3 × 24" and 4 × 24". Generally, larger sanders remove stock more quickly, although other factors, such as belt speed, platen size, and tool weight also determine sanding efficiency. Belt sanders can weigh anywhere from 5 to 16 pounds. Large, heavy sanders are less fatiguing to use on large, horizontal panels and glue-ups because the weight of the tool is usually enough to do the job. However, these same tools will quickly wear out your arms when used on vertical surfaces, and are harder to control with smaller workpieces, or when sanding the edge of a board. Many pro's and avid do-it-yourselfers own two belt sanders: a lightweight 3 × 21" model for finer work, and a 4 × 24" sander for the occasional big job. For general use, a 3 × 24" model is a good compromise.

Speed and power. Belt sanders are classified by no-load speed ratings and motor size (measurements are taken when the belt is allowed to spin freely). No-load belt speeds range from about 900 to 1,500 surface feet per minute (SFPM). The faster the speed, the faster the stock is removed. But the motor must be powerful enough to maintain the top-end speed without bogging down. In some applications, though, a belt sander can be too aggressive when running at

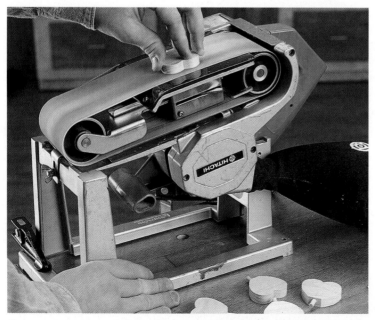

You can convert your belt sander into a stationary sanding station by mounting the sander in a bench-mounted inversion stand.

top speed. In this case, it helps to have variable speed control to slow things down, especially when sanding thin-veneered plywood, or touching up smaller workpieces with fine-grit belts.

Platen size. The platen is the base plate between the belt rollers. Larger platens put more of the belt surface in contact with the workpiece, creating more efficient sanding. In some cases, the platen surface area of a 3 × 24" sander may be nearly equal to that of a 4 × 24" sander; however the platen on a 4 × 24" sander is wider for greater stability.

Dust control. Belt sanders kick up more fine dust than any other portable power tool, so practically all models include dust-collection bags. Many sanders have an adapter so you can connect it to a shop vacuum hose.

Sanding belts

Sanding belts come in a variety of grits, labeled by standard grit numbers (from #36 to #180-grit). Generally, suppliers designate #36- to #60-grit belts as "coarse"; #80- to #100-grit belts as "medium", and #120- to #150 belts as "fine"—these categories are a little different from those used with sandpaper sheets *(See page 70)*. Better sanding belts have a sturdy, flexible cloth backing and butted seams to increase belt life and improve tracking. Pay attention to how you install the sanding belts; most are designed to run in one direction only, and have printed arrows on the backside to indicate proper mounting direction.

Accessories

In addition to a good selection of belts and a dust bag, you'll find several accessories worth owning. A bench-mounted inversion stand *(See photo previous page, bottom)* or mounting clamps enable you to use the portable belt sander as a stationary tool for sanding or shaping small parts. Many stands include a small table or fence to support the workpiece. A belt-cleaning stick *(See photo, right)* will increase belt life considerably, since most sanding belts gum up with sawdust and wood resin well before the abrasive grit wears out. To use the stick, simply rub it over the moving belt.

TIP:

When sanding the edge of a narrow board, clamp a scrap board to each side, flush with the point to which you're sanding. This provides additional stability for the tool, and leaves a good, crisp edge when the boards are removed.

Using a belt sander

Because a belt sander is an aggressive machine, you'll need to develop a firm grip, combined with a light touch to prevent sideways tipping, which can gouge the work. Also, keep the sander moving at all times, using long, even strokes. When working on large surfaces, maintain a firm, balanced, erect stance with both feet planted firmly on the ground. In short, don't overreach or put yourself in an awkward position. Also be aware of the cord location at all times. Don't bear down on the tool, as its weight alone should be enough to do the job. Bogging down the tool will slow down the cutting action, stress the tool's motor and possibly cause gouges or burn marks. When sanding a large surface, use a diagonal sanding path.

A belt cleaning stick removes compacted sawdust and resin from the belt, prolonging its useful life. With the sander running at its lowest speed setting, simply hold the stick against the spinning belt and move it from side to side. You can also use the sanding stick on other types of sanding pads.

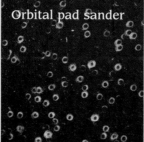

Orbital pad sander

Random-orbit sander

The shape of the sanding patterns created by orbital and random-orbit sanders is the main difference between the tools. With orbital sanders, the individual grits move in tight regular circles more likely to leave noticeable sanding marks than the sporadic, nonrepeating grit marks of the random-orbit sander.

TIP:

Don't press down too hard when sanding, especially if you're using a hook-and-loop sanding pad. If you apply too much pressure on the sander, the friction will create heat, which may "melt" the delicate plastic "hooks" on the pad, thus ruining it (this is usually more of a problem when using fine-grit papers on metals or other dense materials).

Random orbit sanders

If you were limited to owning just one portable power sander, this would be the choice. With its circular sanding pad, this tool combines the rotary action of a disc sander with the orbital action of a finishing sander to produce a virtually scratch-free finish, no matter which direction you run it—with or across the grain.

This dual sanding action makes random-orbit sanders aggressive enough for quick stock removal with coarser-grit papers, yet provides an exceptionally smooth finish when used with finer grit papers. Because these sanders provide a relatively scratch-free surface, even with coarse-grit papers, you won't need as many intermediate grits to arrive at a surface smooth enough for finishing. If you haven't used a random-orbit sander, it's definitely worth the experience. The tool will most likely change your notions on how wood should be sanded.

Random-orbit sander basics

Although random-orbit sanders come in several types, the ones used most frequently by home handymen are the palm-grip random-orbit sanders. These lightweight, compact tools work well for sanding smaller projects, from start to finish. Most have a 4½"- or 5"-dia. sanding pad.

Speed and power. As with other portable power tools, speed combined with motor amperage plays a big part in how quickly the tool will remove stock. Typically, random-orbit sanders operate on 2 to 3 amps, although some of the heavier-duty tools get into the 5-plus amperage range.

The speed at which the pad spins is usually around 1,000 rpm. Some random-orbit sanders have variable speed control, which allows you to slow down the action when sanding thin veneers, or performing delicate operations. The second speed rating is the rate at which the pad orbits, expressed in orbits-per-minute *(opm)*.

Most random-orbit sanders have a top speed from 10,000 to 12,000 opm. Both of these speed ratings can be a little misleading, since the pad quickly slows down when you apply the tool to the work.

Sanding Pads. Random-orbit sanders come with one of two pad types *(See photo below)*. Some are equipped with pressure-sensitive adhesive *(PSA)* pads that accept self-sticking sandpaper discs. Others use a hook-and-loop (Velcro®-type) fastening system. Most sanders can easily be converted to accept both types of fastening systems, simply by changing the pads. The pads are easily replaceable when they wear out.

Although hook-and-loop sanding discs are more expensive, you can easily

turer or an authorized dealer. Most sanders with a dust extraction feature will remove 70% to 80% of all the dust generated by the tool. For greater efficiency, you can install a rubber dust shroud that attaches to a shop vac hose.

Accessories

Random-orbit sanders can also be used as polishing and buffing tools. Add-on attachments include felt and lamb's wool buffing pads; sponge pads for applying waxes and rubbing compounds to

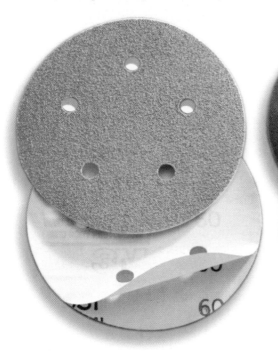

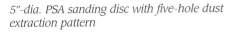

5"-dia. PSA sanding disc with five-hole dust extraction pattern

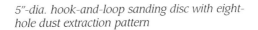

5"-dia. hook-and-loop sanding disc with eight-hole dust extraction pattern

remove and reuse them. They come in handy on small projects where you need to switch grits frequently. And because they can be reinstalled easily, you can reuse them, rather than discarding them as you must after removing PSA pads. PSA pads eventually become glazed over with dried adhesive from the discs, and must be cleaned with mineral spirits.

Dust control. On a random-orbit sander with a dust collection feature, dust is extracted though holes in the sanding pad, then sucked by the motor fan through the tool body and deposited in a dust bag or a small canister. To take advantage of this feature, you must buy sanding disks with matching hole patterns, usually directly from the manufac-

woods and metal; and nonwoven abrasive pads for cleaning and polishing, light sanding between finish coats, and even stripping paint.

Using random orbit sanders

As with other tools, it will take some practice to achieve the best results. Always start with the finest-grit paper that will do the job. Keep the pad as flat as possible when applying the tool to the work, and while sanding— tilting the tool can cause gouges. Keep the sander moving at all times, and always lift it off the work before shutting it off. When sanding along edges, always keep at least ¾ of the pad surface on the workpiece to avoid rounding over the edge.

Sandpaper.
Selecting the right sandpaper or sanding belt is at least half the battle in getting the best use from your portable electric sanders. The paper coarseness generally ranges from #36- to #600-grit.

KEY: Sample sandpapers shown include:
(A) Emery cloth
(B) #40-grit aluminum oxide
(C) #100-grit aluminum oxide
(D) #220-grit aluminum oxide
(E) #400-grit wet/dry silicone carbide

The most common abrasive materials used are garnet and aluminum oxide, although others are used (but mostly for non woodworking applications). Sandpaper is either "open coat" or "closed coat." Open-coat papers sand wood more aggressively and are less likely to clog, but the abrasive grit generally wears out faster than on closed-coat versions.

Orbital finishing sanders

Also called *pad sanders,* these tools have square or rectangular soft pads that can be fitted with conventional sheet sandpaper, or self-stick PSA (pressure-sensitive adhesive) paper. As the name implies, finishing sanders are used for final sanding with fine-grit papers. The orbital or circular action of the pad enables you to move the sander in any direction, with or across the grain, producing the same results.

Orbital finishing sanders have the advantage of using a square pad, which enables you to sand flush into corners. Also, because the sanding action is less aggressive on a finish sander, you have finer control over stock removal. And, as opposed to random-orbit sanders, finish sanders transmit much less vibration and virtually no sideways torque, significantly reducing wrist and arm fatigue.

Orbital finishing sander basics

Finishing sanders are categorized according to the size of the pad area, which is based on fractions of a standard 9 × 11" sheet of sandpaper—½ sheet, ⅓ sheet, or ¼ sheet. The actual usable surface area of the pad takes into account the amount of extra paper required to wrap around the sander base to be secured by clamps at the front and back of the base. The most popular orbital finishing sanders are the ¼-sheet sanders, also called *palm-grip* sanders or *block sanders.* They're relatively inexpensive, compact, lightweight, and are designed for one-handed use, making them perfect tools for most home handyman projects.

Speed and power. A combination of several factors determines how fast these tools will remove stock. Obviously, pad size is a major factor. Beyond that, speed and power are two major factors. Higher motor speeds, measured in orbits per minute (OPM), contribute to faster sanding, provided the motor can maintain speed under load. Most finishing sanders operate at 10,000 to 20,000 OPM. Motors on ¼-sheet palm sanders range from 1.2 to 2 amps; while ⅓- and ½-sheet sanders have motors up to 5 amps.

The most popular orbital finishing sander is the 1/4-sheet palm sander (below). The 1/3-sheet pad sander (above) can cover more surface than the palm sander, but is tougher to fit into tight spaces.

Sanding pads. Finishing sanders come with replaceable rubber or felt sanding pads. Although felt pads are cheaper to replace, they don't last as long as rubber pads. Some companies give you an option of a hard rubber pad or a soft sponge-rubber pad. Soft pads are used for fine sanding of curved or irregular surfaces; hard pads provide crisper edges on flat, squared stock.

Dust control. As with random-orbit sanders, some orbital finishing sanders have "through the pad" dust control. You match up the holes in the pad with holes punched in the sandpaper (a hole punch is often provided with the tool). The motor fan draws dust through the sander body to a dust bag or hose port.

Accessories

Other than sandpaper and replacement pads, you won't find much in the way of accessories for these tools. If you decide to go with the self-stick paper in rolls, several companies offer convenient dispensers for these. Similar to tape dispensers, you just pull out and neatly rip off the amount of paper needed.

Using finishing sanders

Do initial rough sanding with a belt sander or random-orbit sander, and use the orbital finishing sander with finer-grit paper to remove sanding marks left by other sanders, and to impart a smooth surface that's ready for finishing. A #220-grit paper is usually adequate for applying most clear finishes (lacquer, varnish, and polyurethane). Finer grits may be used when applying a penetrating oil finish or sanding between coats of other finishes.

Detail Sanders

A fairly recent addition to the family of portable power sanders, the detail sander (also called a *corner sander*) employs a small, oscillating triangular pad that will squeak into tight spots that other sanders miss *(See photo, right)*. While you may consider a detail sander to be a luxury, it will save you hours of tedious, meticulous hand-sanding. For woodworking, you can use one to sand right up to a corner, or to touch up moldings, carvings, and other curved or intricate surfaces. Around the house, you can use a detail sander for polishing, paint stripping, automotive detailing, and even for rust removal in tight spots.

Detail sander basics

All detail sanders work pretty much the same way. The triangular pad is connected at a right angle to the motor via a set of gears and an eccentric cam that creates an oscillating motion. The actual pad movement (which establishes the sanding pattern) will vary slightly from one tool to the next. No one type of movement is decidedly "better" than another when it comes to sanding efficiency or smoothness, although sanders with relatively little movement at the front tip of the pad will enable you to get farther into a right-angle corner.

Power and performance. Due to the small size of the pad, detail sanders don't require gutsy motors. Amperages range from slightly under ¼ amp on low-end models, up to about 1.5 amps on high-end machines. The advantage of a larger motor lies more in extended tool life, plus having a bit of power in reserve for the occasional tough job. Also, tools with larger motors usually have better quality gears, bearings and other components. They also run at higher speeds (measured in oscillations per minute, or orbits per minute, as the case may be), thus will remove stock more quickly.

Sanding pads. Because of the relatively small pad surface area (less than 6 square inches, in most cases), you'll often find yourself changing sandpaper frequently. Also, because most detail sanding is done with the front portion of the triangular pad, this portion will wear out first, requiring you to rotate the paper

A detail sander is an efficient tool for sanding those hard-to-reach spots that would otherwise require hand sanding.

on the pad (or the pad itself) to gain maximum use of the entire surface. Like random-orbit sanders, some detail sanders have a hook-and-loop fastening system, while others have PSA systems—a few offer both options.

Dust control. Despite their small size, detail sanders can generate enough dust that a dust control feature is worthwhile. As with random-orbit and orbital finishing sanders, some detail sanders come with "through the pad" dust collection devices that draw dust up and into a dust collection bag or canister.

3½" triangular hook-and-loop sandpaper sheet with dust extraction holes.

Accessories

When you buy a detail sander, it usually comes with a half-dozen or so abrasive sanding sheets—not nearly enough to do anything significant. So, pick up plenty of extras in each grit. Beyond paper, you'll find felt and foam polishing pads, nonwoven abrasive pads, and metal scraper attachments for removing paint splatters from windows and other surfaces.

Using detail sanders

Only a light touch is required to perform most tasks done with a detail sander. If you do bear down on the tool, you'll only reduce its sanding speed and efficiency. If you notice that the sander is overheating, stop work and give it a rest. When using a detail sander to complete a sanding job begun by another tool, try to match the sandpaper grit used on the last pass with the preceding sander.

TIP:

Attach a foam pad to the sanding pad on your detail sander, and use it to remove excess car wax or polish from around the trim strips and other hard-to-reach areas of your car.

Biscuit Joiners

Biscuit joiners (sometimes called *plate joiners*) are single-purpose tools designed to do just one thing: cut matching semicircular slots that accept football-shaped biscuits used to reinforce wood joints. If you frequently build furniture, cabinets, picture frames, bookcases and other woodworking projects, you'll find that using biscuits creates a stronger joint than using dowels or most other conventional fasteners. You can use this system to reinforce a variety of butt joints, corner joints, miter joints, edge-glued joints, and more. In addition to reinforcing joints, biscuits also give you a near-foolproof method for aligning mating parts.

Standard biscuit sizes are #0, #10 and #20 (biscuits shown actual size).

Biscuit joiner basics

A biscuit joiner consists of a small circular saw blade (about 4″ in diameter) mounted at a right angle to the motor shaft at the front of the tool. The blade is enclosed in a spring-loaded housing; plunging the tool into the workpiece exposes a portion of the blade, which cuts a semicircular slot in each of the mating wood pieces. Into each pair of slots, you glue a flat, football-shaped biscuit. The biscuit swells as the glue hardens, creating a tight, secure joint.

Reference marks on the tool face and an adjustable fence enable you to accurately locate the biscuit slots in mating surfaces. Most biscuit joiners have a three-position depth of cut adjustment that enables you to cut slots to the correct depth and length for standard-size biscuits (marked #0, #10, and #20). Some also cut deeper slots for larger biscuits and biscuit-shaped hardware (hinges and knock-down fasteners, for example). After cutting matching slots in the pieces to be joined, you glue the slightly undersized biscuits into the slots with yellow woodworker's glue.

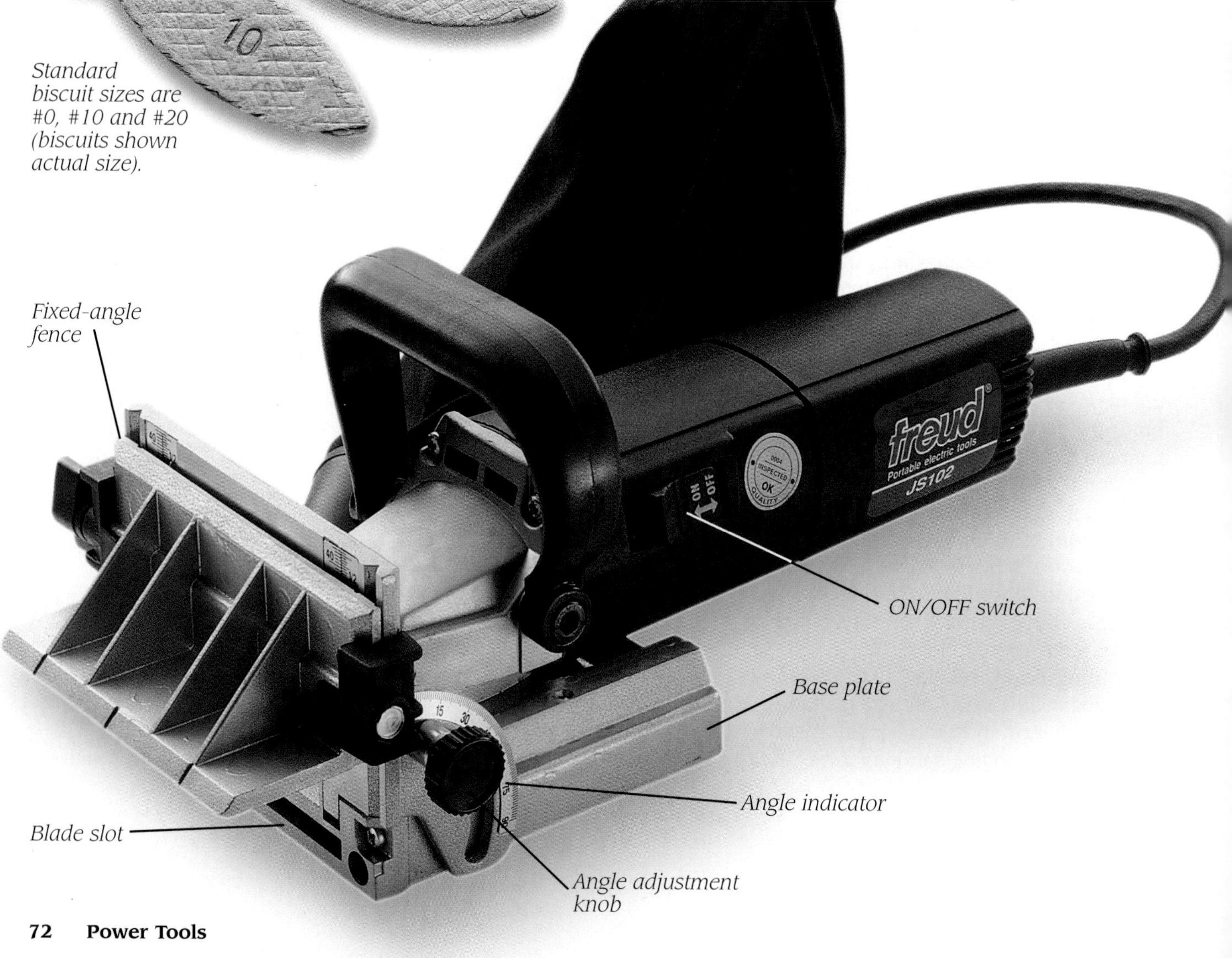

Fixed-angle fence

ON/OFF switch

Base plate

Angle indicator

Angle adjustment knob

Blade slot

Power and speed. Motor sizes on biscuit joiners range from 3.5 to 6 amps, with the average being about 5 amps. Blade speeds range from 8,000 to 12,000 rpm (the average is 10,000 rpm). Even those with the smallest motors usually have more than enough power to drive their small blades to cut slots into even the densest wood. Biscuit joiners with larger motors are designed for everyday production use. The more powerful machines are also more durable and more accurate.

Fences. The versatility, accuracy and ease of use of a biscuit joiner is a product of its fence. It's the fence that allows you to precisely locate the biscuit slots. Fences have two basic adjustments for slot location: *height and angle.* The fence height determines the vertical slot position on the edge of the board. On all joiners, the fence moves up or down in relation to the face of the tool and is locked in position with a lever, knob, or large allen screw.

Biscuit joiners have either a fixed fence or an adjustable fence for cutting slots in angled joints. Most fixed fences work on 90° and 135° angles in reference to the vertical face of the tool; the 135° setting enables you to cut slots in 45° miters by registering against the inside surface of the workpiece.

Antislip pins and pads. All biscuit joiners have some sort of antislip device to keep the joiner from slipping sideways as the circular blade completes the cut. On many joiners, these consist of rubber knobs or pointed, spring-loaded metal pins on each side of the blade slot to grip the work. Better models employ a "full-face" rubber pad to prevent sideways slippage. This style is best for gripping pieces that are too narrow to be captured by knobs or pins.

Dust collection. Even though biscuit joining doesn't create as much sawdust as some other power tools, most models come equipped with a dust bag. On large jobs, the bag will fill up rather quickly.

Blades

All biscuit joiners come with a 4"-dia., 6- or 12-tooth carbide-tipped blade. The 12-tooth blades are more expensive, but make a smoother cut. Several companies also offer antikickback or "chip limiting" blades; these have shoulders behind the cutting edges that prevent overfeeding by slowing down the cutting action. This feature is primarily a safety consideration to help keep the blade from jamming or kicking out of the cut.

Biscuits

Most biscuit joiners cut slots for three standard biscuit sizes: #0 (3⁄8 × 1¼"), #10 (3⁄4 × 2⅛") and #20 (1 × 2⅜"). The biscuits are made of compressed wood. When they come in contact with the wet glue, they swell up in the slots to make a strong, tight joint. Biscuits are generally sold in standard packages of 250 or 1,000. You can also buy temporary plastic clamping biscuits that are inserted into the joint without glue to aid in alignment. These clear plastic biscuits are used mostly for installing countertops.

1. Mark mating parts across joint.

2. Cut slots at reference points.

3. Glue in biscuit and make joint.

Using biscuit joiners

You don't need to go through complicated layout procedures to use a biscuit joiner. The following sequence shows the basic procedure used to make a biscuit-reinforced butt joint.

1. *Dry-fit the pieces to be joined. Find the center of the biscuit location and draw a simple pencil line across the joint to mark both pieces.*

2. *Separate the pieces and secure each to the bench. Set the depth of cut for the biscuit size you're using. The fence height should center the biscuit slot on the side of the board. Hold the joiner with one hand on the handle and the other on the joiner body, then press the face of the joiner lightly against the workpiece, aligning the center reference mark on the joiner face with the layout line on the stock. Switch on the motor, then push the spring-loaded body forward so the blade enters the workpiece. When the cut is complete, the blade will automatically retract when you release pressure.*

3. *After slotting both pieces, squeeze glue into each slot, insert a biscuit, and immediately join the pieces. Make any final adjustments in alignment, then apply the appropriate clamping device. Clean off any glue squeeze-out in the joint. Because the biscuits will quickly swell to lock the joint, clamping time should take only 10 to 15 minutes, in most cases.*

Stationary Power Tools

Equipped with precise guides and fences and a cutting tool that stays in one place, stationary tools have a great advantage over portable tools in both accuracy and power. It's with these tools that you make the step from general *do-it-yourselfer* to *woodworker*.

There are about a half-dozen stationary power tools common to most woodworkers. At the head of the list is the table saw—the focal point of most workshops today. The drill press is not too far behind, mostly because it's function is so radically different form the table saw's. Despite declining popularity, the radial arm saw is still a very common tool in many workshops. A stationary sander is a welcome addition to any shop for its many abilities, including precise shaping of small parts.

After the table saw and the radial arm saw, the band saw is perhaps the most popular stationary saw, particularly among woodworkers who enjoy preparing their own stock. In that vein, the jointer and power planer are also key tools for getting rough stock dressed for use in furnituremaking.

If your interest in detailed woodcrafting takes off, you'll want to add a scroll saw to your tool collection. And for a completely different direction in woodworking, look toward the lathe and its unique capabilities. Anyone who owns a fair number of tools will need a bench grinder or a sharpening center to keep blade edges sharp.

Benchtop vs. floorstanding tools

Almost every stationary power tool is available in two sizes: benchtop and floorstanding. On some tools, such as the drill press, the only real difference between the types is in the height of the tool. The power numbers are often indistinguishable. But with other tools, such as the band saw, the benchtop versions are typically less powerful and are limited in the types of tasks they can perform. Regardless, many handymen appreciate benchtop tools because they don't need dedicated space on the shop floor—not to mention their price tags, which are usually a good deal lower then floorstanding tools.

TIP:

Combination tools

For those of us who are fascinated by clever, efficient design, combination power tools have an intriguing appeal. Just about everyone has run across them at some time, perhaps at a woodworking show or even in a kiosk in the common area of your local shopping mall. At first glance, these clever multi-function tools appear to be a gangly blur of polished steel rails and pivot housings. But in actuality, most of them are quite sturdy. The combination of tools varies among machines. One popular combo is a table saw, drill press, lathe, and sander/grinder—all driven by the same motor. Although each separate tool is normally a little less powerful than its single-purpose counterpart, in total the combination tool can pack quite a punch.

Table Saws

Acquiring a table saw is a milestone event for any handyman. In most workshops it's the first power tool to represent a major investment of money and space. And more than that, it signals a strong commitment to the do-it-yourself and woodworking crafts.

Accuracy, speed and versatility are the primary benefits of a table saw. It can make crosscuts, rip cuts, miter-cuts and bevel-cuts with only the most basic guides—a miter gauge and a rip fence. The more advanced woodworker can make dadoes, tapers, profile cuts and even cove cuts with the correct guide, jig, blade or cutter.

From humble origins as a homemade tool that was usually rigged up by industrious, mechanically inclined craftsmen, the table saw has evolved to become the focal point of most modern workshops. In the process, it's become more compact, more powerful, and much safer to use than in the past. One primary improvement to become standardized over the years is the table itself. It wasn't too many years ago that the motor and blade were fixed, and adjustments to the cutting depth or angle were made by moving the table.

A few tilting-table saws survive today, but most manufacturers have converted exclusively to models where the table remains fixed and the height and angle of the blade are adjusted. Vast differences still remain between table saws, but from the lowliest benchtop table saw to the most exalted cabinet saw, the basic features and techniques are remarkably similar.

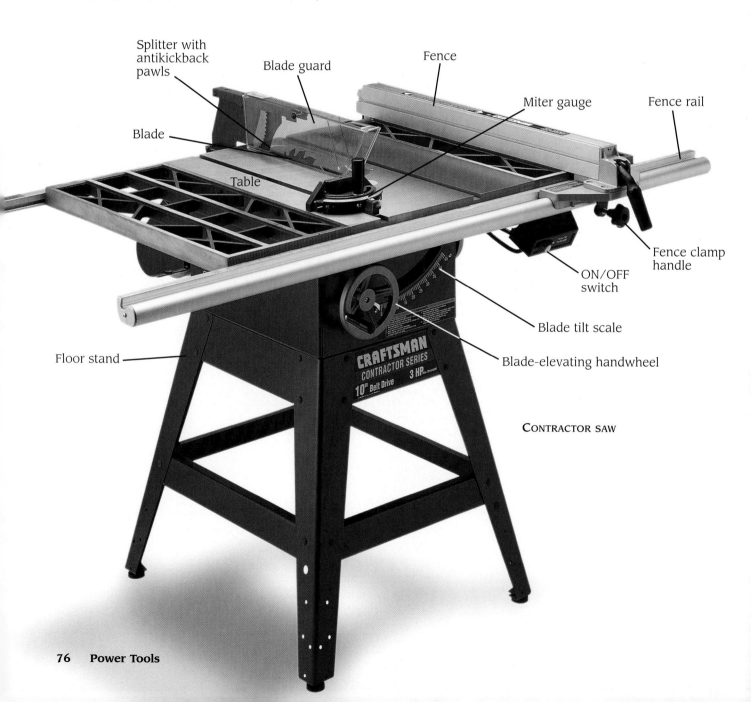

Splitter with antikickback pawls

Blade guard

Fence

Miter gauge

Fence rail

Blade

Table

Fence clamp handle

ON/OFF switch

Blade tilt scale

Floor stand

Blade-elevating handwheel

CRAFTSMAN
CONTRACTOR SERIES
10" Belt Drive   3 HP

CONTRACTOR SAW

Table Saw Fact Sheet

Application	Tool Recommendation	Accessories
Light Use	10" benchtop model with 2½ hp, 12- to 15-amp motor, sliding miter gauge, lockable fence, adjustable arbor tilt, and clear blade guard with splitter.	Set-up table; vacuum for dust collection; sturdy base that can be clamped to worksurface; outfeed rollers; push sticks, featherboards, hold-downs.
Moderate Use	Contractor's saw with 2- to 3-hp, 15- to18-amp motor (8- to 10-amps at 230-volt service), cast-iron table with extension rails; auxiliary fence; 4"-dia. dust collection port; keyed switch; single belt-drive motor; handwheel depth and cutting angle adjustment; T-slot miter gauge grooves.	Hold-down clamp for miter gauge; dado-blade set; table extension; dust collector with 4"-dia. hose; taper cutting jig; auxiliary table inserts.
Heavy Use	Cabinet saw with 2- to 3-hp motor running on 230-volt service, enclosed cabinet; belt-drive motor with 2 or 3 belts, table extension wings, precision rip fence and miter gauge.	Side-mount, overarm blade guard; tenoning jig; molding head with variety of cutters; hold-down rollers for rip fence; dial indicator for fine tuning; sliding table.

Table saw types

There are three primary table saw types: the *benchtop table saw,* the *contractor's saw,* and the *cabinet table saw.* Generally, the size and accuracy increase as you move up the ladder from benchtop saws to state-of-the-art cabinet saws. But there are many other factors to consider when judging table saws: a sturdy, well-made benchtop saw may be more accurate or even more powerful than an entry-level contractor's saw.

Benchtop table saws. Typically, the most inexpensive table saw is the benchtop type, which is lightweight, portable and usually comparable to a professional-quality circular saw in power. Even if you already own a stationary table saw, you may want to consider purchasing a benchtop saw simply because of its portability. Clamped or screwed to a stable worksurface, it brings the advantages of a home workshop right to the jobsite. When mounted in a sheet of plywood that serves as an auxiliary table, it can be used to cut down sheet goods to more manageable sizes.

Benchtop table saws bring most of the advantages of a full-size table saw right to the jobsite. The model shown here weighs less than 40 pounds. Be sure to clamp or bolt your benchtop saw to a secure worksurface before operating it.

The main drawback to benchtop saws is that they're generally less accurate and less powerful than stationary saws. The table on a benchtop saw is usually made from pressed aluminum or another lightweight alloy that is more prone to warping than the milled steel tables found on most stationary table saws. The smaller size of the table is also a disadvantage when it comes to accuracy,

mostly because the smaller tables are equipped with lighter, flimsier rip fences and miter gauges that cannot effectively be micro-adjusted for highly accurate work. And because the blade is turned directly by the motor, not by a drive belt, the benchtop saw vibrates more, which can cause the blade to wander.

Because most benchtop saws are equipped with a 10"-dia. blade, the cutting capacity is comparable to that of a stationary table saw.

Contractor's saws. The contractor's saw is by far the most common type of table saw. With a full-sized table and precision-ground slots for the miter gauge, these saws can be tuned for extreme accuracy. They can also be fitted with a very precise after-market rip fence, although the stock rip fence provided with the saw is perfectly suitable for most purposes.

Contractor's saws are stationary tools, featuring an *arbor* (the spindle turned by the motor and connected to the blade) driven by a single V-belt. However, they're called *contractor's saws* because they can be disassembled and moved (with some effort) for set-up on the jobsite. Most contractor's saws operate on 115 volts and draw from 12 to 18

amps. However, some can be converted easily to 230-volt power for efficient operation that causes less heat buildup in the motor. The size of the table, the fence quality, and the power of the motor are the main variables among contractor's saws. For most users, an average-sized table of about 27 × 40" and a 1½ hp motor are more than adequate.

Cabinet saw. At first glance, the cabinet saw is almost indistinguishable from the contractor's saw—the table is generally a little larger, but the standard-issue fence and guard are usually quite similar to those found on a contractor's saw. Inside, however, in the base and power transmission, the great advantage of the cabinet saw becomes apparent.

The enclosed base of a cabinet saw is quite stable. The interior of the cabinet can be used to collect sawdust if you don't have a dust-removal system. The motor (almost always 230-volt) is located inside the cabinet and has two or three V-belts that drive the arbor in nearly vibration-free power. Because cabinet saws aren't moved frequently, many owners add table extensions and a large auxiliary rip fence. You can expect to pay at least twice as much for a cabinet saw than for a contractor's saw, however.

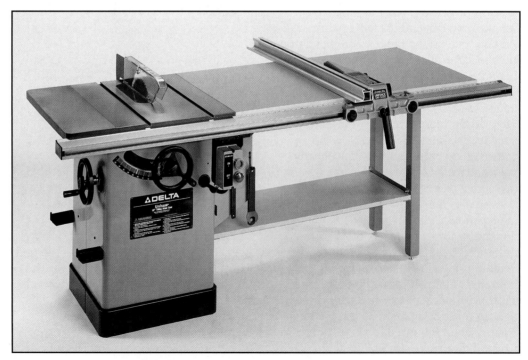

The cabinet saw is a top-of-the-line stationary power tool favored by advanced woodworkers and professional cabinetmakers.

Tuning your table saw

Check the various alignment relationships on your table saw regularly. Especially if you change blades frequently or move your saw around the shop, you should pay close attention to the relationships between the blade arbor, miter gauge slots and rip fence. You should also check to make sure the table is even, the throat plate covering the blade opening is at the correct height, and that all gauges and scales are accurately adjusted.

Check for parallels. The accuracy of your table saw depends on a parallel relationship between the blade, the miter gauge slots and the rip fence. The variable in this relationship is the position of the arbor (the part of the saw to which the blade is attached). It doesn't happen often, but if the arbor falls out of alignment, then any other tuning procedures you attempt will be ineffective.

Test the arbor. To check if the arbor is square to the table, set the handle of a combination square in the miter slot and adjust the blade so the end just touches the tooth closest to the infeed side of the saw. Then, rotate the blade by hand until the same tooth is at the point farthest from the infeed side. Slide the square along the miter slot until the blade touches the tooth *(See photo, above right).* If the blade doesn't meet the tooth precisely as it did before you spun it, then the blade is not parallel to the slot (with this test, as with any, you should perform it more than once to make sure your readings are accurate). *Note: Before you get too involved trying to correct the arbor alignment, try re-testing with a different blade—the alignment problem could be as simple as a warped saw blade.*

The probable cause of the arbor being out of square, however, is a misalignment of the parts that support the arbor: the *trunnions* and the *cradle*. A front and rear trunnion are bolted to the underside of the table. Each contains a semicircular slot that houses one end of the cradle—the part that supports the saw arbor. When you adjust the bevel angle of the blade, the cradle pivots in the trunnion slots. If one or both of the trunnions are out of alignment, the cradle (and hence the blade) will be out of square with the

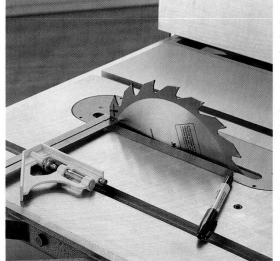

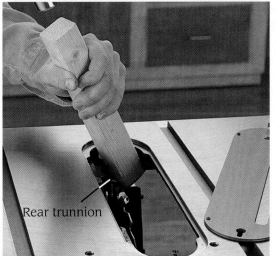

Rear trunnion

Top photo. Test to see if the arbor is square to the table slots by measuring the distance from the same blade tooth to the slot at two or more points. Mark one tooth with a marker to keep track of it, then measure the distance from the slot to the tooth at the front. Rotate the blade and measure the distance at the back. If the distances are identical, the arbor is square to the table slot.

Bottom photo. If the arbor is not precisely parallel to the miter slots in the table, loosen the bolts that hold the trunnions to the table and rap the trunnion with a wood scrap until the trunnions and cradle are positioned so the arbor is square to the miter slots.

table. To correct the problem, simply loosen the bolts that hold the trunnion to the table *slightly*, then rap on the trunnion with a wood block until it's back in line *(See photo above),* then secure the bolts.

Check the miter gauge. Once the miter slots are parallel to the blade, insert the miter gauge into a slot and check with a square to make sure the gauge is exactly 90° to the blade. Reset the head of the miter gauge if necessary.

Check the rip fence. Next, check to make sure the rip fence is parallel to the miter slots. This test should be performed each time you adjust the position of the rip fence. To make the test as quick and easy as possible, use a board the same thickness as the miter slot (usually ¾"). Clamp the fence in position, then slip the board into the miter slot. Use a try square to make sure the board is perfectly

Slip a ¾"-wide board into the miter slot (it should be a good tight fit) and measure the distance to the rip fence at several points. If the distances are off, unclamp then reset the rip fence.

upright in the slot. Then, measure from the board to the rip fence in several spots *(See photo above).* If the measurements are not identical, loosen the fence, adjust it as needed, and clamp it back down.

Check the table. Once in a while, you should check the table itself to make sure it hasn't warped. This is especially important when your saw is new. Like wood, steel can move or warp as it cures. To check the table, remove the fence and lower the blade below table level. Then

Use a long straightedge to check the table surface for dips or crowns. Brand-new saws are the most likely to develop warps or other forms of unevenness.

pass a long straightedge over the table in many spots, checking for any valleys or crowns *(See photo below).* If you find significant unevenness, check your warranty: you may be able to get a replacement table from the manufacturer. If your saw is not under warranty, your options aren't very appealing. You can get the table ground back to level at a machine shop, but that can be fairly expensive. A cheaper (but less effective) alternative is to use polymer-based floor leveling compound (epoxy-based is best) to fill in any dips. Sand the filler with fine sandpaper.

Adjust the throat plate. The throat plate covers the oval-shaped opening in the table where the blade is inserted. The plate should be adjusted so it's very

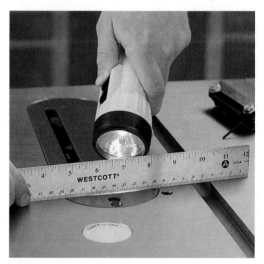

Shine a flashlight between the throat plate and a steel rule to check fpr small gaps. The throat plate should be slightly below the table surface in front, and slightly above it in back.

slightly below the table surface at the infeed end and very slightly above the surface at the outfeed end—the difference in height should be about the thickness of a sheet of copier paper.

To check the height of the throat plate, set a steel rule so it spans the plate and the throat opening, then shine a flashlight from behind the rule. In front, you should see a thin band of light between the rule and the plate *(See photo above).* In back, you should see light between the rule and the table (on both sides of the throat plate). On most saws, the throat plate is adjusted with set screws that are tightened with an allen wrench. Adjust the plate as needed.

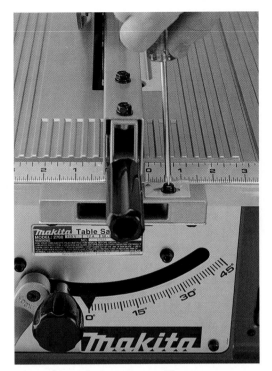

The scales and gauges on a table saw are designed so they can be reset to match the actual readings of the machine. For example, if the rip fence distance indicator says the fence is ¼" away from the blade when it's actually flush against the blade, leave the fence flush against the blade, loosen the indicator screw and reset the indicator to the zero point.

Check gauges & scales. Most table saws have preset gauges and scales that indicate blade tilt for bevel-cutting, the distance of the rip fence from the blade, and blade height (cutting depth). Even when they are set accurately, use the gauges and scales only for rough positioning. Most gauges and scales are constructed so they can be reset to the actual positions of the saw *(See photo above)*. To make sure these items are set correctly, use reliable measuring devices to set the blade or fence to the desired setting, then adjust the gauge or scale, if needed, to match. When setting the blade tilt, be sure to test the blade angle at several settings, using a protractor. And always make a test cut in a piece of scrap to confirm that the angle is correct before you cut your actual workpiece.

Blade guard & splitter. Modern table saws are always equipped with a factory-installed blade guard for your safety. Whenever possible, leave the guard in place while cutting. The guard itself

doesn't require much tuning, other than to make sure it's securely fastened to the saw. But most blade guards include a splitter that needs occasional adjusting. The splitter is a metal blade in the center of the guard that is aligned with the saw blade. When the workpiece comes in contact with the guard, a properly adjusted splitter fits into the saw kerf as the workpiece is fed through the saw blade. This helps keep the workpiece from binding on the blade if the saw kerf closes up. Before operating the table saw, use a straightedge to make sure the splitter is aligned with the saw blade. Also, use a try square to make sure the splitter is exactly vertical *(See photo above)*. And check to make sure the antikickback pawls on each side of the splitter have a minimal amount of play from side to side but are still able to move freely back and forth.

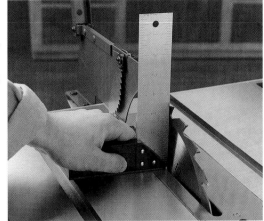

Use a try square to make sure the saw blade is exactly vertical when the tilt gauge is set at zero. Make sure the square is pressing cleanly against the body of the blade, away from the tips of the teeth.

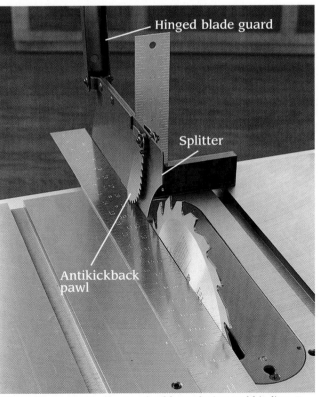

Hinged blade guard

Splitter

Antikickback pawl

The splitter prevents the saw kerf from closing and binding. It should be vertical and aligned exactly with the saw blade—check with a square to make sure it's correct.

Table saw blades

Once your table saw is tuned up and ready to go, direct your attention to the blade. If the blade is dull or inappropriate for the type of cut you're making, even the most powerful saws on the market can bog down or make overly rough cuts. Most of the basic information that applies to choosing blades for your table saw applies to all saws that use a circular blade *(See page 21 in the circular saw chapter).* But because table saws can be used to make such a wide variety of cuts and in many different material, blade selection is of particular importance.

Choosing the best saw blade for a particular job is becoming more and more complicated—as anyone who's browsed through a tool catalog lately can tell you. An increasingly competitive marketplace brings innovations in blade technology every year. Carbide-tipped blades, for example, are now available in at least four very different styles designed for specific purposes: triple-chip grind, alternate top bevel (with or without straight

raker blades), and flat-top ground. Many blades now have an antikickback feature—an unsharpened nub pointing in the opposite direction of the tooth. You can buy teflon-coated blades, thin-kerf blades, hollow-ground blades, abrasive blades, negative hook angle blades, extra-deep gullet blades . . . the list is seemingly endless.

Many of the innovations in blade design are worthy of serious consideration. But don't get hung up on it. The fact is, as long as the blade is sharp, clean and reasonably well-suited for the task you're asking it to do, it will be fine. For a short list of the most basic blade types you should probably own for your table saw, see the *Tip* to the left.

If you decide to add a hollow-ground blade to your collection (and you probably should), look into getting a set of *blade stabilizers* to use with it. Blade stabilizers are heavy washer-like pieces of hardware about 4" in diameter. They sandwich the blade on each side where it is attached to the arbor, helping to prevent wobbling and runout, especially on thin-bodied blades *(See photo below).*

Replacing blades. To remove or install a blade on your table saw, first raise the blade to full height. Next, set the teeth of the blade against a block of wood to keep the blade from moving *(See photo, left).* Then, loosen the arbor bolt and remove the blade. Keep an eye on the washers—they're very easy to lose.

Use a wood scrap to prevent the saw blade from moving while you loosen or tighten the arbor bolt that secures the blade to the arbor.

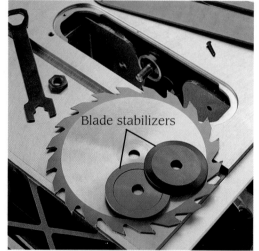

Blade stabilizers

Blade stabilizers give some extra body to thin blades, like this hollow-ground blade, making them less likely to wobble or run out when used.

Auxiliary fences & tables

While there is almost no limit to the jobs you can do with a table saw using only the equipment provided by the factory, most saw owners assemble an arsenal of auxiliary tables and fences that make different operations faster, more accurate, and safer. Some auxiliary tables or fences also help protect the saw, extending its life and minimizing repairs and upkeep.

Auxiliary fences. No matter how carefully you work, the rip fence on a table saw is right in the line of fire where nicks and gouges are almost inevitable. Unfortunately, most fences do not withstand blade contact well. And in addition, their low profile makes them almost useless for clamping featherboards and other accessories. That's why anyone who's been around a table saw for a while usually ends up making an auxiliary fence.

With a wooden auxiliary fence (hard maple is a good choice for this job), you'll spend a lot less time replacing or repairing the metal or nylon sides of your rip fence. In fact, some rip fences are designed with an auxiliary fence in mind.

A board attached to the head of your miter gauge works as an extension, creating a more stable surface for controlling your workpiece as you crosscut it on the table saw.

A homemade auxiliary fence is much easier to repair or replace than the factory side of your rip fence if blade contact occurs. Use hard maple to make the auxiliary fence, and make sure it's held in place securely and that no fasteners are exposed on the blade side.

In the model shown here *(See photo, left)* screws are driven into the back face of the auxiliary fence, then the screw heads are fitted into the T-slot in the rip fence. If you make your auxiliary fence so it's an inch or two higher than the original fence, the upper edge will create a good spot for clamping stopblocks, featherboards and jigs.

You can also make an auxiliary fence for your miter gauge. Most miter gauges have guide holes for screws so you can attach a board to the miter gauge before using it to guide wide workpieces *(See photo above)*. This miter gauge extension gives the workpiece added stability for crosscutting. You can also clamp your workpiece to an auxiliary miter gauge, which increases both the safety and the accuracy of crosscutting or miter-cutting on the table saw.

Molding Heads

If you do quite a bit of finish carpentry or are interested in making custom millwork, look into getting a *molding head* with profile blades for your table saw. Functioning like a shaper, the table saw version is a very aggressive profiling tool that can make quick work of heavier stock. The molding head is a metal hub with three slots that accept interchangeable cutting blades. The blades vary according to the profile being cut. Common uses for the molding head are making decorative edge profiles, cutting grooves or veins in the face of a workpiece, and some advanced types of wood joinery.

When using a molding head, make sure the set screws (called *gibs*) that hold the blades are securely fastened, then remove the throat plate and mount the molding head on your saw arbor. Because it would be difficult to find custom throat plates (and working without one is very dangerous) it's a common practice to make your own throat plate from a piece of ¼"-thick plywood. First, lower the cutter below the surface of the table. Then, position the plywood over the saw throat, flush against the rip fence. Clamp a board to the fence, pressing down on the plywood (this board will become your auxiliary fence). Turn on the saw and slowly raise the cutter up until it breaks all the way through the stock *(See photo below)*. Also allow the cutter to partially cut out the auxiliary fence so the cutter is recessed slightly in the fence.

Adjust the fence to make a cut of the correct width, then feed your workpiece past the cutter, using a pushstick and hold-down. **CAUTION: This procedure requires that the blade guard be removed. Use extreme care.**

The shape of the interchangeable molding head blades determines the profile you can cut. Here, a sampling of shapes is shown. In use, the molding head is fitted with three blades that all have the same shape.

Molding head

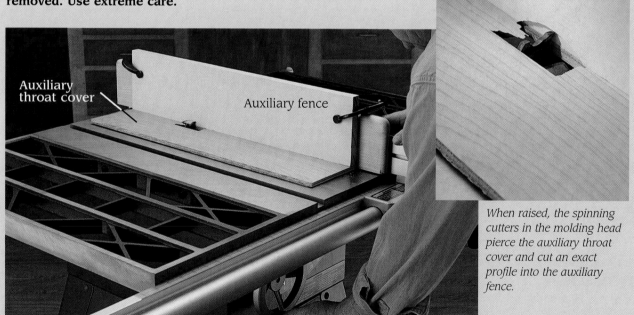

Auxiliary throat cover

Auxiliary fence

When raised, the spinning cutters in the molding head pierce the auxiliary throat cover and cut an exact profile into the auxiliary fence.

Held in place by an auxiliary fence, the auxiliary throat cover provides protection for you and a sturdy guide surface for your workpiece as you shape it with the molding head.

Auxiliary tables. If you do a lot of panel cutting or tend to crosscut longer stock, you'll probably want to look into getting a table extension for your saw. Contractor's saws and cabinet saws usually can be fitted with manufactured table extensions attached to the rails at the front and back edges of the table. Cabinet saws, in particular, are well designed for accepting long table extensions to support sheet goods. But for most people, the easier solution is simply to position your saw next to a work-surface that's the same height as your saw table. Or you can use one or more auxiliary work supports, like the roller type shown on page 87.

Larger saws can be equipped with sliding tables that support the workpiece and move along with it as it's fed into the blade. Sliding tables are very useful for panel cutting. Another form of auxiliary table is the special-purpose table that's really more of a customized throat cover than a table. When working with unusual blades or cutters, or with very thin stock, you can make a special-purpose table by carefully raising a specialty blade or cutter up into a piece of 1/4" plywood (See Advanced Workshop Tip, left).

Accessories

There is an everchanging array of table saw accessories available for sale at woodworking stores. Some are tried-and-true classics, and others are fly-by-night gimmicks that disappear quickly. In addition to the commercially made saw accessories, you can find book after book packed full of plans for table saw jigs designed to help you accomplish just about any kind of cutting or shaping exercise known to man. As you continue using your saw, you'll quickly learn to determine which accessories are truly useful to you. If you're just getting started, here are a couple of accessories that no shop should be without.

Dado-blade set. Table saws can be used to cut very accurate dadoes, rabbets and grooves. The simplest way is to make multiple passes over the blade, moving the stock further from the blade with each pass. But anyone who has used this method with any frequency will attest to the value of blades that are specially designed for cutting dadoes. The

cheapest dado blade is called a *wobble blade*. Blades of this type have a built-in offset so they wobble wildly from side to side as they spin, creating a wide cutting path. Wobble blades are okay for rough cuts in soft material, but they have little value beyond that.

The more accurate and cleaner accessory is the *dado-blade set*. These sets consist of a pair of circular blades and an assortment of *chippers* that fit between the blades for removing waste wood (See photo above). The more chippers you add, the wider the dado. Because dado-blade sets are so much wider than a single saw blade, you usually need to install an auxiliary throat plate with an extra-wide opening (See photo below). To use the set,

The most popular dado-blade sets can be adjusted to cut dadoes up to 7/8" wide. They consist of a pair of circular blades surrounding chippers used to adjust the width of the set. It isn't necessary that you find and purchase a 10"-dia. blade set for your 10" saw; a 6" or 8" set will cut dadoes as deep as you'll likely need.

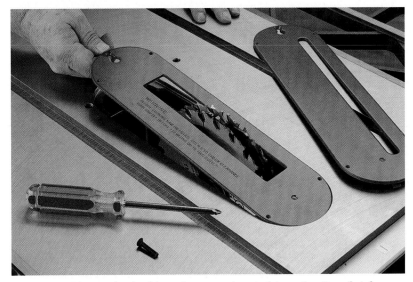

The extra-wide opening in this replacement throat plate makes it perfect for use with a dado-blade set.

Some table saws can be retrofitted with dust collection devices, like the broad plate with 4" hose port installed in this saw.

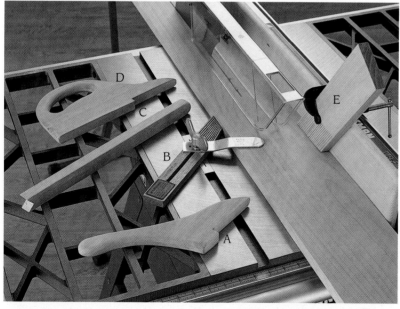

Create an assortment of pushsticks, pushblocks and featherboards for your most common table saw operations. (A) pushstick with 45° handle for ripping; (B) commercial hold-down fits in miter slot; (C) long-handle pushstick to be used only with a featherboard; (D) handle pushstick for cutting dadoes and rabbets; (E) featherboard clamped to rip fence.

follow the manufacturer's guidelines to get the correct combination of chippers for the width of the cut you want. When cutting long grooves or cutting hardwood, make the cuts in multiple passes, raising the blade slightly after each pass until the finished depth is achieved.

Miter-gauge hold-down. As you feed stock into the saw blade using your miter gauge, it has a tendency to slip toward the blade. In addition to being a common cause of kickback, this slipping usually ruins your workpiece. A good way to prevent the stock from slipping when crosscutting an angle is to use a miter-gauge hold-down. Attached at the back of the miter gauge head, the hold-down contains a threaded rod that screws down to apply pressure to the top of the workpiece. If the hold-down that's right for your saw isn't available at your local woodworking or tool store, you can usually order one directly from the saw's manufacturer.

Dust collection. As awareness of the importance of dust collection increases, more and more table saws are sold with standard or optional dust collection capability. If your table saw is not set up to accept a dust collection hose, some universal accessories might be of use. Most woodworking stores carry after-market plates designed to fit between a contractor-saw stand and the base *(See photo, left top).* The plate has a port for a 4" dust collection hose. Some benchtop saws have built-in dust ports. Cabinet saws are designed to catch sawdust inside the cabinet, but they can also be connected to a more elaborate dust control system.

Pushsticks & featherboards. Most accidents that occur with a table saw result from careless technique when feeding stock into the blade. The best way to guard against accidents of this type is to make good use of pushsticks and pushblocks to move the workpiece and featherboards to prevent it from kicking back out of the saw. You can buy pushsticks and pushblocks in a variety of shapes and sizes. But many woodworkers prefer to make their own. Some of the most popular types of homemade pushsticks and featherboards are shown here *(See photo, left).*

Featherboards are simply boards that are kerfed to create wooden tines. When positioned correctly, the featherboard flexes with the workpiece as it goes past, but will stiffen and resist the board if it catches on the blade and starts to kick back. Maintaining a full set of pushsticks, pushblocks and featherboards is a very important responsibility. If you're unsure how to make them, check at your local library for plan books.

Table saw technique & safety

More major shop accidents occur on the table saw than on any other power tool, not because the table saw is particularly dangerous, but simply because it's used so much more frequently than other power tools. Still, table saws are powerful cutting machines that demand respect and care when used.

You should know and follow a few basic safety rules when using a table saw: always wear ear and eye protection; do not operate the saw wearing gloves; make sure all shirt cuffs and jewelry are well out of the way; be sure to have adequate light and ventilation. But beyond that, avoiding injury basically comes down to common sense and using good techniques.

Rip-cutting. The table saw is perhaps the best tool ever created for ripping stock to width (although some band saw fans might argue the point). The main techniques for safe and effective rip-cutting are:

- Never stand directly behind the stock as you feed it into the blade (kickback occurs most frequently when ripping).
- Make sure the rip fence is securely fastened and parallel to the saw blade.

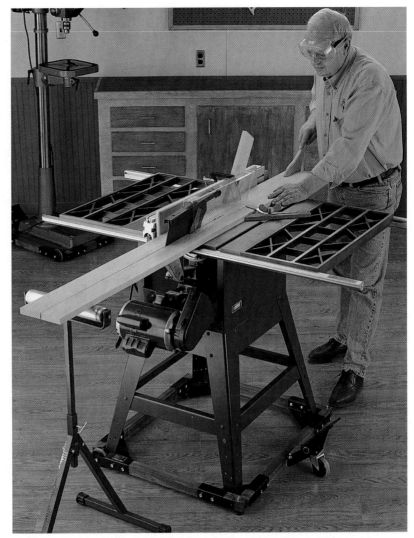

Keep out of the path of the workpiece when rip-cutting on the table saw. Rip-cutting has a higher potential for kickback than most other table saw operations. Use extra work supports, like this roller-type support, when ripping long workpieces.

- Use a featherboard to hold down the stock close to the point where it meets the saw blade.
- Use featherboards on the side opposite the rip fence to help keep the workpiece from binding.
- Have adequate support for the workpiece on the infeed and outfeed sides of the table. If using a roller-type of work support like the one shown above, make certain that it's exactly the same height as the table.
- Don't make rip cuts less than 1" wide.
- Make sure the narrower wood strip is between the blade and the fence, and don't remove the strip until the saw is turned off.
- Never put your hand behind the saw blade or even allow it to get within 6".

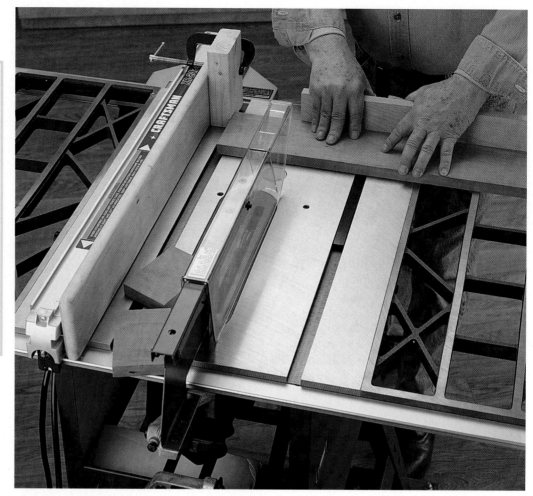

Clamp a stopblock to your rip fence as a guide when making repetitive crosscuts. Make sure the stopblock is well back from the blade, and use it to position the workpiece against the miter gauge.

Crosscutting. Although there are other tools better suited for crosscutting (like the radial arm saw or the power miter box), this is a frequent operation on the table saw. Most of the same safety rules for rip-cutting also apply to cross-cutting. But because you're using a miter gauge rather than a rip fence to guide your work, the potential for binding and kickback is far less than when rip-cutting.

The key to successful crosscutting is keeping the workpiece stable. This can be accomplished by clamping or even screwing the board to the miter gauge. At the very least, use one hand to hold the workpiece tight against the miter gauge, and use the other hand to guide the gauge along the miter slot. Here are more tips for crosscutting on a table saw:

• Attach an auxiliary fence extension to the miter gauge head to create a stable surface for the workpiece to press against.

• Use a hold-down or clamp to secure the workpiece to the miter gauge when making mitered crosscuts (the blade wants to pull the workpiece toward the cut as it's being made).

• Make sure the miter slot is clean and well lubricated.

A hold-down accessory is used to apply downward pressure onto a workpiece when crosscutting with a miter gauge. The hold-down keeps the workpiece from slipping toward the blade, especially when miter-cutting.

• Keep the rip fence well out of the way of the workpiece.
• Clamp a stopblock to the rip fence well in advance of the blade for making repetitive cuts (use the stop–block as a gauge for positioning the workpiece against the miter gauge).

Other techniques. *Double-cutting* to prevent tearout. If you're concerned about getting a ragged cut at the end of your workpiece, make the cut in two passes. First, set your rip fence to the correct width. Then make a cut about 2″ deep at one end of the cutting line. Turn off the saw and allow the blade to come to a stop, then remove the workpiece, flip it end for end, and finish the cut.

Gang-cutting. Cutting multiple work-pieces in one pass (gang-cutting) isn't as easy on a table saw as it is with some other power saws, mostly because you bring the workpiece to the tool when using a table saw. But there will be some occasions where you can save yourself a lot of time and hassle by gang-cutting. The trick is to find a way to attach the workpieces so they don't slip (masking tape can work well for this).

You also must make sure the work-pieces are well supported, feeding them with a pushblock or using a miter gauge extension.

TIP:
Reduce vibration of the saw arbor by clamping the front and back trunnion to the saddle in your saw's undercarriage. A moving trunnion causes side-to-side wobble (known as *runout*) that widens the saw kerf, slowing down the saw.

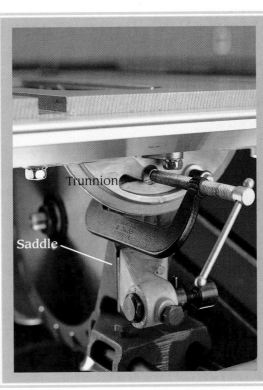

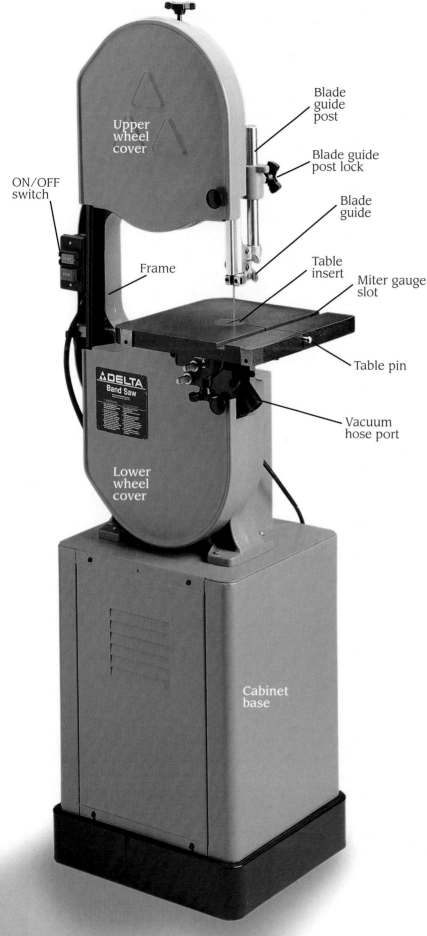

Upper wheel cover

ON/OFF switch

Frame

DELTA Band Saw

Lower wheel cover

Cabinet base

Blade guide post

Blade guide post lock

Blade guide

Table insert

Miter gauge slot

Table pin

Vacuum hose port

Band Saws

Simple, quiet and unassuming, the band saw is the favorite stationary power tool in many woodworking shops. It cuts with deliberate precision and smooth, controllable power that's a natural fit for woodworkers who pride themselves on careful, accurate work.

The better known functions of the band saw include cutting curves and resawing thick or very rough, uneven wood into usable boards. In addition to these functions, the band saw can be used to rip-cut just about any stock, to slice wood veneer, and to cut tenons for mortise-and-tenon joints. Special blades let you use the band saw to cut metal and even as a sander. Most wood-cutting band saws will cut light-gauge nonferrous metals if you install a fine-toothed metal cutting blade. But if you want to cut heavier metals, you'll need to buy a band saw with multiple-speed settings—the blades on wood-cutting band saws spin too fast (up to 3,000 feet per minute) for heavy metal.

Among its many benefits, the band saw enjoys the reputation of being a very safe power cutting tool. The continuous downstroke of the steel band cuts with a one-directional cutting motion, eliminating the counterforces that can cause kickback when using a circular blade. And the straight-line cutting path won't pull stray fingers into the blade as a circular blade can. The relatively thin kerf created by a band saw blade is a popular attraction for woodworkers who strive to eliminate waste in their work.

As with all other tools, keeping your band saw well tuned and aligned is essential to getting good performance. The condition of the blade is also critical to getting smooth, fast cuts that follow your cutting line with minimal wandering.

One word of caution: Once you get to know the band saw and its relaxed versatility, you may never want to go back to using your other power saws.

Band Saw Fact Sheet		
Application	Tool Recommendation	Accessories
Light Use	8″ to 10″ benchtop band saw with ⅕- to ½ hp motor, metal guide blocks, tilting table, and die-cast aluminum frame.	Miter gauge, rip fence, ¼″ and ⅜″ blades.
Moderate Use	10″ to 14″ benchtop or floor-standing models with ½- to 1- hp motor capacity to accept ½″-wide blade, 5″ to 8″ resaw capacity, and cast iron frame and table.	½″ blade, hook-tooth blade for resawing.
Heavy Use	Floor-standing cabinet saw with at least 14″ throat capacity and 1½+ hp motor, accepts blade up to 1″ wide, two-direction table adjustments for compound cuts.	Riser block throat extension, full selection of blades, including 1″ blade and sanding band, dust collection, various special-purpose jigs as needed.

Band saw basics

The essential parts of a band saw are the *steel-band blade*, the *rubber-clad wheels* that turn the blade, the *frame* that supports the wheels, the *tilting table,* and the *blade guides* that keep the blade aligned. The lower wheel is driven by either a direct-drive or belt-drive motor, and the upper wheel (on two-wheel models) can be raised or lowered to adjust the tension of the blade. Allowances for different cutting chores are usually made by changing the blade, although some band saws have multiple speed settings.

Band saw types. The basic menu of band saws has changed little in recent years, with a wide variety available, from lightweight benchtop saws, to portable handheld band saws used in the building trades, to huge, gas-powered industrial band saws designed to resaw logs on-site. But for most home handymen the choice basically comes down to selecting a benchtop saw or a cabinet saw—which is essentially a question of dollars, capacity, and features.

Benchtop band saws. If most of the cutting you'll do with your band saw is limited to curves or pattern-following in light or small stock that's just a little too big for your scroll saw, you can probably get by with a small benchtop band saw. Due to the limited size of their throats and the fact that most can't handle a blade more than ⅜″ wide, many of these saws are viewed primarily by more serious woodworkers as crafting tools. Some benchtop saws, as well as some floor models, feature a third wheel that creates a triangular blade path. Three-wheel saws can yield greater throat capacity in a small space, but they're usually a little more difficult to align. The triangular configuration also places greater stress on the blade, often leading to breakage. All but top-of-the-line benchtop saws have a fairly small (⅕- to ½- hp) motor.

Floor-model band saws. Larger and more powerful than benchtop band saws, floor-model saws can perform the full range of activities the band saw is capable of—including many of the cutting chores typically associated with table saws or radial arm saws. Many of the more popular saws are mounted on a cabinet-style stand; others have a lower wheel that extends all the way to the base at floor level.

Most cabinet saws for home use have the same basic features: a ½- to 1-hp motor, a resaw capacity of about 6″, a tilting table that may have positive preset stops, and a maximum blade width of 1″ to 1½″. But if you're shopping for a saw, you'll find quite a range of prices among these saws. The basic factors that determine the cost of a band saw are the precision with which the components are made, the sturdiness of the frame, and the quality of the adjustable blade guides.

TIP:

For best results, select the widest band saw blade that will cut the tightest curve on your project. Here are some general guidelines for the minimum radius that the common blade widths can cut. Actual results will vary slightly based on the set and style of the teeth, and on the manufacturer of the blade.

Blade width	Smallest radius cut
⅛"	3/16"
3/16"	⅜"
¼"	⅝"
⅜"	1 ¼"
½"	3"
¾"	5"
1"	8"

Band saw blades

Band saw blades for cutting wood are made of tempered, high-carbon steel strips welded together at the ends to form a band. Although the weld is filed down to the point that it can be difficult to locate, it's still the weakest spot in the blade. *Bimetal blades* have carbide or high-speed steel tips on the teeth to stay sharp longer. The blades for most floor-standing home-use saws are .020" thick, while benchtop saws with wheel diameters of 12" or less usually can accept a .014"-thick blade.

The blade length varies depending on the size and configuration of the wheels. The width ranges from ⅛" (used for making delicate, curved cuts) to 1" (used for resawing thick stock). A few saws designed for home use can drive blades up to 1½" wide, and industrial saws used in production-style resawing can handle blades as wide as 3".

Tooth style. In addition to width, band saw blades vary by tooth style *(See photo above)*. The three tooth styles available today are *regular* or *standard*, *skip-tooth*, and *hook-tooth*. The evenly spaced, contiguous teeth on standard blades have their cutting faces perpendicular to the

body of the blade (a 0° rake angle). Standard blades are good general-purpose blades, well suited for making curved cuts through cross grain and with the grain.

Skip-tooth blades also have a 0° rake angle, but the teeth are set apart by a flat-bottomed gap. Skip-tooth blades remove waste wood more quickly than standard blades, allowing you to make faster, somewhat rougher crosscuts than with a standard blade. The teeth on hook-tooth blades have a slight, 10° downward angle that helps keep the blade from wandering to follow the grain of the wood. This feature makes hook-tooth blades ideal for rip-cutting and resawing.

Pitch. The number of *teeth per inch* (tpi) on a blade is known as the *pitch* of the blade. Common band saw blades for wood-cutting range from 4 tpi to 14 tpi (The 14 tpi blades can be also be used for cutting light-gauge, nonferrous metals). Generally, blades with fewer tpi cut faster and rougher than blades with more tpi. When applied to your work, this makes a 4- to 6- tpi blade a good choice for rough, fast cutting, while an 8- to 14- tpi blade is better suited for cutting curves.

Tooth set. On band saw blades, as with most other types of saw blades, the teeth aren't aligned with the body of the blade. The amount and type of offset of the teeth is known as the *set* of the blade. The three basic set types include: *alternate-bevel set, raker set,* and *wavy set (See photo, previous page, and photo below).*

Alternate-bevel teeth are commonly found on general-purpose, standard-tooth blades. With this type, teeth are set to one side of the blade or the other in alternating fashion. This maximizes the number of teeth striking each side of the saw kerf, resulting in smooth cuts.

Raker-set teeth (not shown below) are similar to alternate-bevel teeth, except that each pair of alternating set teeth is separated by a straight tooth with no set at all. This raker tooth cleans waste from the cutting kerf, reducing resistance and speeding up the cut.

Wavy-set teeth are offset in a wavy, serpentine fashion. These blades are used most frequently for cutting metal.

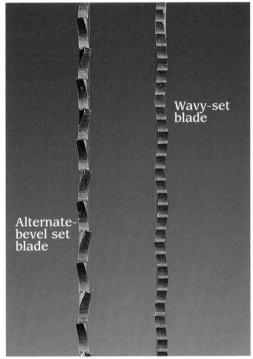

The set of the sawteeth affects the speed and smoothness of the cut. Alternate-bevel set teeth cut faster than wavy-set teeth, which are most commonly found on metal-cutting blades. A third set type, the raker-set blade, is similar to the alternate-set blade, but it has one straight raker blade with no set between each pair of alternating-set teeth.

TIP:

Round over the back edge of a new blade on both sides after it's installed. Press a silicone carbide sharpening stone (most woodworking supplies retailers sell stones designed specifically for use with a band saw blade) against the back edges of the blade, with the saw running *(See photo below).* File the edges until they have a slight roundover: this helps the blade move more cleanly through the saw kerf by reducing friction, and it also lets you cut tighter curves.

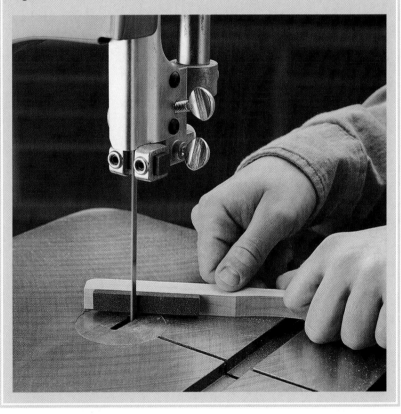

POWER TOOLS BY THE NUMBERS

Wheel diameter is the primary measure for gauging band saw size. Typical home-use cabinet saws have a 14" wheel diameter, and benchtop saws generally range from 8" to 10" in diameter. In most cases, the throat capacity or resaw capacity (which gauges the maximum thickness of stock the saw will cut) increases with wheel diameter. The majority of benchtop saws can resaw wood from 3" to 5" thick, but some higher-end benchtop saws can manage stock up to 8" thick. Most cabinet saws can resaw stock up to about 6" thick, although some industrial models with 18"- or 20"- diameter wheels will accept stock up to 12" thick.

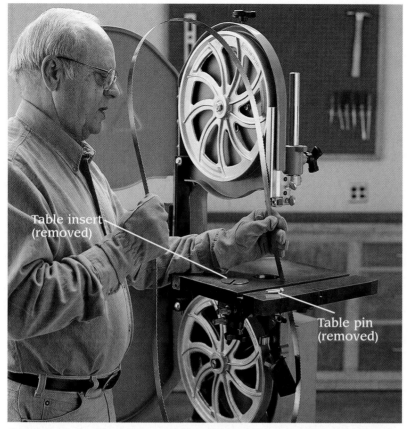

Table insert
(removed)

Table pin
(removed)

To remove or install a band saw blade, slide the blade through the slot that runs from the center to the edge of the table. You'll need to remove the table insert and the table pin to get access to the slot.

Blade selection guide:

Here are a few suggestions for matching band saw blades to cutting tasks:

Task	Width	Pitch	Style	Set*
Scrollwork, joinery	⅛"	14 tpi	ST	AB or R
Cutting light metal	⅛"	14 tpi	ST	W
Tight curves in thick wood	⅛"	6 tpi	SK	AB
Smooth curves	3⁄16"	10 tpi	ST	AB
General purpose	¼"	6 to 8 tpi	ST or SK	AB
Ripping, some resawing	¼"	4 to 6 tpi	H	AB or R
General crosscutting	⅜"	8 to 10 tpi	ST or SK	AB or R
Fast crosscutting	⅜"	4 tpi	SK	AB
Resawing larger stock	½"	4 tpi	H	AB
Slicing veneer	½" or ¾"	6 tpi	H	AB
Crosscutting thick stock	¾"	6 tpi	ST	AB
Resawing extra large stock	¾"	4 tpi	H	AB
Resawing logs, blocks	¾" or 1"	3 tpi	H	AB

*Key: ST=standard   SK=skip-tooth   H=hook-tooth
        AB=alternate-bevel   R=raker   W=wavy

TIP:

Regularly clean the rubber band saw tires lining the wheel rim. Unplug the saw, remove the blade, then hold a piece of sandpaper or steel wool against the tire as you rotate it by hand.

Installing blades

To install a blade in your band saw, first lower the top wheel near its lowest position. Remove the slotted table insert and the table pin that fits into the end of the slot in the saw table. Wearing gloves, unfold the saw blade so it's free of kinks, and orient it so the cutting edges of the teeth are facing downward. Slip the blade through the groove in the table and into the round opening for the insert *(See photo, above left)*. Wrap the blade around the top of the tire on the upper wheel, then position it over the tire on the lower wheel. Raise the upper wheel until the blade is snug. Replace the table insert, making sure that any locking nibs are aligned with the appropriate slots. Replace the table pin in the table slot. At this point, the blade is in rough position only. Don't use the saw until the tune-up is complete.

Storing blades

When you purchase a new band saw blade, it usually comes folded into a three-ring loop. To store the blade, fold it back into the same configuration. This is a fairly simple procedure once you get the hang of it. Wearing gloves, spread out your arms and hold the blade in a full loop. Rotate one of your wrists to fold the blade into a figure eight. Then, draw your hands together slowly and the blade should fold itself into a third loop. Tie strings or twist-ties around the loops to hold them in place for storage.

Setting up & tuning your band saw

Even a top-of-the line cabinet saw requires regular tuning and adjusting to hit peak performance. At first, tuning your saw may seem like a time-consuming chore, but as you gain experience it will become a quick process that's almost second nature. Whether you're setting up your saw for the first time, or giving it a routine once-over, adjust it in the following sequence.

Check the plane of the wheels. Before you make any adjustments on the saw blade or guides, make sure the wheels are aligned and in the same plane. With the wheel guards open, position a long metal straightedge so it contacts each wheel at two points *(See photo, right)*. Try to position the straightedge so it falls at or near the hubs of the wheels—in some cases, you may need to tilt the table up and out of the way.

If the wheels are in correct position, the straightedge will be straight up and down, and there will be no gaps between it and the wheels at any points. If gaps are detected, adjust the wheels as needed until the gaps are no longer present. The technique for moving the wheels to alter the plane differs from model to model: in some cases, the bottom has an adjustment feature; in other cases, you'll need to add or remove thin washers between the top wheel and the support frame. Check your owner's manual.

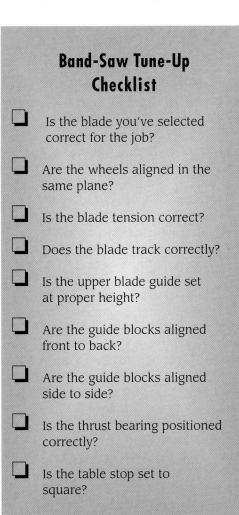

Band-Saw Tune-Up Checklist

- [ ] Is the blade you've selected correct for the job?

- [ ] Are the wheels aligned in the same plane?

- [ ] Is the blade tension correct?

- [ ] Does the blade track correctly?

- [ ] Is the upper blade guide set at proper height?

- [ ] Are the guide blocks aligned front to back?

- [ ] Are the guide blocks aligned side to side?

- [ ] Is the thrust bearing positioned correctly?

- [ ] Is the table stop set to square?

Use a long metal straightedge to test the band saw wheels to make certain they're coplanar (aligned in the same plane as they spin). Try to get the straightedge as close to the hub of each wheel as possible and check for gaps at all four points where the straightedge contacts a wheel rim.

Extending the saw throat

Most floor-standing workshop band saws are powerful enough to resaw lumber that is more than 6" thick, but many just don't have enough throat capacity. One solution is called a *riser block.* These kits are inserted into the back column on the frame of the band saw, effectively raising the height of the upper wheel by about 6". This, in turn, increases the throat capacity by the same amount. But if you decide to use a riser block, be aware that rigging it up is no small effort: you'll need to do some rewiring, as well as replace the post that supports the guide. And you can also plan on replacing all of your band saw blades with longer ones.

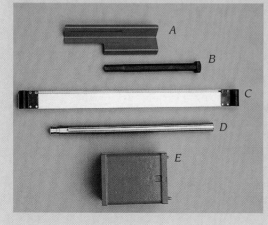

Riser block

Use the adjustment knob at the top of the upper wheel cover to set the band saw tension indicator to match the width of your blade.

Above: A throat extension block, or riser block, is fitted between the parts of the band saw frame to increase cutting capacity by up to 6".

Left: The main parts of a throat extension kit include (A) guard assembly, (B) ¾ × 9" square-head screw, (C) guard, (D) post, (E) riser block.

Set the blade tension. Most band saws have preset calibration points to help you adjust the blade to the correct tension for its blade width. Typically, a knob located on the upper wheel guard is turned to dial the tension to the correct calibration mark *(See photo above).* Some experienced woodworkers prefer to set blade tension by plucking the blade and listening to the pitch of the resonance. Others simply apply side pressure to the blade to gauge the deflection—the blade should not move more than ¼". Whichever method you prefer, make sure the blade tension is set correctly before moving on to tracking the blade (the next step in your band saw tune-up).

Adjust the blade tracking. On almost all band saws, the blade should be centered on the upper and lower wheels as they spin. This is absolutely critical to making good, clean cuts. Before you check and adjust the tracking of the blade, move the upper and lower guide blocks and bearings well out of the way of the path of the blade.

The first test is simply to rotate the wheels by hand and watch for any signs of side-to-side blade movement against the tire. If the blade creeps at all as you spin, you'll need to make an adjustment. The devices for adjusting the blade tracking are usually located very near (or are part of) the blade tension adjuster—a wing nut and thumb screw or an allen key are two common methods for making tracking adjustments. Make the tracking adjustments only in very small increments until the blade stays in the centers of the tires when the wheels are spun *(See photos, right top and bottom)*. Tighten the fasteners to lock the tracking mechanism in place.

Check the table stop. The table stop is a bolt or metal rod between the underside of the table and the table support frame. It's purpose is to create a secure resting point that supports the tilting table so it's precisely square with the saw blade. To check to see if the table stop is set correctly, position a small try square with one leg against the flat of the blade and the other on the table surface. If the two parts are not square to one another, lift the table and raise or lower the table stop until a square relationship is achieved *(See photo, bottom left)*.

The band saw blade should be centered on both the upper and lower wheels. Hand-turn the wheels and watch the movement of the blade. If it drifts from side to side, you'll need to make an adjustment to the tracking.

Adjust the height of the table stop bolt with an open-end wrench. When the table is lowered and comes to rest on top of the table-stop bolt, the table should be perfectly horizontal and square to the band saw blade.

Adjust the tracking by turning the blade tracking lever, usually located on the side of the upper wheel cover.

Set the blade guides. You'll find a set of blade guides above and below the table. The guides perform two valuable functions: they minimize blade movement when cutting, and the upper blade guide combines with the guide post to create a blade guard. The guides are equipped with either ball-bearing rollers or solid-material blocks that are pushed together to create a narrow channel for the blade. The majority of home-use band saws have solid blocks, usually made of metal (you can buy special heat-absorbing blocks that reduce blade stress caused by friction).

The blocks on the blade guides should be forward just enough to line up with the bottom of the blade gullets (the valleys in the blade).

The blade guides support the saw blade above and below the table. Before cutting, set the upper blade guide so it's no more than ¼" away from the workpiece.

The first guide adjustment is to position the upper guide so it's within ¼" of the top of the material you'll be cutting *(See photo above).* A gap greater than this will expose more of the blade, creating a safety hazard and allowing the blade to wander as it cuts.

Next, make sure the guide blocks on both the upper and lower guides are aligned with the flat of the blade—you'll usually find a set screw on the back of the guide mechanism that allows you to rotate it when loosened. Now, adjust the guide blocks front-to-back so the front edges are even with the bottoms of the sawtooth gullets *(See photo, above right).* There should be a gap about the thick-

ness of a sheet of paper between the guide blocks and the blade. To adjust the blocks side to side, slip a paper shim between each block and the blade, shift each block so it pins the paper against the blade, then adjust the blocks back slowly until the paper can be pulled out.

Set the thrust bearings. Both the upper and lower blade guide assemblies have a thrust bearing (also called a *blade support bearing*) that prevents the blade from deflecting away from the stock as you feed it into the blade. These roller-type bearings should be set as close to the blade as possible, without touching the blade while it turns. With the blade stationary, move the bearings backward or forward into the correct position *(See photo, below).* (You can use a pair of paper shims to set the gap, if you wish.)

Adjust the thrust bearing so it just touches the still blade at the spot of the blade weld.

Using a band saw

The primary cutting operations done on a band saw are crosscutting, miter-cutting, ripping, bevel-ripping, and resawing. Most basic cuts can be done using a miter gauge or rip fence.

Crosscutting and miter-cutting. For the most part, a table saw, radial arm saw, or power miter saw will perform these operations faster than a band saw. However, you can certainly accomplish them on the band saw if you choose. Simply use the miter gauge that comes with the saw as a guide and feed the workpiece into the blade *(See photo, right middle).* A ⅜"-wide, 8- to 10- tpi standard or skip-tooth blade is a good choice for making these cuts.

Ripping, bevel-ripping, and resawing. While rip-cutting and bevel-rip-cutting can be done effectively on other power tools, a band saw is ideal for resawing lumber into usable boards or even veneer. For standard ripping, use a rip fence clamped to the band saw table. (Most saws come equipped with a rip fence.) Use a 4- to 6- tpi standard hook-tooth blade for best results. You can also use the rip fence as a guide for resawing *(See photo, lower right).* Using a wider blade will give you a straighter cut. To resaw veneer, however, you're better off either free-handing the cut or clamping a pivot point near the blade. This allows you to maintain a relatively even cut, making adjustments as you go to compensate for the tendency of the blade to follow the grain of the wood.

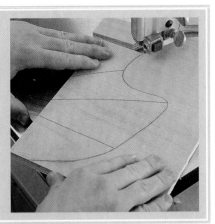

TIP:

Making relief cuts. When cutting complex curves with your band saw, make a few relief cuts through the waste area and up to the cutting line. This will make the workpiece much easier to manage and the blade less likely to bind.

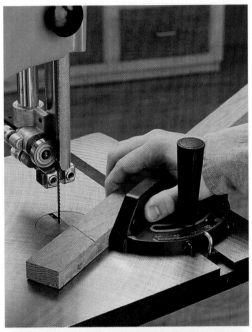

To make mitered crosscuts with a band saw, hold the workpiece against the miter gauge and feed the stock through the blade.

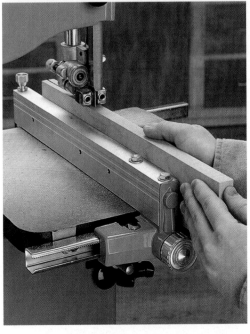

The rip fence supplied with your band saw can be used as a guide for resawing lumber.

Radial Arm Saws

The radial arm saw was once viewed as a "must-have" power tool for any respectable workshop. In fact, it wasn't too long ago that weekend woodworkers engaged in a running debate over which is the better tool to build a shop around, the table saw or the radial-arm saw. But two factors have combined to reduce the stature of this powerful saw in recent years. The first, and most notable, is the advent of the power miter box. Inexpensive and portable, the "chop saw" can perform most of the crosscutting operations that were once the exclusive territory of the radial saw.

The other factor in the decline in popularity of the radial saw is its reputation as being dangerous. The high number of accidents that occur on a radial saw can be blamed mostly on carelessness or misuse, but most woodworkers would agree that the dangerous reputation is well earned.

If you're considering buying a new radial-arm saw, don't rule it out just on the basis of these two factors. Despite the safety concerns, this saw can perform several functions faster and with greater accuracy than power miter saws. A great advantage to the radial saw is that it can cut to varying depths, making it useful for dadoes, rabbets, grooves, and kerfing. It can cut compound miters. And by spinning the yoke that holds the motor so the blade is parallel to the saw fence, you can even use the radial-arm saw to rip boards—something not even the sliding compound miter saw could hope to accomplish. Also, radial arm saws are generally more powerful than power miter saws.

Compared to table saws, one advantage to the radial arm saw is that you apply the blade to the workpiece: this lets you keep the workpiece securely positioned, eliminating errors that can occur while feeding stock into the blade. Another benefit to the radial arm saw is good visibility —cutting lines are in plain sight as you make your cuts. On table saws, they're often obscured by the blade guard.

Arm

Column

Split collar

Hold-down knob

Blade guard

Rear table

Spacer table

Fence

Yoke

Miter/arm lock lever

Bevel-index lever

Front table

Bevel-lock lever

Elevation crank

Base

SINGLE-ARM
RADIAL ARM SAW

Radial Arm Saw Fact Sheet		
Application	**Tool Recommendation**	**Accessories and Blades**
Light Use	8¼" benchtop model with 12- to 13-amp motor.	General-purpose crosscutting blade with low rake angle (less than 5°) teeth, push-sticks and featherboards.
Moderate Use	10" floor-standing model with 12- to 16-amp motor and electric brake.	Smooth-cutting crosscut blade, dado-blade set, work supports.
Heavy Use	10" double-arm (turret) saw; 12" or 14" single-arm saw.	Dust collection system, rip-cutting blade, sanding discs and spindles.

Radial arm saw types

The number of manufacturers producing radial arm saws has dwindled in recent years, reducing significantly the number of options for home use. The basic choices boil down to: a lower-cost benchtop model, a floor model with a single arm running front-to-back; and a floor model with a second arm (called a *double-arm* or *turret saw*) mounted in the upper arm. The other significant variable is maximum blade diameter.

Benchtop radial arm saws. A handful of manufacturers still make a scaled-down version of the radial-arm saw that's mounted on a benchtop or other worksurface. Slightly lower in cost than floor models, they usually have an 8¼"-dia. blade and a crosscutting capacity in the 10" to 12" range. They're a little cheaper than a good sliding compound miter saw and might be a good choice if you don't have much workshop space.

Floor models. Most radial arm saws in use today are floor-standing (*See photo, previous page*). The primary differences between floor models are in power, blade diameter (which determines cutting depth capacity), and arm configuration. *Single-arm saws* have a radial arm that can be adjusted for depth and swung from side to side on the back column. Most have a 1½ to 2 hp motor and draw from 12 to 16 amps. *Double-arm saws* (*See photo, right*) give you the ability to make miter cuts at maximum capacity from the right or the left. (On single-arm saws, the ability to miter-cut from the left is limited.) Typically, double-arm saws are more expensive than single-arm saws, and most require 230-volt service.

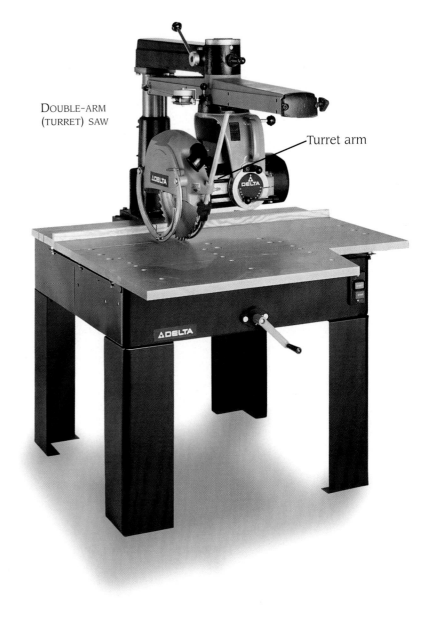

DOUBLE-ARM (TURRET) SAW

Turret arm

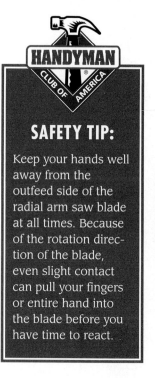

Radial arm saw basics

Radial arm saws tend to require frequent tune-ups, since the major parts of the saw are not fixed. This is especially true if you use your radial saw for multiple machining operations. You'll save yourself quite a bit of time and decrease the need for readjustments if you provide your radial arm saw with a dedicated space in your shop. Most people prefer to locate it up against a wall, with some kind of work support on each side. This allows you to take advantage of one the saw's primary benefits: the ability to make precise crosscuts on stock that's too long to be cut on a table saw.

The head. The business end of the radial arm saw is the *head* of the saw, made up of the *blade and arbor*, the motor in its housing, the *yoke* that suspends the motor, and the rollers that fit into the roller track on the underside of the arm. The head is swung from side to side to set cutting angles.

The column and base. The framework that supports the radial arm saw consists of a polished steel cylinder (*the column*) attached to a *base*—a floor stand or a flat subtable that's clamped to a workbench. The column is fitted into a metal *split collar* bolted to the base.

The arm. Attached to the column, the arm contains tracks that house the rollers on the head, supporting it. Depth of cut is set by raising or lowering the arm on the fixed column at the back of the saw.

Cut kerfs in the saw fence at the cutting angles you use most frequently.

The table and fence. Unlike table saw tables, the table and fence on a radial arm saw are made of wood so you can kerf the table slightly when cutting

clean through a workpiece. In fact, the first cut you make on your radial saw should be a kerf cut through the fence and slightly into the table to establish cutting lines *(See photo, below)*. Make a straight cut and additional cuts at 45° and other common settings.

Blades. The best blade for a radial arm saw is a crosscutting blade with a rake angle of less then 5°. These blades have teeth that are nearly perpendicular to a line drawn out from the center of the blade. Blades with a high positive rake angle (sometimes called the *hook*) are likely to yield a rough cut. The crosscutting blade will handle most cutting tasks performed by a radial arm saw. Use a rip-cutting blade for making rip cuts. For more information, see the chapters on circular saws, table saws and power miter saws.

Tuning your radial arm saw

Even top-of-the-line industrial radial arm saws require careful, frequent tune-ups. Because different saws employ different adjustment devices, consult your owner's manual for more information. The general instructions below pertain mostly to single-arm radial saws. Double-arm saws require additional checks—consult your owner's manual.

Test clamps and locks. Before tuning up your saw, check the accuracy of the clamps and locks.

• Start by checking the lever-lock that secures the arm at various cutting angles. Release the lock and pivot the arm to cut at an angle of about 30°. Lock the arm in place, then apply pressure to the sides to make sure the arm doesn't slip. If it moves easily, you can usually increase the holding power of the lock by making an adjustment on the underside of the arm, beneath the lock lever.

• Next, check the yoke locking mechanism that holds the saw head in place. When the locking mechanism is released, you can pivot the saw head in the arm to position the blade parallel to the fence for rip-cutting. Release the lock, pivot the head slightly, then lock the yoke in place. There should be no movement when you push against the saw head. If movement happens, you'll need to remove the saw head from the arm so you can tighten the fasteners that secure the locking mechanism at the top of the yoke.

• Make sure the bevel adjustment lock is secure. Set the saw head at an angle, as you would for making a bevel-cut. Lock the head in place, and test to make sure it's easy to lock and the head doesn't move. If the lock is too tight or too loose, disassemble the locking mechanism, make adjustments to the tension on the bolt that secures the lock to the saw head, then reassemble the mechanism and test again. Repeat if needed.

• Check the split collar that houses the bottom of the steel column. The column should fit tightly enough into the collar so it can be raised or lowered without too much difficulty, but not so loose that there is play between the two. Make adjustments by tightening or loosening the tension bolts that draw the halves of the split collar together.

Test relationships. To ensure accurate cuts, a radial saw must be tuned so: (a) the arm is parallel to the table, (b) the arm is perpendicular to the fence, and (c) the blade is perpendicular to the table.

The arm to the table. The saw table needs to be perfectly level and parallel to the radial arm. To test the table, first remove the blade, then rotate the motor in the yoke so the arbor spindle points straight down. Set a piece of paper onto the table to use as a feeler gauge, and lower the arm until the spindle presses against the paper just enough so it resists when you try to pull it out *(See photo below)*. Lock the yoke in position. Move

To see if the saw table is level, pivot the head of the saw so the arbor spindle points down. Slip a paper feeler gauge beneath the spindle and lower the spindle until it presses against the paper. Swing the arm to several positions, checking the feeler gauge to identify high or low spots.

TIP:

A quick test for tuning up

Before you spend a lot of time adjusting your saw, do a simple test to see if it's producing square cuts. Checking the squareness of actual cuts made by the saw is the most reliable indicator of how well tuned your saw is.

Step one: Set the saw at 0° and lock the arm in place. Then choose a square-cornered board that's at least 5″ or 6″ wide, and draw a crosscutting line midway through the board. Draw an "X" so the intersection point falls on the cutting line. Position the test board squarely against the fence, and crosscut the board in two, following the cutting line.

Step two: Push the saw head back past the fence and out of the way, then flip one of the board sections upside down. Butt the cut ends together and check to see if the ends of the board are flush—this reveals whether or not your saw blade is set exactly perpendicular to the table. If it's not, there will be a gap between the boards, as there is in the photo shown here. To correct this, you'll either need to adjust the table or the arm.

Step three: Flip one of the board sections so the opposite long edge is flush against the fence, and butt the ends together. If the ends do not fit together flush, that means the path of travel of the blade is not perpendicular to the fence, so you're actually cutting a slight miter. The easier correction is made by adjusting the table and fence, although the better, more permanent solution is to reset the arm so the blade travel is perpendicular to the fence, then reset the miter indicator to the zero point once everything is square.

the saw head so the spindle strikes the table at several different points around the table surface, testing with the feeler gauge (don't change the depth setting). If you encounter high or low points in the table, you can usually adjust for them by tightening or loosening the countersunk bolts that hold the table to the saw frame. In some cases, you may need to insert shims beneath the table.

The arm to the column. To make accurate cuts, the arm (which governs the line of blade travel) must be exactly perpendicular to the back column when set at 0°. Set the miter indicator to 0° but don't lock it in place. With the blade guard removed and the saw unplugged, position a framing square up against the rip fence, with the other leg aligned with the blade. Move the saw blade forward, checking to make sure the blade travel parallels the leg of the square *(See photo below).* Be sure to use the same saw tooth as a ref-

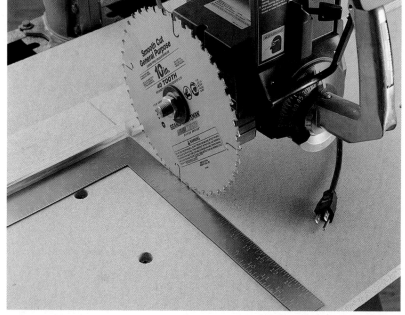

A framing square is a primary tool when checking the alignment of your radial arm saw blade. Here, it's being used to determine if the line of blade travel is perpendicular to the saw fence. Using one saw tooth as a reference, check for square at many points.

erence at all points. If needed, loosen the set screws at the rear of the arm and shift the arm slightly until the blade travel is exactly parallel to the square, then reset the miter indicator at the 0° mark.

The blade to the fence. Once you're certain the table is level, check the bevel and the line of the saw blade to see if the blade itself is exactly perpendicular to the fence and table.

To check the bevel, simply press the long leg of a framing square up against

the fence and press the shorter leg against the unguarded blade. If the blade isn't perfectly vertical, locate the adjustment screws that control the plane of the saw arbor (usually located near the yoke where it is joined to the saw motor). Tighten or loosen as needed until the blade is exactly vertical.

Also check to make sure the cutting line the blade follows is vertical—even if it's set with a 0° bevel and the path of travel is perpendicular to the fence, the blade itself could be offset slightly if the spindle is not parallel to the fence. This causes wobble (called *heeling*) that widens the kerf and can cause kickback. With the long leg of a framing square flush against the fence, raise the short leg a few inches and press it against the blade, checking for gaps. Spin the blade in quarter turns, checking for gaps with the square. If you find gaps, you'll need to locate the indexing pins that set the yoke position and adjust the yoke until the spindle is exactly parallel to the fence.

Checklist for tuning your radial arm saw:

❏ **1.** Secure arm lock lever?

❏ **2.** Secure yoke clamp?

❏ **3.** Secure bevel adjustment lock?

❏ **4.** Good fit between column and split collar on base?

❏ **5.** Table level and parallel to arm?

❏ **6.** Arm square to column at 0°?

❏ **7.** Blade perpendicular to fence and table?

❏ **8.** Blade vertical at 0° bevel?

❏ **9.** All moving parts clean and well lubricated?

Using radial arm saws

Many woodworkers who own radial arm saws use them almost exclusively for one purpose: making straight crosscuts in boards. The single-purpose approach dramatically reduces the amount of time and energy needed to keep a radial saw in tune. And making straight, repeated crosscuts is what radial arm saws do best. But if, like most people, you want to make your tools work as hard as they can, there are a number of other operations you can perform with a radial arm saw. You can expand on straight crosscutting to include making miter cuts and compound miter cuts. You'll find the radial saw to be well equipped for these cuts, and the procedures used to make them are relatively non-threatening.

Traditionally, woodworkers also use their radial saw to rip-cut boards. While this is certainly an achievable cut for the radial saw to make, the danger quotient goes up significantly when you turn the blade parallel to the fence and actually feed stock into it. If you own a table saw or a bandsaw, use either of these tools for your rip cuts. If circumstances demand that you rip on your radial saw, use extra precautions and read the section on rip-cutting that follows. With the appropriate accessories or jigs, you can also use your radial arm saw as a sander, shaper, or even a drill. But again, avoid these uses unless you don't have any other tool-choice options.

Crosscutting. First, set up your cut, making sure the workpiece is pressed flush against the fence and the saw kerf is on the waste side of the cutting line. If you're using a stopblock clamped to the fence, do not position it on the waste side: this could cause the cutoff piece to bind and kick out. Grasp the workpiece securely with your left hand, keeping the hand well away from the line of blade travel. Use a wood scrap or a clamp to hold shorter workpieces in place *(See photo, right)*. Turn on the saw and take firm hold of the handle on the saw head with your right hand. Let the blade reach full speed, then pull it forward through the cut. Push the blade back behind the fence before removing the workpiece and the cutoff piece.

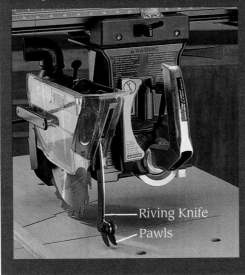

SAFETY TIP:

Perhaps even more than other stationary power tools, the blade guard on a radial arm saw is a critical element to safe use of the tool. Because the blade is movable, the chance for accidents is increased. Blade guards on most radial arm saws are equipped with antikickback pawls and a riving knife at the front that works the same way as a splitter on a table saw guard. These safety features can usually be adjusted up or down and locked in place so you can position them as close to the workpiece as possible. Before using your saw, make sure the riving knife is aligned exactly with the saw blade to enable the knife to fit into the saw kerf as you cut. To adjust the knife alignment, loosen the screw that holds the bracket or housing in place, adjust as necessary, then re-tighten the screw.

Riving Knife
Pawls

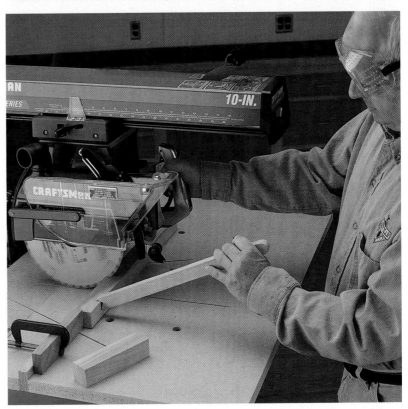

Secure the workpiece with your left hand and operate the saw with your right hand when crosscutting.

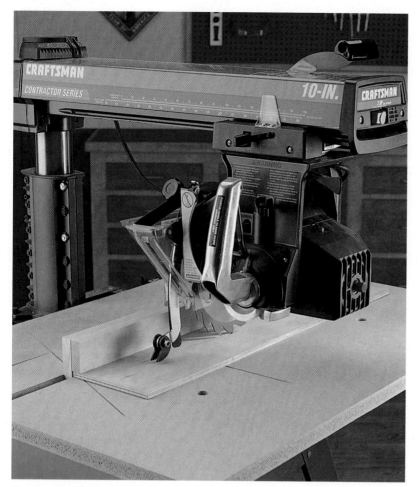

Miter-cutting. Raise the arm, then release the arm lock and pivot the arm until the miter indicator shows the desired angle. This will be accurate enough for a rough cut. For greater accuracy, use a sliding T-bevel or an angle-cutting guide to set the blade position. Secure the arm lock and make a test cut on a piece of scrap, double-checking the angle of the cut. Adjust as needed, then proceed as you would with a straight crosscut. Whenever possible, make miter cuts from the right-hand side of the radial arm saw table.

Rip-cutting. Before starting a rip cut, replace the kerfed fence on the saw with a straight, uncut fence: the stock can get caught on the kerfs in the fence as you feed it through the blade. Rip cuts are made by pivoting the blade so it's parallel to the saw fence, then feeding the stock into the blade *(See photo, left)*.

To set up for a rip cut, first determine if the cut you need is an *in-rip* or an *out-rip* cut *(See photos below)*. For narrower rip cuts (between 2" and 12" on most saws), the saw should be set in the in-rip position, with the blade closer to the back of the saw. Wider rip cuts should be made in the out-rip position, with the blade closer to the front of the saw.

Proper setup for a rip cut includes swiveling the yoke so the blade is parallel to the fence and replacing the saw fence with a clean, uncut auxiliary fence.

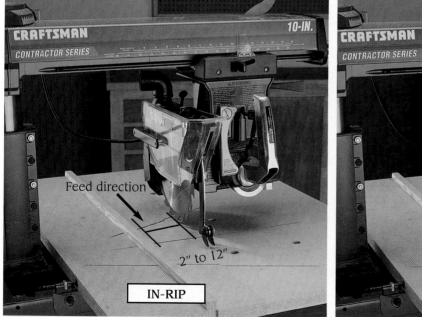

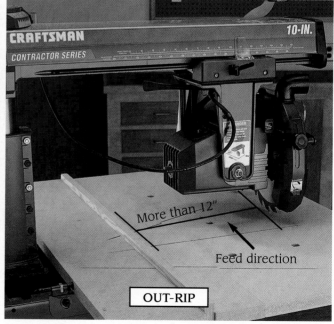

Because the saw head can be spun in either direction, you have the option of making ripcuts in the in-rip (left) or out-rip (right) position. Use the in-rip position, with the blade closer to the column, for all ripcuts up to the maximum in-rip capacity

(usually around 12"). Use the out-rip position, where the blade is closer to the front of the saw, for ripcuts where width of the board is greater than the in-rip capacity.

Once you've determined the correct position for the blade, release the yoke lock and any indexing pins and spin the yoke so the blade is parallel to the fence. Lock the yoke. Now, confirm from which direction you should feed the stock into the blade *(See Safety Tip, right)*. **This is extremely important:** if you feed the board following the direction of the blade rotation, the blade can catch the workpiece and drive it forward and out of the saw with enough force to puncture walls. Be certain you're feeding the board against the rotation of the blade.

Before proceeding, adjust the position of the riving knife and antikickback pawls so they'll engage positively with the stock as you feed it through the blade. (See your owner's manual for adjusting these safety devices correctly.) Set the blade the correct distance from the fence for your cut. Position the stock so it's flush against the fence, a few inches away from the blade. Clamp a featherboard to the table, pressed firmly, but not too tightly, against the board. Brace the featherboard with a support stick clamped against the outside edge of the featherboard *(See photo, below)*. With your body aside from the line of the cut, turn on the saw. When the blade has reached full speed, feed the workpiece

Rotation of blade

Rip feed direction

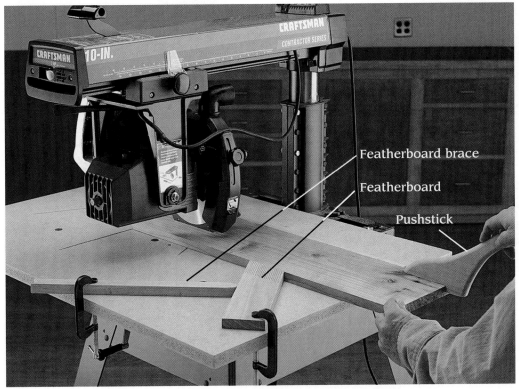

Featherboard brace

Featherboard

Pushstick

SAFETY TIP:

Always feed the stock **AGAINST** the rotation of the blade when rip-cutting. Feeding the board into the blade following the direction of blade rotation is an extreme safety hazard. The improperly fed board can shoot out of the saw at high velocity, causing extensive damage or injury.

into the blade, using a pushstick or push-block. Feed the board through the blade at a steady pace. Turn off the saw and allow the blade to come to a complete stop before removing the workpiece.

To make beveled rip cuts, set up as you would for a straight cut, but set the blade to the correct bevel. Make sure the blade is beveled toward the saw fence to prevent the workpiece from binding.

When rip-cutting, hold the workpiece in place with a featherboard and featherboard brace set up on the infeed side of the saw blade.

Scroll Saws

The scroll saw may not be the most glamorous or versatile workshop tool, but for some types of cutting, it's the only game in town short of a hand coping saw. It's used heavily by handymen with an interest in puzzlemaking, marquetry, fretwork, inlaying, and other precise crafts. Furnituremakers often use a scroll saw to cut templates for production-style work, as well as to make decorative cutouts and intricate contours on their projects.

The basic appeal of the scroll saw is its ability to make incredibly tight cuts that no other power saw, not even a band saw or a portable jig saw, can duplicate. And because it's a stationary tool with a sturdy table, you bring the work to the blade for pleasing, professional-quality results.

The scroll saw cuts with a reciprocating action using a fine blade that's chucked both above and below the cutting table. Though not powerful, a scroll saw can still accomplish highly intricate cuts in a variety of materials, including plastics and light-gauge, nonferrous metals like copper, aluminum and brass. Scroll saws are among the safest power tools to use, making them very popular with beginning woodworkers or crafters who aren't familiar with most workshop tools. Like any power tool, however, a scroll saw should be treated with respect and care.

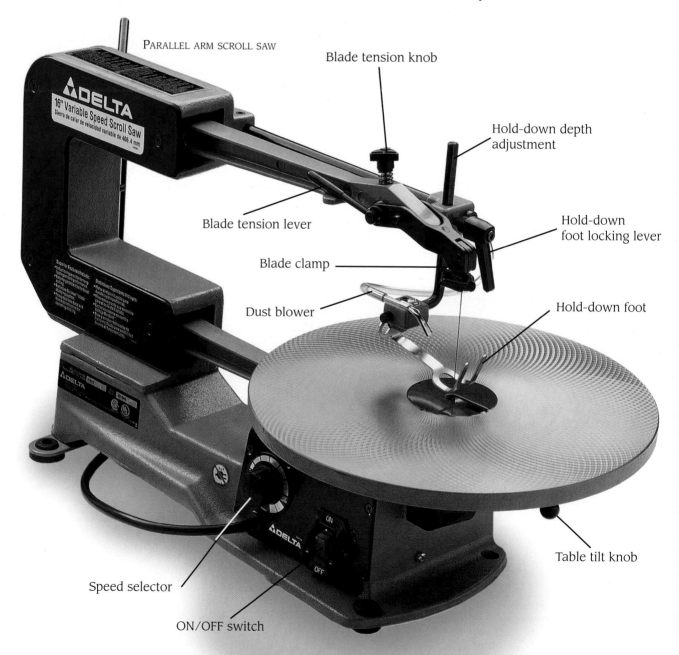

PARALLEL ARM SCROLL SAW

Blade tension knob

Hold-down depth adjustment

Blade tension lever

Hold-down foot locking lever

Blade clamp

Dust blower

Hold-down foot

Table tilt knob

Speed selector

ON/OFF switch

Scroll saw types

The greatest variation between scroll saw designs is in the style of the arm. Saws designed for the home workshop come in two basic styles: *parallel arm* and *C-arm*. Parallel arm saws, like the one shown on the previous page, have two separate arms that reciprocate up and down in unison to move the blade in a fairly tight cutting path. The lower arm is driven up and down by the motor, and because it's linked to the upper arm at the back of the saw, the upper arm mimics the lower arm's motion. Most new scroll saws sold today are parallel arm saws.

The C-arm scroll saw has a single C-shaped arm. One end of the blade is attached to each end of the arm, and the entire arm is rocked up and down by the motor. This type of cutting action is suitable for making fast, semi-smooth cuts, but for more delicate work, the parallel arm saw has an advantage.

Scroll saw basics

The scroll saw is a very simple tool to understand and use. Basically, a thin blade is moved up and down in a reciprocating pattern. The stock is set onto a table and fed into the blade. By moving the stock, you change the direction of the cut—the angle of the blade doesn't change. On some saws, however, you can mount the blade sideways in the chucks to enable you to feed longer stock through the blade teeth without striking the back of the saw throat.

Size & power. All home workshop scroll saws have a motor so small that the manufacturers seldom even bother to list its size in their product literature. The primary measure for a scroll saw is the throat capacity and the thickness of stock it can cut. Measured from the inside edge of the throat to the back edge of the blade, saw capacities range from 13" up to 16" on the most popular models. Larger saws designed for professionals and dedicated enthusiasts have throat capacities from 16" all the way up to 30". Almost all scroll saws you're likely to find at your local tool retailer will cut stock up to 2" thick. The larger saws may cut up to 2½"-thick stock, but at this point you've already entered territory that's better covered by a band saw.

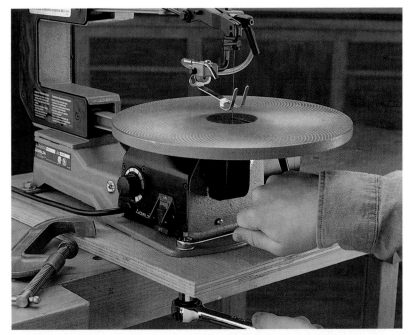

Bolt your benchtop scroll saw to a piece of sturdy plywood. By bolting a piece of plywood to the base (be sure to countersink the heads of the bolts), you make the saw easier to transport and provide a good surface for clamping the saw to your worksurface. Scroll saws vibrate quite a bit when they cut, so you should always fasten them down.

Speed. Most scroll saws in use today cut at only one speed—around 1700 *strokes per minute* (spm). Others give you two speed options: approximately 900 or 1800 spm. But advancing technology and increasing competition from foreign manufacturers have caused some variable speed saws to be priced down to nearly the same price range as one-or two-speed units. Most of these can be adjusted anywhere between 400 and 1800 spm.

Tables. Scroll saw tables can be tilted up to 45° for making bevel cuts. Some feature positive stops at common bevel angles. On inexpensive saws, the tables tend to be made from cast aluminum, while higher-quality saws have cast-iron tables. The shape of the table differs among manufacturers, from circular to rectangular to five-sided polygons.

Other features. Generally, more expensive saws have more bells and whistles. Among the more helpful are built-in blowers to keep the cutting area dust free, a dust-collection port, a clear blade guard, and a built-in worklight. But perhaps the most useful feature is a quick-release blade change system that allows you to easily disconnect and reconnect the blade when making repeated inside cuts.

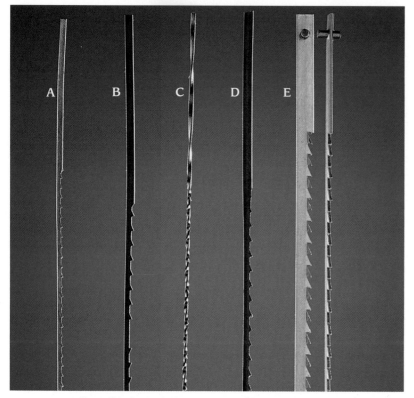

Common scroll saw blades include: (A) #7, 12 tpi scrolling blade; (B) #7, 11.5 tpi reverse-tooth fret blade; (C) #2, 41 tpi spiral-tooth blade, (D) #9, 11.5 tpi fret blade; (E) #5, 15 tpi pinned scrolling blade (side and front views).

TIPS:

Buy precision-ground blades. Most inexpensive scroll saw blades are made of stamped steel—scroll saw blades are quite prone to breakage, so woodworkers as a rule don't care to invest much money in them. The main drawback to stamped blades is that one side is usually rougher than the other, which can cause the blade to pull toward the rough side when you cut with it. For a little more money, you can purchase precision-ground scroll saw blades that are machined to produce two sides of equal smoothness. These will make cleaner cuts than stamped blades, and because they're less likely to get hung up in the workpiece, they usually last longer.

Follow these guidelines to preventing premature blade breakage:
- Keep an eye on blade tension—a blade that's too loose or too tight is the leading cause of broken blades.
- Use the best blade for the task.
- Don't try to cut a curve that's tighter than your blade can cut.
- Slow down the speed on variable speed saws if the stock is resisting the cut.
- Don't force the workpiece into the blade.
- Release blade tension when the saw is not in use.

BUYING TIP:

Because there are so many scroll saw blade options, choosing the right blade can be a little dizzying. The safest way to choose blades is simply to read the suggested use information on the blade package. As you gain more experience, make notes on each type of blade and keep the information in the same place you store your blades.

Scroll saw blades

Scroll saws blades are almost exclusively special-purpose blades. When you switch patterns or materials, you'll usually need to switch blades to get the best cutting results. The blade shanks come in two basic varieties: *pin end* and *plain end (See photo above).* Many saws will accept either style, but check your owner's manual to make sure. Scroll saw blades are listed with a gauge number from #0 to #12, referring to blade thickness (from 0.10" to 0.024").

Pin-end blades resemble coping saw blades, with a short pin embedded in each shank. The pin provides some auxiliary support for the clamps that hold the blade in place. The main difference between pin-end blades is the number of teeth per inch (tpi). The tooth configuration is quite similar from blade to blade.

Plain-end blades simply have a flat shank at each end. They're available in a greater variety of types and sizes than pin-end blades, and are used more frequently for finer work. Plain-end blades fall into three general categories:

scrolling blades, for making faster cuts; *fret blades*, with a skip-tooth design for finer cutting (some fret blades have a reverse tooth pattern at the bottom to minimize tearout); and *spiral blades*, which are twisted so the teeth sprout out from the blades in all directions—this allows them to make very tight cuts, although the thickness of the kerf is increased. To cut nonferrous metal, use a hardened steel *jeweler's blade* with teeth that resemble those on a hacksaw blade.

Setting up a scroll saw

Because scroll saws are basically single-purpose tools, they don't require as much tune-up as other power saws. One important consideration is making sure the table is square to the blade path when set at 0°. Set the saw for a straight cut, then check the blade with a square. Make adjustments as necessary, then reset the bevel indicator to 0° when the blade and table are exactly perpendicular.

Also make sure the blade tension is correct. Most scroll saw users do this by tightening the blade tension knob, then plucking the blade with a finger and listening for a high, steady tone. Also inspect the adjustable hold-down clamp (it should move freely but hold fast against the top surface of the workpiece (See photo below). Check to make sure the dust blower tube is free of clogs.

Using a scroll saw

Getting good results from your scroll saw is simply a matter of practice. In most cases, you don't use a straightedge or fence with a scroll saw—the tool is intended to be used freehand. If the saw is equipped with a blade guard, make sure it's in place. Adjust the hold-down to keep the workpiece from bouncing, and start cutting. If you're just learning to use the scroll saw, practice on wood scraps until you get a feel for the machine.

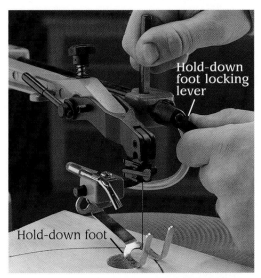

Hold-down foot locking lever

Hold-down foot

Adjust the height of the hold-down foot so it is resting securely on the top of the workpiece—but not with so much tension it mars the the wood. Lock the foot in place with the hold-down foot locking lever or knob.

TIPS:

Gang-cutting. Gang-cut thin workpieces for uniform results. Because the scroll saw is not a very aggressive machine, you can usually get by with using double-sided carpet tape to hold multiple workpieces together. When gang-cutting, it's especially important to make sure the table is square to the blade, and pay special attention to your feed rate.

Cutting metal. For clean cuts in nonferrous metal, sandwich the metal between two pieces of scrap stock before cutting. With a jeweler's blade installed, set your variable speed scroll saw for around 600 spm, and make your cut (it's okay to hold the scraps and workpiece together with masking tape, as long as it doesn't obscure the cutting line).

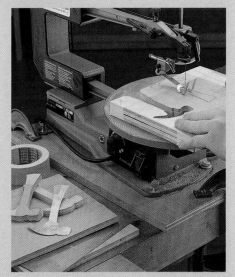

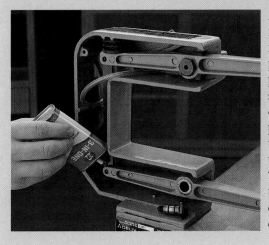

Maintenance. The most important maintenance procedure for parallel-arm scroll saws is to periodically lubricate the pivot points where the arms are linked, using machine oil. This allows the saw to run more efficiently and quietly.

Drill Presses

Over the years the drill press has evolved from being simply a hardworking metal-boring tool to become one of the most important tools used in wood joinery. It can drill precise holes for dowel joints, perfectly positioned counterbored pilot holes for fastening screws, and it's often used to remove most of the waste in a mortise.

But its usefulness in the shop goes well beyond simply joinery. You can use a drill press to drill guide holes for everything from hardware, to spindles and axles, to lamp cords. With the proper bits you can make perfect flat-bottomed holes. It can cut wood plugs that are a perfect match for your woodworking projects. And with special jigs and accessories you can sand, grind, polish and even rout profiles and grooves with a drill press. And on top of everything, the drill press is still the only tool that can effectively bore clean holes in metal and other hard materials.

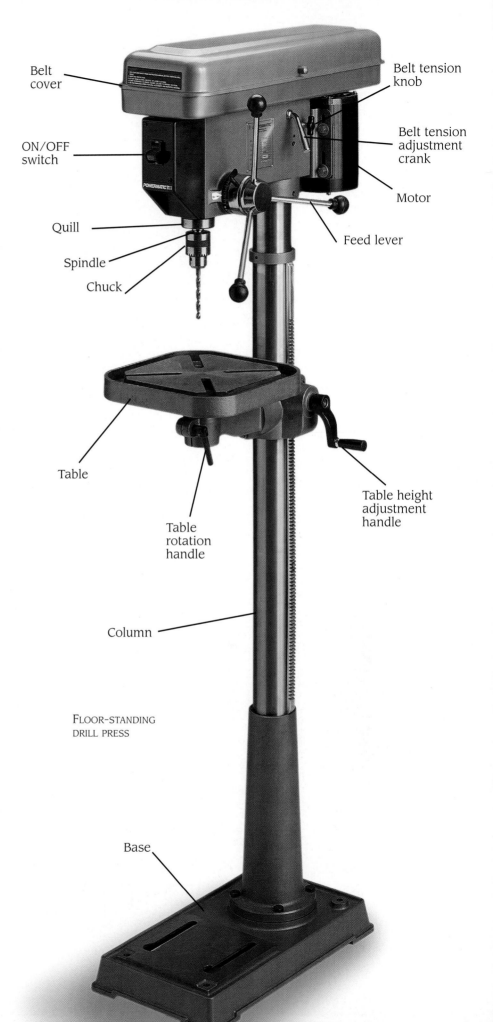

Belt cover

ON/OFF switch

Quill

Spindle

Chuck

Belt tension knob

Belt tension adjustment crank

Motor

Feed lever

Table

Table rotation handle

Table height adjustment handle

Column

FLOOR-STANDING DRILL PRESS

Base

Drill Press Fact Sheet		
Application	**Tool Recommendation**	**Accessories**
Light Use	Benchtop model with ⅙- to½-hp motor, tilting table, variable speed from 620 to 3000 rpm, and 4″ to 7″ throat capacity.	Common sizes of twist bits, brad-point bits and Forstner bits, sanding drum, auxiliary table (wood).
Moderate Use	Floor-standing model with ¾- to 1-hp motor, variable speeds from 250 to 3000 rpm, and 8″ throat capacity.	Full sets of brad-point and Forstner bits, vix bits, additional sanding accessories, hole saws, fly wheel, plug cutter, dowel cutter, mortising attachment.
Heavy Use	High-end floor-standing model with 1- to 1½-hp motor, variable speeds from 150 to 4000 rpm, 8″- to 10″-throat capacity. Radial drill press for drilling compound angles.	Auxiliary compound-angle drilling jig, dust collection system, full set of carbide coated twist bits for metal.

Drill press basics

The drill press consists of four principal components: the *base and column,* which support the tool; *the head,* which is attached to the column; a *motor* mounted at the back of the head; and an *adjustable table,* which supports the workpiece.

The base and column. The cast-iron base of the drill is aligned with the normal position of the head and table for maximum stability with a small footprint. The base has guide holes for anchor bolts—always bolt or clamp a benchtop drill press securely to your worksurface. The polished steel column secured in the base varies in height depending on the tool type and manufacturer. It's connected to the table with a vertical height adjustment mechanism (usually rack-and-pinion style) so the table can be raised or lowered and locked into position.

The head. The head of the drill press includes the motor and drive mechanism, the housings and covers, and the lever that lowers the drill bit. One or two rubber V-belts are stretched between cone-type (sometimes called *step*) pulleys inside the head to transfer power to the *quill* (the quill is a tubular housing fitted with ball bearings that contains the drill spindle). By adjusting the position of the V-belt(s) in the pulleys, you control the speed of the drill. Drilling action is created when the V-belts turn the quill inside the head: A *chuck* is attached to the exposed end of the *spindle,* and a drill

bit or another cutting instrument is inserted into the chuck at the base of the quill. To drill, the quill is lowered with a lever to contact the workpiece on the table. A drill press is usually equipped with a rod-style depth stop to control drilling depth precisely.

The motor. Workshop drill presses don't require large motors. Most are ½ or ¾ hp, and draw anywhere from 8- to 16-amps. Benchtop drill presses may have motors as small as ⅙ hp, with some drawing less than 3 amps of power.

The adjustable table. Drill press tables vary somewhat in size and in the arrangement of the slots. All have a 1″- to 2″-diameter hole for the drill bits to pass through. Most are made of cast-iron, although lower-end models often have a cast aluminum table. The table can be tilted 90° on most machines, allowing you to clamp longer workpieces to increase the capacity of the drill *(See photo, right).* Most tables have an angle indicator calibrated up to 45°.

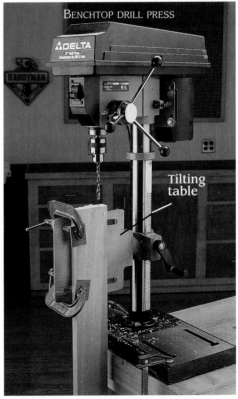

BENCHTOP DRILL PRESS

Tilting table

Tilt the table to vertical and use it as a clamping surface when drilling large or awkward workpieces.

Drill press types

Drill presses are available in benchtop and floor-standing versions. The primary difference is in the greater distance from the drill to the drill table on floor models, which allows you to work on larger projects. If you own a benchtop drill press, you can usually get around the limited working depth by spinning the drill so the quill overhangs your workbench. If you tilt the table out of the way, this lets you work on workpieces that are resting on the floor or clamped vertically to the table *(See photo, previous page)*.

The size of the drill press is usually listed by the *throat capacity*, which is determined by doubling the distance from the chuck to the front of the column. Benchtop drill presses start at 8″ throat capacity; models with 10″, 12″ and 14″ throat capacity are readily available. Some manufacturers make benchtop drill presses with a throat capacity as large as 18″. Floor models start out around 12″ in throat capacity, and 14″ models are the most common. You can buy tools with a throat capacity as great as 30″.

Radial drill presses. A less common drill press type is the radial drill press. On this tool, the head is mounted on the end of a horizontal ram cylinder that moves back and forth in a collar at the top of the column. The head pivots on the ram, allowing you to drill angled holes. By tilting both the table and the head, you can drill compound angles. A radial drill press normally has a larger throat capacity than standard models. If you build a lot of spindle-type furniture, this tool can be useful.

Bits & accessories

Bits. Any bit that's suitable for a portable drill can also be used in a drill press (for a sampling of common bits, see the chapter on *Portable Drills*). About the only bits that won't work are square-shank bits used in some hand drills. The best bits for drilling wood are brad-point bits and Forstner bits. Both are excellent for accurately engaging the wood at a drilling point and piercing the wood without creating tearout as a twist bit or standard spade bit will.

Brad-point bits (sometimes called *spur bits*) have a sharp spur at the tip and additional cutting spurs at the end of each *flute* to enter the wood cleanly. Forstner bits *(See photo, left)* are designed for drilling holes with very smooth sides and flat bottoms. In some cases, you won't be able to avoid using a twist bit or spade bit in woodworking, since they're available in a much greater range of sizes than brad-point or Forstner bits.

If you're drilling metal, use a carbide- or cobalt-tipped twist bit—be sure to punch a depression at the drilling point with an awl to prevent the drill bit from skating as it seeks to engage the metal. And if you do use a spade bit, try to find one that has cutting spurs at both edges to cut the wood fibers without tearing.

Hole saws and fly cutters. Hole saws and fly cutters can cut large holes by slicing out the perimeter of the hole. Hole saws are used and mounted in the same manner as when they're used in a portable drill *(See page 49 in* Portable Drills *section)*. Fly cutters are simply two round shafts joined together in a T-shape. One shaft resembling a twist bit fits into the chuck. The other shaft contains an adjustable cutting tip that cuts the wood as it spins around the center shaft. With both hole saws and fly cutters, set the drill press at a very slow speed setting.

Mortising attachments. These fairly complex drill press accessories are used to cut near-square mortises. To use them, remove the chuck from your drill press and attach the bracket of the accessory to the spindle. When the attachment is lowered into the wood, a hollow chisel compresses the edges of the mortise while a spinning auger inside the chisel clears away the waste wood. Even if you don't own a mortising attachment, you can cut mortises simply by drilling a series of holes the same diameter as the width of the mortise, then cleaning up the edges of the holes with a wood chisel.

Forstner bits are ideally suited for woodworking because they cut holes with smooth sides, flat bottoms, and no tearout.

Plug cutters. A plug cutter is used to make custom wood plugs for filling screw-hole counterbores in woodworking projects. A standard plug cutter cuts out ⅜"-diameter plugs. To use a plug cutter, simply set the depth stop of the drill press to make a cut about ½" deep, then cut as many plugs as you'll need from a piece of wood that matches the wood you're using in your project *(See photo, right)*. To release the plugs, resaw the board to about ⅜" thickness on your band saw.

Drum sanders. Drum sanders are sanding cylinders with a central shaft that mounts in the chuck of a drill. Their main use is in smoothing out contours or circular cutouts. You can buy drum sanders in a wide range of diameters, from ½" up to 2" or 3". Most sizes are available in several grits. Because sanding creates so much dust, you may want to make yourself a dust collection box like the one shown in the photo below. Drum sanders (sometimes called *spindle sanders*) can be purchased individually or in sets. Some sets have a single arbor that fits in the chuck, with interchangeable drums so you can sand in progressively finer grits without having to constantly loosen and tighten the chuck.

A plug cutter lets you make your own wood plugs for filling screw hole counterbores. By cutting the plug from the same stock as the workpiece, you can create a perfect match. Resaw the board on your band saw after the plug cutter holes are drilled.

TIP:

Build a dust collection box to help contain dust generated from a drum sander attachment mounted in your drill press. Make a sturdy box, about 12 × 12" and at least 4" deep. Make sure the top of the box is strong and smooth, since it will become a sanding table. Leave a lip that's at least 1" wide on the bottom of the box so you can clamp the box to your drill press table. Drill a hole in one side to accommodate a port for your dust collector or shop vacuum hose (usually 2½" or 4" in diameter). Using a hole cutter, drill a 2½"-dia. hole in the center of the top (this will accept a sanding drum up to 2" in diameter). Lower the drum so the bottom is below the top of the box.

Tuning up your drill press

A drill press requires considerably less tune-up than many other stationary power tools. Other than occasional resetting of the angle indicator on the table, the main exercise is to check the various spinning parts to make sure they're true and spinning in a tight pattern. If the quill, spindle, or chuck is worn or bent, the drill bit will move in a slight elliptical pattern, making it impossible to drill precise holes—this is called *runout*. If you notice runout as the bit spins or cuts, first try installing another bit. Bits are more likely to bend than parts of the drill.

Testing the chuck. If more than one of the bits you install in your drill spins off center, test the chuck to make sure it's not worn out or damaged. The most accurate way to do this is to install a precision-milled metal rod into the chuck. The most widely available type of rod is a polished steel, pointed rod known as a *know bit.* You can find these at some tool supply stores or at a supplier of metal-working machinery. Insert the know bit (or another straight rod about ½" in diameter) into the chuck and tighten the chuck securely.

Then, clamp a straight board to your drill press table so the edge is butted up against the side of the know bit. Rotate the spindle by hand-turning the V-belts at the top of the drill press. Watch the know bit as it rotates—it should stay in contact with the board, without any gaps. If you see a gap, even a very tiny one, as the bit spins, you'll need to measure the gap to find out if it's within the acceptable toler-

ance for the machine—most woodworkers consider 0.01" as the tolerance for the chuck and spindle.

There are two ways to measure the gap: you can simply insert a feeler gauge into the gap and take a manual reading *(See photo, left)* or you can use a precise *dial indicator,* like the one being used to test the spindle in photo below. If the gap is greater than 0.01", the next step is to determine if the runout is being created by the chuck or by the spindle.

Testing the spindle. To test the spindle for runout, first remove the chuck. In some cases, this is a pretty simple procedure. But if you've got an older drill press with the original chuck in place, it may be a bit of a battle. Your owner's manual should contain information on removing the chuck. If you're unable to get the chuck off, don't try to force it—you will only worsen any problems you may have. The safest bet is to remove the quill that contains the spindle and chuck and bring it to a tool service center to have the chuck removed. With the chuck removed, test the spindle for runout, using either a feeler gauge or a dial indicator *(See photo below).* If the spindle is true, you know the chuck is the culprit and it requires replacement. If the spindle shows runout, order and install a replacement spindle.

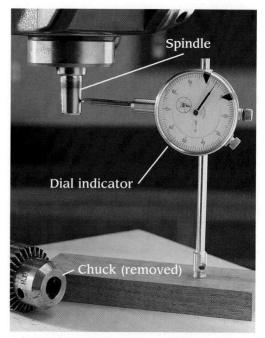

If the chuck is free of runout, remove it and test the spindle with a dial indicator or feeler gauge.

Use a know bit and feeler gauge to test your chuck for runout. Rotate the quill and check for gaps of more than 0.01" between the know bit and a straight board. You can also use a dial indicator for this test.

TIP:

When using hole saws or other accessories that are larger than the hole in the center of your drill press table, cut an auxiliary table from ¾" plywood and clamp it on top of the metal table. Or, you can attach it more permanently to the table by screwing it in place through the holes or slots in the drill press table.

Check the table angle indicator. To see if the tilt angle indicator on your drill press is calibrated correctly, you need to chuck a straight bit or rod into the drill. Once you've done this, tilt the table to several different angles, according to the indicator. Measure the angle between the bit or rod and your table, using a T-bevel and protractor. If the angles differ, reset the indicator on your drill to match the angle shown by the measuring tools.

Using your drill press

The most important factors when using a drill press are choosing the best bit for the job, and setting the drill to the correct speed. Inside the cover of your drill press, you should find a chart that shows the appropriate drilling speed for

Build a compound angle jig. Because the head of a regular drill press doesn't tilt, build an adjustable jig if you want to drill holes at a compound angle. Hinge together two pieces of ¾ × 12 × 12" plywood on one edge. On the edges adjacent to the hinged side, install locking chest lid supports. Clamp the jig to your drill press table and tilt the table to one of the angles in the compound angle. Use a protractor to set the two pieces of the jig so they are at the same angle as the second angle in the compound angle. Lock the lid supports in position. Drill a test hole before drilling your workpiece.

TIP:

Seating the chuck. Here's a good way to install a chuck on your drill press (except if your drill press has a screw-on chuck). Insert the spindle into the opening at the top of the chuck with just enough tension to hold it in place. Then, place a piece of plywood on the drill press table. Raise the table so the plywood just touches the bottom of the chuck. Pull down on the feed lever to seat the chuck, then turn on the drill press at its lowest speed setting and continue to apply downward pressure on the feed lever.

just about any task. A basic rule of drill press operation is: *The bigger the bit, the slower the speed.* Harder materials also require slower speeds than softer woods and plastics. Along with the speed suggestions, you should find a series of symbols that show you how to position the V-belt or (V-belts) to get the correct speed. There should be one or two levers or bolts on the side of the drill press cover that release the tension in the belt or belts so you can change their position without stressing them. Always unplug your drill before making any adjustments.

Keep a few basic rules in mind when operating a drill press:
- Don't force the bit into the material; apply gentle, even pressure when lowering the feed lever.
- Always wear eye protection when operating a drill press.
- Make sure the workpiece is securely clamped to the table. This is especially important when machining metal.

Jointers

The jointer is seldom the first power tool purchased when setting up a workshop, and you can probably get along without one—for a while. You can build many fine woodworking projects using lumber that is sold already planed and surfaced to standard thickness, and ripped to standard widths. But eventually you'll want to add a jointer and a power planer *(See next chapter)* to your tool collection. With these tools, you can prepare and size your wood stock from rough lumber much more quickly and accurately than you can using hand planes. Having this capability will greatly increase your lumber selection options, as well as save you money. Lumber sold in the rough or with only one side surfaced, and in random widths, is considerably cheaper than premilled wood.

The primary purpose of the jointer is to cut flat, square edges in wood stock. This ensures that the lumber will be square when you plane it, shape it and make joints. This is usually the first operation you perform on rough stock. The process of squaring and sizing is known as *dressing* a rough board. If the rough stock is much wider than the workpiece you need, rip it to a slightly oversized width on your band saw or table saw before jointing it. Once you've created

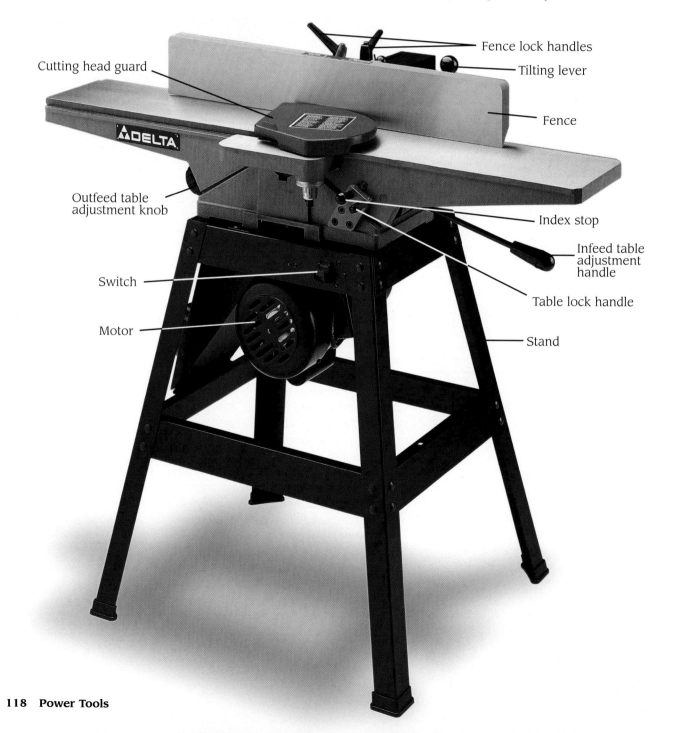

Cutting head guard

Fence lock handles

Tilting lever

Fence

Outfeed table adjustment knob

Index stop

Switch

Infeed table adjustment handle

Table lock handle

Motor

Stand

smooth, straight edges on two adjacent sides of the board, you can use a planer or table saw to size it.

The jointer isn't used exclusively on rough lumber. Any time you need a smooth, straight edge on a workpiece, look to the jointer first. For example, it's good practice to run the mating edges of two boards through the jointer before edge-gluing them. Some jointers feature a protruding ledge next to the cutting head that supports the workpiece when cutting rabbets or tongues. You can also use a jointer to cut bevels, chamfers and tapers, as well as to salvage warped or bowed wood.

If you already own a jointer or intend to buy one, you should also make sure your shop is equipped with a power planer. Together, these two tools can convert an ordinary workshop into a mini-lumber mill.

Jointer types

Although jointers are sold in both benchtop and stationary floor models, the vast majority in service and for sale today are of the floor-standing variety. Typically, these have longer infeed and outfeed tables than benchtop models, making them more accurate when jointing stock of any significant length. Floor-standing jointers can have much greater cutting-width capacity, with some models able to machine stock as wide as 12″ or even 16″ (these are industrial tools, however, with hefty price tags). Most jointers for home use have a maximum cutting width of 6″. With floor-standing jointers, you have the option of purchasing a cabinet-type stand. The cabinet protects the motor while giving the tool better stability, and it can also be used to collect shavings.

Jointer basics

The jointer is essentially a power version of the jointing plane. It has four important parts: a cylindrical cutting head with slots that accept cutting knives; an infeed table that's adjusted up or down to set the cutting depth; an outfeed table, usually stationary, that supports the workpiece after it passes through the cutter; and an adjustable fence. A spring-loaded metal guard covers the exposed cutting knives as they spin.

The cutting head. The cutting head is a machined metal cylinder with milled longitudinal slots that hold the cutting knives. Lower-end jointers have two knives on opposite sides of the cylinder, but usually you'll find three evenly spaced knives. Some models have four cutting knives. The fewer knives a cutting head has, the faster it must spin to produce a clean cut. Two-knife jointers usually spin between 8,000 and 11,000 rpm, while most three-knife and four-knife jointers spin at about 4,500 rpm. In general, faster cutting-head speeds yield smoother cuts, but the real test is the number of cuts per minute, which is figured by multiplying the rpm rating by the number of blades. Keep in mind, however, that in order for any of these numbers to be meaningful, the knives must be precisely adjusted to the same cutting height. Otherwise, the highest knife will be the only one cutting, which tends to cause noticeable rippling in the cut.

The infeed and outfeed tables. The jointer tables, sometimes called *beds,* are usually made of cast iron with smooth, milled surfaces on top. The outfeed table is not designed to be adjusted on most modern models, although many older machines allow you to raise or lower the outfeed table. The height of the infeed table is always adjustable. By raising or lowering it, you control the depth of the cut. The peak cutting height of the knives must be level with the outfeed table. Then, as the workpiece is fed along the infeed table, it contacts the exposed portion of the knives, which shave off enough material so the machined surface rides smoothly along the outfeed table.

The fence. The fence on a good jointer is also made of cast iron with a polished surface on the cutting side. A fence that's exactly perpendicular to the table and to the cutting head is critical to making accurate, square cuts. Most fences can be tilted and locked in place for cutting bevels. The center of the fence features a semicircular cutout so the fence can be positioned over the spinning cutting head.

Power. A typical floor-standing jointer has a ¾-or 1-hp motor. Benchtop models approach that range in hp, but more often than not they're equipped with a *universal*

TIP:

Keep your jointer adjusted to remove about 1/16" to 1/32" of material. For deeper cuts, make multiple passes, measuring the workpiece after each cut, until it's the correct width.

motor. Universal motors make more noise than the *induction motors* usually found on floor-standing models, plus they're more apt to bog down when cutting heavier stock. Industrial jointers feature 2-hp to 3-hp motors that normally run on 230-volt service.

Features. If you're in the market for a jointer, the first features you should examine are the table and fence adjustment devices. Many woodworkers prefer jointers that have locking handwheels for easy, precise adjusting. Also check the cutting head to see how the knives are held in place. Some cutting heads have spring-loaded slots that exert upward pressure on the knives—this makes setting the height a much easier process *(see Align the cutting knives)*. A built-in dust collection port, a lockable or removable ON/OFF switch, and a rabetting ledge are also useful.

infeed side—the end of the table further from the cutting head is prone to sagging.

To raise the infeed table so it's parallel with the outfeed table, you need to adjust the screws that secure the *gib* that draws the bottom edges of the table together with the jointer base. On many machines, these parts mate together in dovetail-shaped slots. Locate the lock nuts that hold the gib fast. With the table-locking mechanism loosened, unscrew the lock-nuts slightly. Then, tighten or loosen the adjustment screws until the gap beneath the straightedge is eliminated *(See photo, left)*. Tighten the lock nuts, supporting the table so it doesn't sag as you work.

Note: Both the infeed and outfeed tables normally are attached to the base the same way. The outfeed table can be adjusted in the same manner as the infeed table.

Raise the outfeed table. Because the cutting knives need to be even with the outfeed table, the table must be slightly higher than the cutting head so the knives have room to extend out from the head. Since the position of the cutting head is not meant to be adjusted, you'll need to raise the outfeed table an amount equal to the recommended reveal of the knives—usually 0.060". You'll need a *feeler gauge* to make this adjustment. Set a straightedge on the outfeed table, then raise the table using the gib bar adjustment screws until a 0.060" feeler gauge fits precisely between the top of the cutting head and the straightedge *(See photo below)*. Be careful to keep the table in the same plane as you raise it. Secure the gib screws.

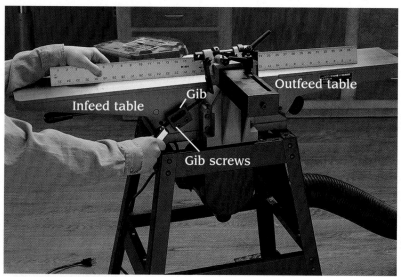

With the fence removed and the cutting head positioned so none of the knives is protruding above the tables, use a long straightedge to check for gaps or dips in the straight line that should be formed between the infeed and outfeed tables when the infeed table is raised to "0" cutting height. Make adjustments by loosening the gib screws, then repositioning the infeed table.

Setting up & tuning your jointer

Check for parallel tables. Start setting up or tuning your jointer by checking to make sure the infeed and outfeed tables are parallel. First, make sure the knives are at or below the height of the outfeed table, then raise the infeed table to its highest point—this should be at the "0" setting on the cutting depth indicator. Remove the fence. Position a long straightedge so it spans both tables. Checking for any gaps beneath the straightedge, test the tables in several spots, including at diagonal angles. If gaps exist, they'll most likely be on the

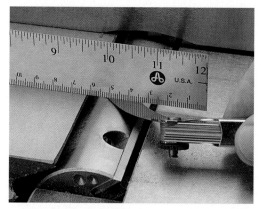

Using a feeler gauge as a guide, set the outfeed table so it's 0.060" higher then the top of the cutting head. Measure down from a straightedge on the outfeed table.

Mark a reference line on the jointer fence at the the highest point of the cutting head. Used to set the height of the knives, this line indicates the spot where the knives will contact the workpiece.

Align the cutting knives. Setting the cutting knives to the correct height can be a disagreeable task at first, but once you get the hang of it, it will become routine. The knives are held in place in the cutting head slots with a *gib bar* system similar to that used to fasten the tables to the base. As the gib bar is tightened, it presses the knife against the edge of the slot, holding it in place.

The knives must be set so they're exactly even with the top of the outfeed table at their peak cutting points. First, clamp the cutting head guard to the table or rabbeting ledge so it's out of the way. Then, slightly loosen the gib screws that hold each knife in place in its slot. To remove a knife, loosen the set screws that press the gib bar against the knife until it can be withdrawn from the slot. Only remove one knife at a time. Also remove the gib bar. Depending on the manufacturer, there may be either a spring-loaded device or adjustable blocks that raise the knife in the slot. Set these devices so they're flush with the bottom of the slot.

Before reinstalling the knife, mark a line on the fence at the same height as the cutting head at its highest cutting

point *(See photo, left)*. You'll use this mark as a reference for installing the knives— the line establishes the point where the knives will contact the workpiece.

Insert a sharpened knife and the gib bar into the slot, so the outside edge of the knife extends slightly past the outside edge of the outfeed table. Tighten the gib screws so they hold the knife in place but are loose enough that the knife can be moved without too much effort. If your jointer has springs in the slot that force the knife upward, position a pair of wooden straightedges on the outfeed table so they contact the knives. The springs will automatically lift the knives to the correct height—make sure the cutting edge of each knife is aligned with the mark you made on the fence when it contacts the straightedges.

If your jointer has adjusting screws that raise the knife, place a straightedge on the outfeed table, and turn each screw to raise the knife until it contacts the straightedge, adjusting the middle screws first *(See photo below)*. Double-check the knife at several spots, making adjustments as needed. Tighten the gib bar screws securely once the knife is set.

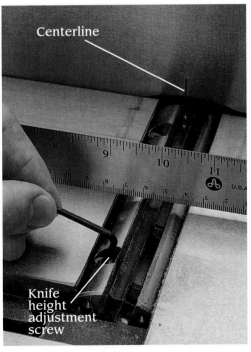

Some jointers have knife height adjustment screws that are used to set the height of each knife so it meets the straightedge at the centerline marking the point where the knife will contact the workpiece.

TIPS:

• **Hone knives.** Use a good whetstone or carborundum stone to hone a nice edge onto the knives— without removing them from the cutting head *(See page 126)*.

• **Spare knife set.** Keep a spare set of sharp jointer knives on hand. Most manufacturers suggest that you remove only one knife at a time, then replace it before removing the next. Having an extra set of knives allows you to replace the knives in short order, instead of making several trips to your local sharpening center to have your knives sharpened one at a time.

A magnetic knife jig draws the loosened knife up to the correct height, even with the outfeed table. These jigs are very useful if your jointer doesn't have spring-loaded knife slots or knife height adjustment screws.

- Make sure the knives are sharp and the machine is adjusted correctly.
- Always feed the workpiece so the knives will remove wood with the grain *(See photo, page 127)*
- Press the workpiece firmly up against the fence.
- Use hold-downs to guide your work-piece past the cutting head. Position one hold-down toward the front of the workpiece, and another toward the rear. Never pass your hands over the cutting head area.
- Do not stand directly in line with the workpiece.
- Always wear ear and eye protection.
- Feed stock into the cutting head at a slow, steady pace, making sure it rides smoothly along the table surfaces.
- Always keep the knife guard in place.
- Make sure the workpiece is completely free of dirt, oil, nails, or any other obstructions.
- Make multiple passes removing small amounts of material.

If the slots in the cutting head of your jointer don't have springs or adjusting screws, setting your knife height can be tricky. One good solution is to purchase a magnetic knife jig *(See photo above).* Place the magnetic jig over the cutting head so the end of the jig rests on the outfeed table. Making sure the cutting edge of the knife is aligned with the center mark on the fence, adjust the tension in the gib bar screws so the magnets can draw the knife up—do this slowly or the force of the knife against the bar magnets could damage the knife. Pressing down on the jig, tighten the gib bar screws.

Check the fence. Use a try square to make sure the fence is perpendicular to the tables when set at *0˚.* If your fence tilts, check with a T-bevel and protractor to see if the angle indicator is accurate, and adjust the indicators as needed. Also check to see that the fence is perpendicular to the cutting head by laying one side of a try square next to one of the knives for a reference point.

Using your jointer

The two most basic jointer operations are edge-jointing and face-jointing. In these, and in all wood-jointing tasks, follow these guidelines *(as demonstrated in the photo, right):*

Standard practices when using a jointer should include: using hold-downs or pushblocks; keeping the cutting head guard in good condition, wearing ear and eye protection, and standing to the side of the workpiece.

Edge jointing. Set the cutting depth to remove the smallest amount of material necessary to get an even surface. Position the better face against the jointer fence, and apply pressure downward and toward the fence as you feed the stock through the cutting head.

Face jointing (also called *surfacing* or *planing*). This action is similar to edge-jointing, except the wider surface is laid flat while an edge runs against the fence. Always use hold-downs or pushblocks. Don't attempt to face-joint stock that's wider than the cutting head.

Rabbeting. A jointer is capable of cutting crisp, clean rabbet grooves in the edges of boards—especially if your jointer has a rabbeting ledge to support the workpiece as it passes the cutting head. The main drawback to using your jointer for these cuts is that you need to remove the knife guard to make the cut, creating a significant safety hazard. To cut a rabbet, adjust the fence so it's the same distance away from the ends of the knives as the planned width of the rabbet. Set the cutting depth—it's best to make multiple passes, deepening the cut each time. Feed the board through the cutting head with extreme care, using pushblocks *(See photo below)*.

Beveling edges. Set the tilting fence to the correct angle and feed the stock as if you were making a straight cut. If your fence tilts either to the left or to the right, tilt the fence to the left whenever possible. Make multiple passes as needed.

Reclaim warped wood

You can reclaim warped or bowed lumber by cutting it back to square on your jointer. To square up a board that has bowed, simply run the crowned edge over the jointer knives until the crown is completely trimmed off. Then trim off the concave edge on your table saw or band saw, with the jointed edge flush against the fence. To reclaim warped wood, joint the face that's warped outward until it's flat, then run the board through a planer to flatten the concave face.

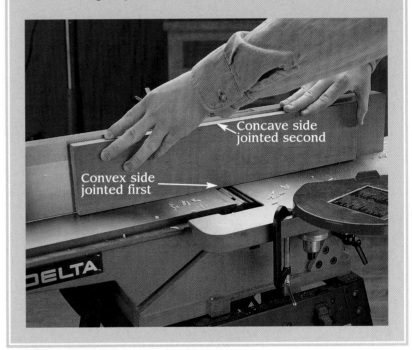

Concave side jointed second

Convex side jointed first

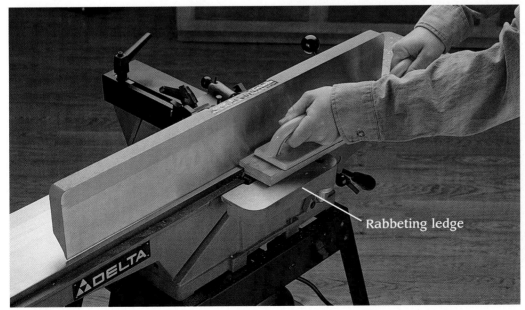

The jointer can cut clean, precise rabbets, but because cutting them forces you to remove the cutting head guard, you must use great care. Always use hold-downs to guide the workpiece past the cutting head, directing pressure both downward and in toward the fence to keep the workpiece from moving side to side.

Rabbeting ledge

Power Planers

Owning a power planer adds a handy dimension to the range of woodworking activities you can do in your shop. Together with the power jointer, it allows you to effectively size and prepare your stock for shaping and joinery. Even if you don't own a jointer, you should read through the preceding chapter on jointers (pages 118 to 123)—you may pick up a few helpful tips for understanding and using your planer.

In many ways, the power planer resembles the jointer. They both feature a metal cylindrical cutting head that's milled with longitudinal slots to accept two or more sharp knives. The knives shave material from the stock as it feeds past, creating a smooth surface.

But the planer differs from the jointer in a few important ways. First, the cutting head is typically about twice the width of the jointer, allowing you to surface stock up to 12" wide on most portable home models. On a planer, the knives shave the stock from above, compared to the jointer, where the workpiece is fed over the cutting knives. And almost all planers today are self-feeding: you simply nudge the workpiece forward until it engages the rollers in the front of the tool, and then the tool takes over.

In addition to drawing the workpiece automatically past the cutting head, the rollers also serve to flatten out any warps in the workpiece. While this may sound like a good thing, the problem is that once the freshly planed workpiece emerges on the outfeed side of the planer, it quickly resumes its previous shape. This leaves behind a workpiece that's perfectly smooth, but no more square than when you started. That's why you should always begin squaring a workpiece by running it through the jointer to get at least two square, flat surfaces.

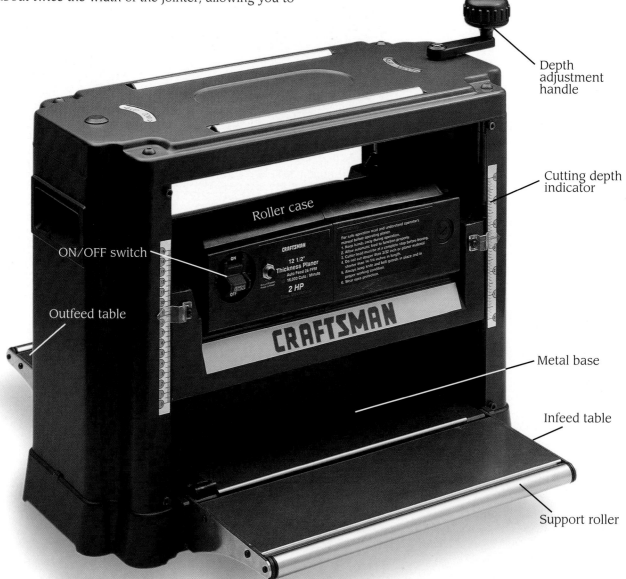

Depth adjustment handle

Cutting depth indicator

Roller case

ON/OFF switch

CRAFTSMAN
12 1/2"
Thickness Planer
Auto Feed 26 FPM
16,000 Cuts / Minute
2 HP

For safe operation read and understand operator's manual before operating planer.
1. Keep hands away during operation.
2. Allow automatic feed to function properly.
3. Cutter head must be at a complete stop before freeing.
4. Do not cut deeper than 3/32 inch or planer material shorter than 14-1/4 inches in length.
5. Always keep knife and belt guards in place and in proper working condition.
6. Wear eyes protection.

CRAFTSMAN

Outfeed table

Metal base

Infeed table

Support roller

Creating a smooth surface and reducing the thickness of a board are the primary purposes of the power planer. As these relatively new shop tools become more commonplace, however, creative handymen continue to find new and interesting uses for them beyond simply shaving off wood in a flat line. By fitting the cutting head with profiled knives, you can convert your planer into a shaper for cutting custom moldings. You can also install a sanding drum on some models, creating a scaled-down version of a *time-saver* stationary surfacing machine. And on some of the more powerful planers, you can purchase a rip-cutting attachment for precise production work.

Power planer basics

The power planer has evolved from a specialty tool found only in lumber mills and woodworking production shops, to a convenient, portable powerhouse of a tool that fits into the space and budget restrictions of most home handymen.

Planer types. Like most stationary tools, planers are available in both *bench-top* and *floor-standing* models. But unlike the others, the portable benchtop versions of the planer are much more common today, mostly due to their lower cost and small footprint. An average portable planer can handle stock up to 6" thick and up to 12" wide, comparable capacities to those for floor-standing models. The main limitation with portable planers is their cutting depth: most max out at around ⅛", while many floor-standing planers can take a bite twice that thick.

Most portable planers have only two knives in their cutting head, compared to three for floor-standing models. To compensate, their cutting head usually rotates at around 8,000 rpm, compared to 4,500 to 5,000 rpm for floor-standing models. A 2 hp motor is standard for portable planers. Floor-standing planers are equipped with motors ranging from 2 to 5 hp, and almost all of them require 230-volt electrical service.

For an average home workshop, a good portable planer should be able to handle most, if not all, of your planing needs. But if you do a lot of stock preparation, it's probably worth investing in a floor model. The deeper cutting capacity of the larger planers means you can get through more work more quickly.

Jointer/planers. Because planers and jointers are normally used in tandem, some manufacturers sell combination tools that do both jobs. These hybrid tools make more efficient use of floor space because they share a motor and base. The cutting capacities are comparable to the single-purpose tools they're designed to replace. The main drawback is the cost: usually at least five times the price of an average portable planer.

Planer features. The two most important parts of the power planer are the *roller case* that houses the cutting head and rollers, and the *parallel infeed and outfeed tables*.

The roller case. The roller case is a broad term that refers to the carriage assembly containing the cutting head and rollers. The case on most planers moves up and down on two or four steel columns to set the cutting depth of the tool. On some planers, however, the roller case is fixed and the table assembly is moved up and down to set the cutting depth. On most home planers, the *cutting head* is 10" to 12½" long, which establishes the maximum-width board the planer can surface.

The *cutting knives* are held in place in slots with a metal bar (called a *gib bar*) that forces the blade up tight against the edge of the slot. The cutting head is shrouded by curved metal plates spanning the entire width of the head. The front plate functions as a chip breaker to prevent splintering, and the main purpose of the back plate is to keep steady downward pressure on the workpiece. The rollers are surfaced with urethane, rubber or serrated metal so they can grip the workpiece. The chain-driven rollers spin independently to draw the workpiece through the tool at a fixed rate (marks made by the roller are removed as the board is planed).

TIP:

Snipe is a noticeable dip that occurs in the last few inches of your workpiece after it's fed through a planer or jointer. It happens when the infeed table is lower than the outfeed table, causing the board to pop up slightly into the cutting head when it clears the infeed table. (Snipe also occurs on jointers when the infeed table is too high.) To eliminate snipe, adjust the tables to parallel.

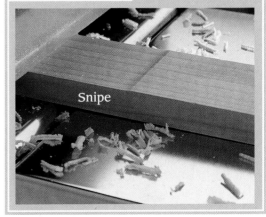

Snipe

Use a carpenter's level to check if the infeed table, outfeed table, and metal base between them are level. Adjust the infeed table to match the base and outfeed table.

Hone knives. Hone the edges of the planer knives with a sharpening stone. The stone should be flat on the bevel of the knife. Sharpen all knives equally. You can hone the knives two or three times without removing them, but eventually you'll need to remove them for resharpening.

The tables and base. Planers have both an infeed and an outfeed table, as well as a metal base that bridges the space between the tables. The tables are usually made from fairly light gauge metal and can be folded up on most portable models for easy transportation of the tool. When the planer is adjusted correctly, the tables and base are parallel and in line. Some planers have passive cylindrical rollers on each side of the base to reduce the resistance from the board as it feeds through the planer. Base rollers should be adjusted so they're top point is between 0.005" and 0.010" above the tables.

Other features. On most planers, the depth of the cut is set with a rotating adjustment lever. Check your owner's manual: each full rotation adjusts the depth by the same amount. The amount is useful to know when resetting the cutting depth. On the sides of the infeed face of the planer, you'll find depth indicators. On models with a movable roller case, "0" cutting depth occurs when the roller case is fully lowered. On models with movable tables, "0" occurs when the table is fully raised.

Buying tips. Look for a planer that adjusts up and down smoothly and has easy-to read depth indicators. Also look for planers with easy-to-use knife adjustment features (*See pages 121 to 122*). Some planer knives are disposable, and many can be reversed when one side gets dull (*See photo, next page*). A dust collection port is a very desirable feature on planers, as are extended infeed and outfeed tables.

Setting up & tuning your planer

Manufacturers recommend that you adjust and reset your planer after every two hours of continuous use. You might want to make a practice of tuning it up more frequently, especially if using it on hardwoods.

Adjust the tables and roller case. The main working parts of the planer need to be parallel to one another to cut squarely. Start by using a carpenter's level to make sure the tables are level and aligned with one another (*See photo, left*). If not, raise or lower the out-of-tune table until level is achieved, using the base as a reference. Then, test to make sure the cutting head is parallel to the tables. If it isn't, your workpiece will end up thicker on one side.

An easy way to gauge this is to feed two boards of the same thickness through the planer at opposite sides (*See photo below*). Compare the boards after planing them: if one board is thicker, adjust the position of the roller case. On models with movable tables, make the adjustment on the tables.

Check the knives and knife height. The knives in the cutting head should all be sharp and set to the same height (if the knives are dull, you'll know from the

Feed boards of the same thickness through opposite sides of the planer opening. After the boards are planed, measure them to find out if the planer is cutting more deeply on one side than the other.

roughness of the cut). To visually inspect the knives, or to replace them, first remove the blade guard portion of the roller case.

NOTE: The technique for setting uniform knife height varies somewhat between planer models. The following information is applicable to most planers, but not all. For more information on setting knives in the cutting head, read your owner's manual and the Align the cutting knives *section in the* Jointer *chapter (pages 121 to 122).*

Use a knife height gauge (a separate gauge that rides on the cutting head) to see if the knives fit into the gap on the underside of the gauge at all points. If not, loosen the gib screws that hold the knife between the gib bar and the slot. Most planers today have spring-loaded knife slots. When the gib screws are loosened, the blade springs up away from the bottom of the slot until it strikes a fixed point—in this case, the knife height gauge. With the knife pressed up against the gauge, tighten the gib screws one at a time to secure the knife at the correct, uniform cutting height. Adjust all knives to the same height.

Check the roller. Periodically check the amount of downward pressure the feed rollers exert on the workpiece. If the pressure is too light, the workpiece will slip. If the pressure is too great, you risk scarring your workpiece. When making deeper cuts or when planing dense hardwood, increase the roller pressure.

Using power planers

Make sure the board is free of dirt, embedded nails, and any other obstructions that could damage the knives. Using the depth adjustment lever, set the planer opening so it's the same thickness as the board. Then, decrease the opening by the amount of material you want to remove—as a general rule, don't remove more than 1/32" of material per pass. Check your feed direction, making sure the workpiece enters the planer so the knives will be cutting with the grain (*See photo above*).

Turn on the planer and let it build to maximum speed. Nudge the board forward on the infeed table, keeping it square to the roller case, until the infeed roller engages the board. Let go and step

Grain direction

back from the planer—don't stand directly behind it. Make sure you have adequate support for the workpiece on both sides of the planer. **Caution: Never handle the workpiece on either the infeed or outfeed side of the planer until the cut is complete and the workpiece is clear of the outfeed roller.** Measure the thickness of the workpiece. If necessary, continue removing material in thin passes until the correct thickness is achieved. Plane equal amounts from both faces of the workpiece to help prevent warping.

Feed boards into the planer so the cutting head knives will be cutting with the grain, as shown in the photo above.

HANDYMAN
CLUB OF AMERICA

TIP:

Cutting head

Reversible knife

Gib screw   Gib bar

Reversible blades. On today's planers, knife blades are often reversible. If the knives are getting dull, simply remove and reverse them so the sharp edge is exposed. Always change or reverse all knives at once. As with a jointer, it's a good idea to obtain a spare set of knives so you can keep working while one set is being sharpened.

Lathes

Because the lathe performs such a unique wood-working function, it's often lumped into the *specialty tools* category by many tool users. And perhaps for good reason. Where other power tools are lauded for their ability to aggressively engage the wood and perform tasks quickly and accurately, the lathe is seen more as a means to an end—and a decorative end at that. The lathe doesn't cut or drill or resurface or even shape wood. It simply spins. The actual work is performed by gouges, skews and other lathe tools.

When secured between the head and the tail of a lathe, wood stock is rotated at speeds that can surpass 4,000 rpm. As the stock spins, it's shaped and shaved with various knives and chisels until a particular size and profile are achieved. Table legs, chair spindles, candlesticks and lamp bases are just a few of the many projects or project parts you can make using a lathe in this way (called *spindle turning*). You can also attach a block of wood directly to the headstock of the lathe and shape it into a bowl, a round base, a wheel, or one of many other shapes possible when *faceplate turning.*

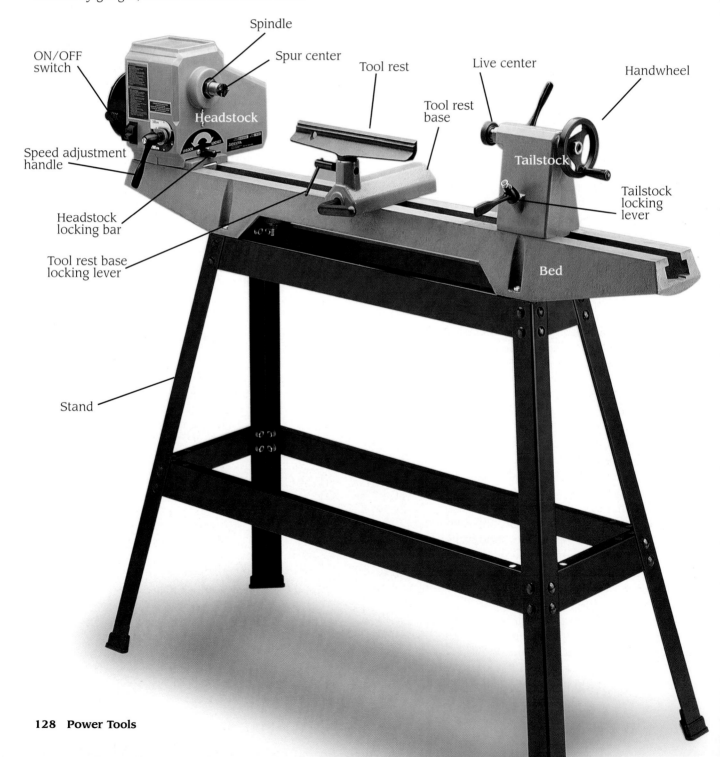

Lathe Fact Sheet		
Application	**Tool Recommendation**	**Accessories**
Light Use	An entry-level benchtop lathe, preferably with at least 12 × 36″ capacity.	Basic lathe tool set, whetstone and gouge slip, sizing tool, sturdy workbench or stand for lathe, face shield.
Moderate Use	Floor-standing model with ¾- to 1hp motor, variable speeds from 500 to 3000 rpm, 12 × 38″ capacity, and live center for tailstock.	Centerfinder, calipers, additional lathe tools in various sizes, power sharpening center or grinding wheel with tool rest.
Heavy Use	1- to 1½-hp motor with electronic variable speed adjustment, 16 × 40″ capacity, heavy-duty cast-iron bed, and heavy-gauge steel floor stand.	Auxiliary chucks with various jaw configurations.

Lathe basics

The lathe has four principal parts: the *headstock,* the *tailstock,* the *tool rest* and the *bed.*

The headstock. Attached to the motor, the headstock is the control center of the lathe. It contains a spindle that drives a *pointed center* that embeds in the workpiece to mount it in the lathe. When doing faceplate turning, a *faceplate* that attaches to the spindle is screwed to the workpiece for mounting. On some lathes, the headstock can be swiveled to an *outboard* position to create access to the faceplate. On others, the headstock is fixed and the faceplate attaches to the other end of the spindle. The headstock may need to be adjusted occasionally to align with the tailstock.

The tailstock. This adjustable assembly contains a spindle that holds the pointed center that's attached to the other end of the workpiece. The tailstock slides back and forth according to the length of the workpiece. The center mounted on the tailstock spindle is simply a sharp, nonrotating metal point on some lathes. Called a *dead center,* it stays in place as the workpiece rotates. On other lathes, the tailstock is equipped with a *live center* containing bearings that allow the pointed center to spin along with the workpiece, eliminating friction.

The tool rest. This critical part of the lathe is made up of a movable base that

supports a horizontal bar. Positioned parallel to the workpiece for spindle turning, or in front of the workpiece for faceplate turning, the tool rest provides a steady surface and pivot point for applying a lathe tool to the workpiece.

The bed. Usually made of cast iron, the bed is the backbone of the lathe, supporting the headstock, tailstock and tool rest base.

Making projects or project parts on a lathe is a pleasurable, satisfying experience. But it can also be very dangerous if you're not careful. When using a lathe, always wear a clear face shield, roll up your shirt sleeves, and never stand directly behind the cutting tool.

A basic set of lathe tools includes: (A) ¼" gouge; (B) ⅝" gouge; (C) ½" round-nose scraper; (D) ½" skew; (E) ½" diamond-point parting tool (spear); (F) ⅞" gouge; (G) 1" skew; (H) ⅛" parting tool.

TIP:

Add stability. Even heavier floor-standing lathes have a tendency to vibrate when the tool is spinning a workpiece. To combat this, many woodworkers simply weigh down the lathe stand with heavy ballast, such as concrete blocks or pieces of heavy-gauge steel. If your lathe stand has lower spreaders, cut a sheet of plywood to rest on top of the spreaders and support the ballast. Make sure the ballast is secure—you don't want it falling off the stand from the vibrations and landing on your foot.

Lathe types & features

The two basic lathe types for the home workshop are standard floor-standing lathes like the one shown on page 128, and benchtop lathes. The more inexpensive benchtop tools usually have less stock size capacity, and because they have no stand, need to be bolted to a sturdy worksurface—even then, it's tough to match the stability of a floor-standing lathe with a cast-iron bed and metal base.

You can also purchase any of a variety of specialty lathes such as *bowl-turning lathes* and *mini-lathes* designed for a specific purpose, such as turning wood pens, or *duplicating lathes* for production use.

The primary differences between lathes are in capacity, power, speed and weight.

Capacity. Most floor-standing lathes can handle workpieces up to 38" long, and 12" in diameter. Lower-end benchtop lathes have capacity as low as 10 × 20", but they move up to 12 × 36" or larger pretty quickly. Mini-lathes usually accept stock up to around 6 × 12".

Power. A ¾- to 1-hp motor is standard for most floor-standing lathes. Benchtop lathes usually are ½ or ¾ hp.

Speed. A typical lathe ranges from 500 or 600 rpm at its slowest setting, up to around 3,000 rpm at top speed. Many lathes use three or four step pulleys to adjust the speed in much the same way as a drill press: by rearranging the location of the V-belt that drives the pulleys. Lathes with this type of speed control are limited to just three or four different running speeds. Other lathes have a mechanical control, usually a lever or crank, that can change the speed anywhere within the range of the tool while it runs. Higher-end lathes have electronic variable speed control where speed changes are dialed in with the turn of a knob or dial.

Weight. Generally speaking, the heavier the lathe is, the less vibration it will produce while running. Many benchtop lathes weigh less than 100 pounds. Floor-standing lathes usually weigh at least 200 pounds, with many of the more popular models tipping the scales at 400 to 600 pounds.

Lathe tools

The chisels, scrapers and gouges used in woodturning are perhaps even more important than the lathe itself. A set of basic lathe tools usually includes at least eight long-handled, sharpened steel chisels of varying widths and cutting profiles *(See photo, previous page)*. Each tool has its own purpose in the wood-turning craft, but the vast majority can be divided into two basic categories: scraping tools and cutting tools.

Better lathe tools are made from high-speed steel that requires less frequent sharpening than plain carbon steel. And sharpening your lathe tools is an essential part of the wood-turning process *(See photo below)*. A dull tool not only produces disappointing results, it's a serious safety hazard.

Note: For a demonstration of how each of these tools is used, see the following sections on using the lathe.

Scraping tools. These tools are used extensively in faceplate turning, as well as to smooth out rough shapes in spindle turning. For beginners, they're much easier to use because they take a fairly non-aggressive bite into the workpiece. Common types are the *skew,* the *round-nose scraper,* and the *square-end scraper.* Scraping tools are used for the final smoothing of the workpiece before it's dismounted.

Cutting tools. Cutting tools do most of the stock removal in spindle turning, from rough-cutting to size, to shaping profiles. Most lathe tool sets contain at least two *gouges,* a *diamond-point parting tool,* and a *narrow parting tool.*

A sharpening center with an adjustable tool rest can be used for periodic sharpening of each tool to the correct angle. For routine honing of the blade, use a whetstone or a gouge slip.

TIP:

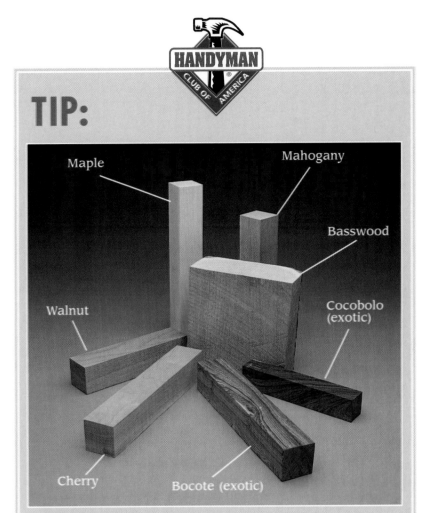

Choosing turning woods. Some wood types respond better than others to spindle turning and faceplate turning. In general, look for straight-grained wood for spindle turning—wood with wild or irregular grain will constantly fight the chisel, making smooth, accurate shaping difficult. When faceplate turning, however, wood with irregular grain isn't usually a problem, and may even create a more interesting project. Choose stock that's air- or kiln-dried and is free of defects and checks.

Generally, softwoods aren't well suited for lathe work. If you want, you can certainly turn softwood projects, but don't expect to be able to do any fancy or decorative cuts. Among the most popular hardwoods, cherry, walnut, maple and mahogany are particularly good for spindle turning projects. Oak, both red and white, will yield less satisfactory results and require quite a bit of sanding.

Exotic woods and fruitwoods are very popular for faceplate turning and for small-scale spindle-turning projects. But they tend to be expensive and difficult to find. Because of the scarcity of exotics, many woodworking stores and catalogs have begun selling pre-glued turning blanks laminated from a variety of exotic species. These blanks make good use of scrap pieces too small to be of use alone, and can create some very striking wood-turning projects.

While not considered an exotic, basswood is one of the most popular turning woods, mostly because it's extremely workable, relatively inexpensive, and takes a finish well.

Suggested Turning Speeds*			
Workpiece dia.	Roughing	Cutting	Finishing
Less than 2"	900 to 1300 rpm	1200 to 2000 rpm	1500 to 2000 rpm
2" to 4"	600 to 1000 rpm	1000 to 2000 rpm	1500 to 2000 rpm
4" to 6"	600 to 800 rpm	1000 to 1800 rpm	1500 to 2000 rpm
6" to 8"	500 to 600 rpm	800 to 1200 rpm	1200 to 1800 rpm
8" to 12"	500 rpm	600 to 800 rpm	900 to 1200 rpm

*Ideal turning speeds can vary from tool to tool; use your lathe manufacturer's speed suggestions, if available.

SAFETY TIP

Wear dust protection whenever doing fine cutting, scraping or sanding. For general use, a high-quality particle mask should be sufficient protection. But if you're doing a large volume of fine work (for example, sanding a large table leg), wear a respirator. You may even want to purchase a special shrouded face shield with an integrated air filtration system.

Tuning up

A lathe is a relatively simple tool that requires very little tuning up beyond basic power tool maintenance *(See pages 8 to 9)*. Periodically, however, you should test the headstock and tailstock to make sure they're properly aligned. To do this, mount a pointed center to the spindle in each part. Then, release the tailstock and slide it toward the headstock until the pointed centers are nearly touching *(See photo below)*. Lock the tailstock in place (locking often changes the position slightly). Inspect the pointed centers. If they're not perfectly aligned, loosen the locking bar at the base of the headstock, adjust the headstock position to match the tailstock, then tighten the locking bar.

After your lathe has been used extensively, you may find that spindles and blanks begin to wobble, even when they're mounted precisely on-center. The likely cause of this problem, called *runout,* is wear on the bearings that surround the spindle inside the headstock or tailstock. To test for runout, the best tool is a dial indicator *(See page 120)*. This machinist's tool can measure gaps as small as one-thousandth of an inch. Position the dial indicator with its point against the spindle, and slowly rotate the spindle by hand-turning the pulleys. If you find a gap of more than 0.005" at any point, you'll need to replace the bearings. If one set of bearings is worn, the bearings for the other spindle are probably not far behind. You might as well replace both sets at the same time.

Spindle turning

Spindle turning is the art of mounting a blank between the headstock and tailstock of your lathe, then shaping it with various lathe tools until it's a finished woodworking project. Common spindle-turning projects include legs, stringers and spreaders for tables and chairs, tool handles, lamp bases, salt-and-pepper shakers—basically, any cylindrical item, usually with a decorative profile.

Prepare the blank. The first step in spindle turning is to cut your blank to length and approximate shape. When cutting the blank to length, allow 2" at each end for waste—never try to shape a blank that's already cut to finished length. Many wood turners prefer to purchase pre-milled cylindrical blanks. If you're starting with a square or rectangular

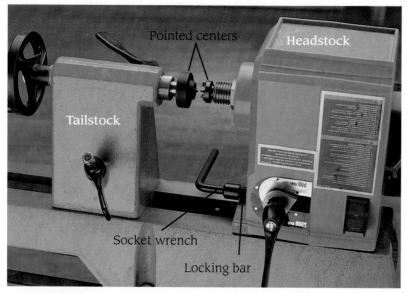

Pointed centers

Headstock

Tailstock

Socket wrench

Locking bar

The headstock and tailstock need to be exactly aligned before mounting a spindle. With a pointed center installed in each part, slide the tailstock forward and check alignment. Loosen the locking bar, if necessary, and adjust the headstock until it aligns with the tailstock.

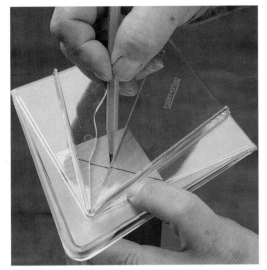

The centerfinder is a handy tool for marking the centers of the ends of square stock. Slip the centerfinder over the end of the stock so two adjacent edges of the stock are flush against the right-angled raised lips on the centerfinder. Trace along the diagonal ledge between the lips. Make a second line to form an "X"—the intersection of the lines is the centerpoint.

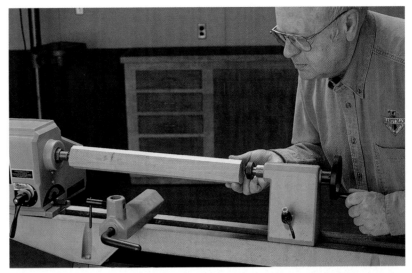

Hold the free end of the blank as you crank the tailstock forward. Make sure the pointed center on the tailstock fits cleanly into the pilot hole you made at the centerpoint of the blank end.

blank, you can save a lot of time and effort by running the edges through your table saw at a 45° bevel, creating an eight-sided "cylinder."

Mount the blank. The blank is held in place over the lathe bed by pointed centers installed on the spindles of the headstock and tailstock. The trick to successfully mounting the blank is finding the exact center of each end of the blank. There are several methods for doing this.

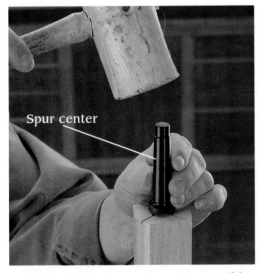

With the point directly over the centerpoint of the blank end, seat the spur center by rapping the end with a wooden mallet.

One of the easiest ways is to use a centerfinder (See photo, above left), but use this tool only if the stock is exactly square or round. If the stock is irregular, draw a line parallel to each edge, forming a box, then connect the corners of the box with diagonal lines.

One end of the blank is attached to the headstock with a *spur center*—a pointed center surrounded by two or four sharp spurs that are driven into the end of the blank. Before attaching the spur center, cut shallow kerfs along the diagonals of the blank to help ensure a fast hold from the spurs. Align the point of the spur center over the centerpoint of the blank end, then rap the end of the spur center with a wood mallet (don't use a hammer) to seat the spur center (See photo, left).

Before mounting the spur center, drill or punch a small pilot hole for the tailstock's pointed center at the centerpoint of the free end of the blank. If you're using a *dead center* on your tail stock (See page 129), place a drop of machine oil or paste wax in the hole to reduce friction.

Install a pointed center on the tailstock spindle. Attach the spur center to the headstock spindle (usually, the spindle is tapered to create a slip fit with the spur center). Then, use the handwheel to crank the tailstock forward until the point aligns with the pilot hole in the end of the stock. Crank the tailstock forward until the blank is held snugly between the points. Lock the tailstock in place.

TIP:

Mounting blanks. Never leave the free end of a blank unsupported after the attached spur center is mounted on the headstock spindle. Hold the blank with one hand as you crank the tailstock forward, using the handwheel, to meet the free end of the blank.

Set the tool rest base so it extends past one edge of the live area of the blank and lock it into position. Then, adjust the horizontal rest so the top is just below the center of the blank, no more than ¼" away.

Position the tool rest. Loosen the base of the tool rest and slide it on the lathe bed until one end of the toolrest extends just past the live area of the blank. Lock the base in position. Loosen the tool rest where it connects with the base, and adjust it so the top edge is slightly below the centerline of the blank, no more than ¼" away. Lock the tool rest in position, and give the blank a quick spin to make sure the blank clears the tool rest at all points. Plug in the lathe.

Rough-in the blank. Now, you're ready to start cutting. The first order of business is to rough-in the blank to create a smooth, even cylinder slightly larger in diameter than the widest diameter of the finished project. The best tool for this job is a ⅞" or 1" *gouge* (often called a *roughing gouge*). Rest the end of the gouge blade on the tool rest, but don't contact the workpiece. Hold the handle securely with one hand. Imagine that the blank is already a cylinder, then pivot the tool until the bevel in the underside of the blade is positioned so it would be resting cleanly on the cylinder.

With the gouge well clear of the blank, turn on the lathe at a relatively low speed (*See chart, page 132*). Grasp the tool firmly with your free hand, near the tip of the blade. Ease the gouge forward until it contacts the spinning blank. Begin scraping away stock, moving the gouge side to side on the tool rest. To increase the depth of the cut, lift the handle upward slightly. Continue moving the gouge back and forth until you've created a rough cylinder in the area in front of the tool rest (if the distance from the tool rest to the blank becomes greater than ¼", stop and move the tool rest forward). Shift the tool rest toward the uncut end of the blank and continue cutting with the gouge until the entire blank is roughed-in.

Use a roughing gouge to trim the blank down to a cylindrical shape slightly larger in diameter than the largest diameter of the finished workpiece.

Use a wide skew to cut the rough cylinder until it's perfectly smooth and even. Adjust the tool rest forward if the gap between it and the blank grows to more than ¼".

Smooth the spindle. Once the cylinder is roughed in (from here forward, we'll refer to it as a *spindle*), scrape it with a 1" or wider *skew* to smooth the surface. Because the blade on a skew is tapered, it has a high point and a low point (called the *heel*) in relation to the handle. To prevent gouging, position the skew so the high point is above the top of the spindle. The blade bevel should be flat with the surface of the spindle. Hold the skew above the spindle, turn on the lathe, and lower the skew until the blade starts to cut *(See photo, previous page, lower right)*.

Cut the spindle with the skew until the surface is smooth and even in all spots. You can test this by resting the shank of the skew blade on the spinning spindle—it the skew clatters, the spindle's not uniformly smooth.

Lay out the profile. If you're a beginning wood turner, start by using *story patterns* from outside sources (a story pattern is a two-dimensional representation of the profile of the part you're making). As your skills develop, you'll be able to create your own story patterns for custom wood-turning projects. It may take you a little while to be able to visualize how the part will look compared to the pattern. Basically, a turned spindle is a series of decorative cuts and shapes of a few types: *coves, beads, grooves* and *tapers* being the most common.

To lay out the profile of your project, center the story pattern against the spindle and make a pencil mark at the edges and top or bottom of each individual shape *(See photo, below left)*. Then remove the pattern, turn on the lathe, and press the pencil against each mark as the spindle spins. This will create full-circle reference marks.

Make sizing cuts. The story pattern tells you what the diameter of the part you're making should be at the low and high point of each shape in the profile. The next step in the spindle-turning process is to cut grooves in the spindle to match the appointed diameters. This is normally done with a *parting tool* positioned on-edge on the tool rest. The parting tool is perhaps the easiest lathe tool to use. You simply align the point of the blade with each reference mark you've made, then press the blade into the spindle until the diameter of the spindle is correct for that point.

To measure the diameter, most wood turners use a *sizing tool*. A sizing tool is an adjustable caliper that attaches directly to the parting tool. Set the sizing tool so the distance from its point to the tip of the parting tool equals the required diameter of the spindle at the point where you're cutting. Then, lower the sizing tool over the reference line, causing the parting tool to begin the cut *(See photo, below right)*. When the correct diameter is achieved, the sizing tool will fall past the spindle, stopping the cutting action of the parting tool. Stop the lathe, remove the sizing tool, and make the rest of your sizing cuts.

Hand position. You have two hand-position options when applying a lathe tool to a blank: palm up, or palm down. Which option you choose is mostly a matter of personal preference. Normally, more experienced wood turners opt for the palm-up position because it makes maneuvering the tool easier. But if you're just learning to use a lathe, you might want to start out with the palm-down grip, especially on rough cuts where you're removing a lot of material: palm-down is generally the more secure grip.

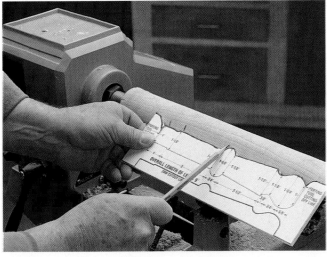

Use a story pattern as a guide for marking the shoulders and top or bottom of each shape in the planned spindle profile.

Sizing tool

Make sizing cuts at the reference marks using a parting tool. A sizing tool attached to the parting tool is similar to a caliper. It automatically stops the cut once the correct depth is achieved.

Shape the profiles. The sizing cuts establish the dimensions of each shape in the project profile. Making the shapes is simply a matter of choosing the right lathe tool and contouring between the sizing cuts. Beads, coves, grooves and tapers are the principal shapes.

Cutting beads. Beads are convex, rounded rings with shoulders nearly perpendicular to the spindle. They can be cut with a small skew or a diamond-point parting tool (also called a *spear*). Round over the shoulders of the stock between the sizing cuts for each bead, staying as uniform as you can (*See photo, top left*).

Cutting coves. Use a small gouge or round-nose scraper to cut these shallow valleys in the spindle (*See photo, top right*).

Cutting grooves. Decorative grooves can be cut with several tools. For straight-sided V-grooves, use a skew or a parting tool. For round grooves, use a round-nose scraper or a gouge.

Cutting tapers. Make a series of regularly spaced, increasingly deep sizing cuts, then remove material from between the cuts until the correct thickness is achieved and the taper is well blended.

Sanding and finishing. Sanding a spindle to prepare for a finish, and even applying the finish, are done easily while the spindle is still mounted in the lathe. With the lathe spinning at its slowest speed, hold strips of cloth-backed sandpaper against the spindle as it spins (*See photo, below left*). Sand in increasingly finer grits (strips of old belt-sander belts work well for this task).

Depending on your project needs, you can also apply a finish to a lathe-mounted spindle. Wipe the spindle free of dust, then dab some rub-on finish onto a small staining cloth and hold it against the spindle, moving from side to side.

Part the spindle. To remove the spindle, cut it to length at each end with a parting tool. Stop the cut with about ½" or so to go, remove the spindle, and finish cutting off the waste ends with a sharp hand saw (*See photo, below right*).

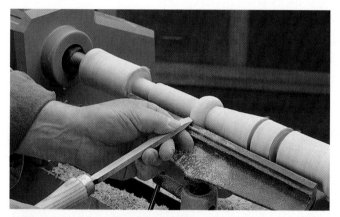

Cut beads in the profile with a small skew or a diamond-point parting tool. Scraping is usually a safer technique than cutting.

Coves are cut with a round-nose scraper or a small gouge, moved from side to side in the cove area.

A strip of an old belt-sander belt pressed up against the spindle as it spins is a very effective sanding device.

Cut through the spindle most of the way through at the ends of the project, using a parting tool.

On some lathes, the headstock is spun 90° on the lathe bed to an outboard position for faceplate turning on extra-large stock.

Faceplate turning

Faceplate turning is used mostly to make bowls. In faceplate turning, the turning blank is screwed to a faceplate, then the faceplate is attached to the spindle on the lathe headstock. So you can mount larger blanks for faceplate turning, either the headstock of the lathe is spun to an outboard position, or the faceplate is attached to the outside end of the headstock spindle.

Faceplate turning is fundamentally a scraping operation, although you can use just about any lathe tool you feel comfortable with for the rough stock removal.

Here's a sample sequence of steps for faceplate turning:

• Start with a square piece of stock—either solid wood or a laminate is fine. Draw diagonals from corner to corner to locate the centerpoint for centering the faceplate. Cut the stock into a round shape with a band saw or jig saw.

• Attach the blank to the faceplate using one of the methods shown in the photos to the right. Mount the face plate on the headstock spindle and position the tool rest around the centerline of the blank, within ¼" from the blank.

• Shape the blank to rough size and shape (See photo, below right), then finish with scraping tool.

• Dismount the blank, then reattach the faceplate on the opposite face. Rough-in the inside of the bowl with a gouge, then finish with a skew.

Before cutting the blank into a circular shape, draw diagonal reference lines for centering the faceplate on the blank. Attach the faceplate to the blank with screws.

OPTION: If you don't want to leave screw holes in the base of your bowl, glue a round piece of scrap to the blank and screw the scrap wood to the faceplate. A piece of paper with a radius about 1" less than the scrap will prevent the scrap and blank from fully bonding, making them easier to break apart when you're done turning.

You can use just about any lathe tool that you're comfortable with for faceplate turning. A wide gouge, like the one shown here, can be used for rough stock removal or, since faceplate turning is basically a scraping operation, you can use a round-nose scraper instead. Use a sharp cutting tool, such as a skew, for making smooth finish cuts as you work the bowl into its finished shape. Note how the tool rest has been shifted in line with the side of the bowl.

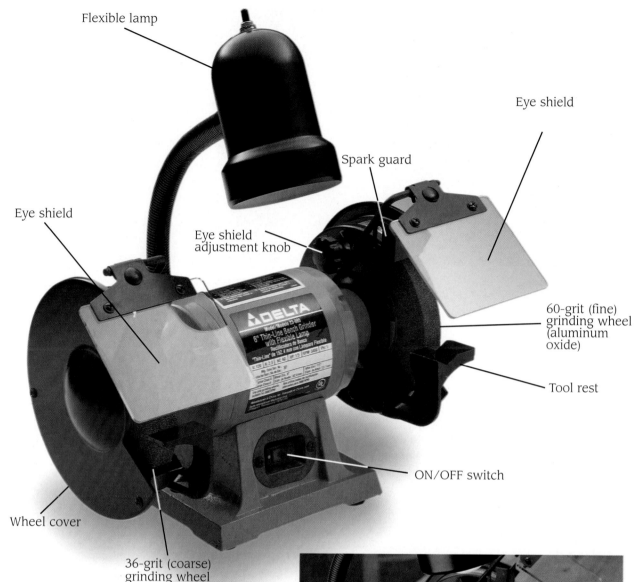

Flexible lamp

Eye shield

Spark guard

Eye shield
adjustment knob

Eye shield

60-grit (fine)
grinding wheel
(aluminum
oxide)

Tool rest

ON/OFF switch

Wheel cover

36-grit (coarse)
grinding wheel
(aluminum oxide)

Bench Grinders

These workshop standards are used to put a nice edge on everything from lawn mower blades to screwdriver blades to pocketknives. They can also remove rust from metal surfaces instantly, or deburr freshly cut metal. If a washer is a little too big for the spot you want to use it, you can grind it down on your bench grinder.

Most bench grinders have two wheels—this creates better balance in the machine, and takes advantage of both ends of the spinning arbor. Typically, one wheel is a coarser grinding stone for rough work, and the other is a little finer, for finishing up. This combination lets you accomplish most grinding chores without switching wheels (but if you do need to switch a wheel, make sure the new wheel is the correct diameter and the right size for the arbor).

"Dress the wheel" regularly with a dressing tool (shown above) or a silicone carbide stick. Dressing cleans hardened residue off the grinding wheel, exposing a fresh grinding surface that yields fast, clean grinding results.

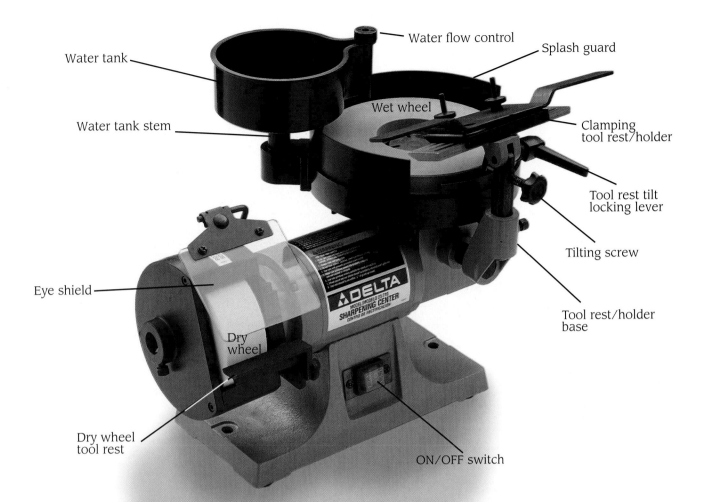

Water tank

Water tank stem

Water flow control

Splash guard

Wet wheel

Clamping tool rest/holder

Tool rest tilt locking lever

Tilting screw

Eye shield

Dry wheel

Tool rest/holder base

Dry wheel tool rest

ON/OFF switch

Use the dry wheel on a sharpening center for everyday sharpening of high-speed steel chisels and other nontempered steel tool blades. Adjust the angle of the tool rest to match the recommended sharpening angle for each tool.

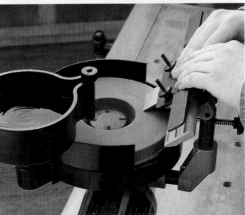

Use the wet wheel for creating a very fine edge on any tool blade and for sharpening plane knives (shown) and tempered steel chisels, secured in the clamping tool holder.

Sharpening Centers

Many woodworkers and handymen who have invested a lot of money in their tools (and that's most of us) choose to do as much of their own sharpening as possible. But keeping up with sharpening can be a very time-consuming effort, especially if you're using plain whetstones, or even a standard bench grinder. And there's nothing more disappointing than spending half an hour putting a razor edge on a chisel, only to find that the bevel angle isn't quite right. For these reasons, the dedicated tool sharpening center is becoming one of the fastest-growing power tools.

Many of the more popular sharpening centers today have two sharpening wheels: one dry wheel and one wet wheel. The dry wheel is used much like a bench grinder: to create a good edge quickly. The wet wheel, usually with an automatic water spigot with a controllable flow, can put a very fine edge on just about any tool. And because the water keeps the blade relatively cool, you won't damage or weaken tempered steel blades with excessive heat.

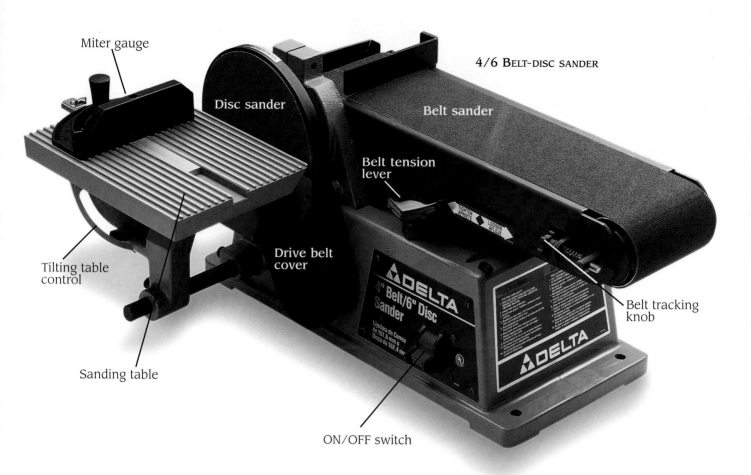

Miter gauge

Disc sander

Belt sander

Belt tension
lever

Tilting table
control

Drive belt
cover

4" Belt/6" Disc
Sander

Sanding table

ON/OFF switch

Belt tracking
knob

Belt-Disc Sanders

A stationary belt-disc sander gives you an amazing
number of wood-shaping and smoothing possibilities in one compact package. Use it to clean up saw
cuts on contours, straight cuts or miters. If the workpiece you just cut is a fraction of an inch too long, end-
sand it to the perfect length using the sanding table
and miter gauge as a guide. Install a coarse-grit belt on
the belt sander, and you can quickly resurface items
that are too small or delicate to attack with a portable
sander. These are just a few of the many ways you can
use the belt-disc sander.

Entry-level belt-disc sanders usually have a 6"-dia.
sanding disc and a 4"-wide sanding belt (if you ever
hear someone refer to a *4/6 sander*, this is the tool
they're talking about). Be sure to look for one with a
dust collection port.

You may find that you outgrow a 4/6 sander pretty
quickly. Not to worry. There are dozens of larger belt-
disc sanders on the market today with discs from 10"
to 12" in diameter and a 6 × 48" sanding belt. Look for
a belt sander that can be tipped up to various angles, a
cast-iron base and table, and a sturdy floor stand.

*The adjustable miter gauge on the sanding table gives you the
ability to fine-tune or smooth out miter cuts until you achieve a
perfect fit. Raise the belt sander to a vertical position, and you
can use the sanding table with it, also.*

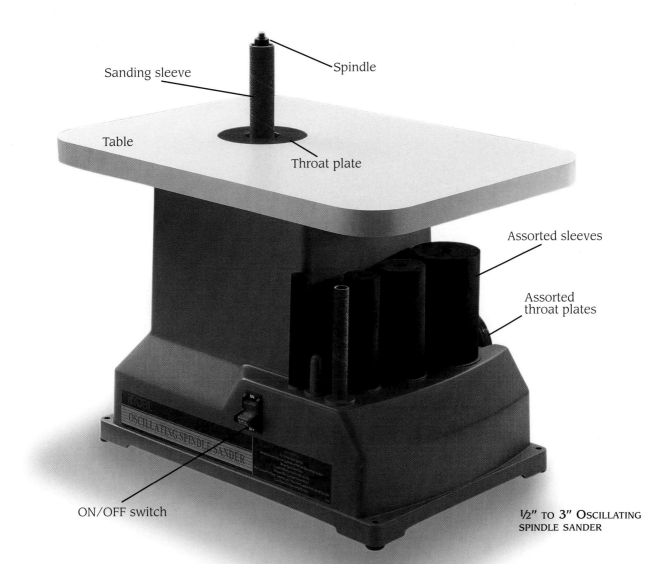

Sanding sleeve

Spindle

Table

Throat plate

Assorted sleeves

Assorted throat plates

ON/OFF switch

½″ TO 3″ OSCILLATING SPINDLE SANDER

The oscillating spindle sander is a favorite tool among woodworkers who enjoy making decorative accessories. But it can also come in handy for furnituremaking chores, like smoothing out round mortises and making replacement parts.

Oscillating Spindle Sanders

The oscillating spindle sander solves one of the more perplexing workshop problems: how do you sand the edges of an inside cut? But the spindle sander is also a great tool for smoothing, or making, contours of just about any size. If you don't do much contour sanding, you may be able to get by with a drum sander attachment in your drill press. But that's not really what a drill press is designed to do best. And most drill presses don't lend themselves to efficient dust collection—a major concern when sanding.

A spindle sander doesn't require a large investment. In fact, you'll probably have enough money left over after your purchase to buy a complete set of sleeves for your sander—a coarse, medium and fine sleeve in each of the most common diameters (½″, ¾″, 1″, 1½″, 2″ and 3″). Make sure to acquire a separate throat plate for each of the sleeve sizes you own.

Workshop Tools

In every workshop you'll find a few tools that aren't easily categorized: they're not exactly stationary tools, but they're not quite portable tools, either. In some cases, they may not strike you as tools at all. The air compressor. The shop vac. The paint sprayer. Wherever you choose to pigeonhole these common machines, they don't quite fit in. But when you put them to use, they can be as important as any other tool you own.

An air compressor by itself isn't of much use. But once you acquire one, a whole new world of power tool possibilities opens up. Pneumatic nailers and staplers, air-powered grinders and sanders, impact wrenches, power washers and many more tools can be driven with a good air compressor. You'll find uses for them in any do-it-yourself pursuit, and even in some woodworking projects.

If stationary tools are the *heart* of your workshop, then a dust collection system is like the *lungs*. From the simplest shop vacuum to a sophisticated, central dust collection system with a two-stage dust collector and a dozen vacuum hoses, dust collection tools make your workshop a safer, more pleasant place to pursue your hobbies and your craft.

Applying a finish is an afterthought for many handymen and woodworkers. The real fun is in making the project—cutting the parts, shaping the joints until they're dead perfect. By the time you've gone through all that, slapping on a little paint or wood stain is almost a let down—and unfortunately it usually shows. But with good paint spraying equipment, you can get the best of both worlds: a professional looking finish that can be applied neatly, easily and, best of all, quickly.

Especially with today's new generation of HVLP (high volume, low pressure) sprayers, a paint sprayer is definitely a tool most serious handymen should investigate.

Of course, there are other "workshop tools" that may not get the glamour and attention heaped onto the latest new router or the groundbreaking new sander. But do your best not to overlook these tools. The bottom line is that they'll help you enjoy your other tools even more.

Dust Collection Tools

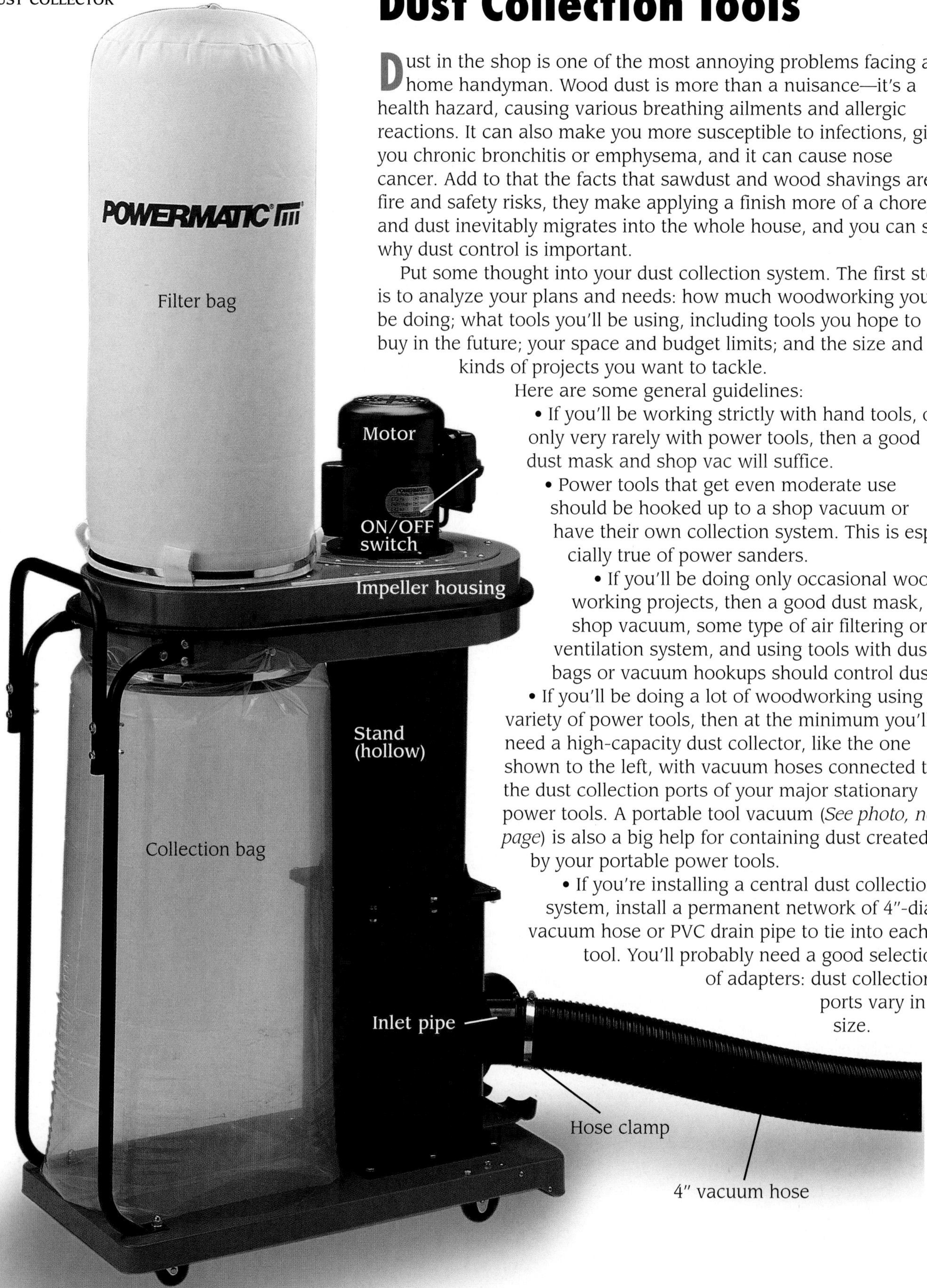

Dust in the shop is one of the most annoying problems facing a home handyman. Wood dust is more than a nuisance—it's a health hazard, causing various breathing ailments and allergic reactions. It can also make you more susceptible to infections, give you chronic bronchitis or emphysema, and it can cause nose cancer. Add to that the facts that sawdust and wood shavings are fire and safety risks, they make applying a finish more of a chore, and dust inevitably migrates into the whole house, and you can see why dust control is important.

Put some thought into your dust collection system. The first step is to analyze your plans and needs: how much woodworking you'll be doing; what tools you'll be using, including tools you hope to buy in the future; your space and budget limits; and the size and kinds of projects you want to tackle.

Here are some general guidelines:

• If you'll be working strictly with hand tools, or only very rarely with power tools, then a good dust mask and shop vac will suffice.

• Power tools that get even moderate use should be hooked up to a shop vacuum or have their own collection system. This is especially true of power sanders.

• If you'll be doing only occasional woodworking projects, then a good dust mask, a shop vacuum, some type of air filtering or ventilation system, and using tools with dust bags or vacuum hookups should control dust.

• If you'll be doing a lot of woodworking using a variety of power tools, then at the minimum you'll need a high-capacity dust collector, like the one shown to the left, with vacuum hoses connected to the dust collection ports of your major stationary power tools. A portable tool vacuum (*See photo, next page*) is also a big help for containing dust created by your portable power tools.

• If you're installing a central dust collection system, install a permanent network of 4"-dia. vacuum hose or PVC drain pipe to tie into each tool. You'll probably need a good selection of adapters: dust collection ports vary in size.

Filter bag

Motor

ON/OFF switch

Impeller housing

Stand (hollow)

Collection bag

Inlet pipe

Hose clamp

4" vacuum hose

Dust Collection Tool Fact Sheet

Application	Tool	System Accessories
Light use	10-gallon or larger wet/dry shop vacuum and reusable pleated dust filter.	Dust bags for portable power tools, dust-collection ports on stationary tools for hook-up to shop vac.
Moderate use	Shop vacuum, tool vacuum, single-stage or two-stage dust collector with 4"-dia. hoses, multiple ports, and 500 cfm capability.	Extra hoses, separate air filtration unit.
Heavy use	Single-stage, two stage or cyclone dust collector with at least 900 cfm capability.	Floor vent for sweepings, dedicated hose or tube permanently mounted to each stationary power tool.

Dust collection tool basics

Dust collection is accomplished with two or three power tools: the wet/dry shop vacuum (See photo, right), the stationary dust collector (*See photo, previous page*), and sometimes a small portable vacuum that is connected to whichever tool you're using (*See photo, below*).

Wet/dry shop vacuum. The most common workshop dust collection tool is the wet-and-dry shop vacuum. These versatile and portable machines can vacuum up dust directly. Or, you can attach the vacuum hose to a dust collection port on any woodworking machine that has one. When vacuuming dry material, make sure the container is fitted with a clean particle filter to prevent fine dust from escaping into the air. Remove the filter when vacuuming wet materials.

The features that really matter are noise level and the unit's pickup power—especially the ability to pick up heavier items, since almost any shop vacuum will handle dust. Look for noise levels in the 80 dB(A) range; avoid anything over 90 dB(A). Look for a hose at least 8 feet long, and a pleated, reusable filter. The tool should be easy to empty, easy to roll around, but hard to tip over (try it in the store), from 3- to 5-hp, with a 10-gallon minimum canister capacity and a straight path (rather than a

**10-GALLON
WET/DRY
SHOP VACUUM**

A portable tool vacuum connects directly to the dust collection ports on your power tools. Some models, like the one shown above, start and stop automatically when the tool is running.

POWER TOOLS BY THE NUMBERS

CFM. Vacuums and dust collectors are rated by the number of cubic feet per minute (CFM) of air they'll draw under steady resistance, usually noted as *"static inches of water lift."* If a tool is rated for 650 CFM @ 8", that means it will draw 650 cfm while encountering enough resistance to raise water 8" into the hose. You may not always find the water lift ratings, but if you do, pay attention. They're a good indicator of how well the tool will perform under actual working conditions.

Tape hardware cloth (medium gauge wire mesh) to the end of your shop vac nozzle. This will keep you from accidentally vacuuming up parts you've left lying around.

A squeegee attachment allows you to make quick, clean work of vacuuming liquids.

Change your shop vacuum filter on a regular basis (if your shop vac has a reusable filter, simply clean it and replace it). Don't forget to remove the filter when you're vacuuming liquids. Another handy trick is to line the canister drum with a plastic garbage bag for easy disposal. You'll need to make a cutout for the inlet opening and duct-tape the bag around the opening.

SAFETY TIPS:

Dust is an extreme fire hazard. Follow these safety guidelines when using dust collection tools, and be sure to read the owner's manual for any specific safety information for each tool.
- Never vacuum metal shavings.
- Never vacuum flammable liquids.
- Ground your dust collection system: vacuum hoses (particularly PVC pipes) can generate static electricity, which can ignite wood dust. Ground the system with bare copper wire connected to a metal ground.
- Empty dust bags and containers before they're half full.

right-angle bend) where the hose enters the drum.

You might want to buy two or three smaller shop vacuums, assigning each to a specific tool's dust port or area of your shop. This makes for a fairly effective and inexpensive dust collection system, besides being more convenient than relying on just one vacuum for all hookups.

Tool vacuums. A new dust-collecting alternative to the standard shop vac is the specialized *tool vacuum* that automatically switches itself on whenever the tool it's connected to is in use (*See photo, previous page*). You simply plug the power cord for the tool into a receptacle mounted on the tool vacuum. You can also buy an electronic switch to give any shop vacuum this instant-on feature.

Dust collectors. Specialized workshop dust collectors are the basis of a whole-shop dust collection system. There are several types of dust collectors on the market today. The most common is the *single-stage* machine, like the one shown on page 144. These typically have a filter bag on top for fine particles, and a lower bag for the bulk of the shavings and wood chips. A dust collector with a 1 hp motor that draws over 500 cfm of air will do the job for most home shops. The main disadvantage to single-stage collec-

Shake the filter bag on single-stage dust collectors so dust falls down into the collection bag below. Do this with the machine turned off.

tors is that when the sawdust enters the machine, it travels right past the impeller blades, causing wear.

Two-stage dust collectors look a lot like shop vacs, but because the blower is mounted on top of the canister, the collected dust doesn't come in contact with it. Instead, the heavier chips and shavings fall into the canister, and the finer dust collects in a separate filter bag.

Cyclone collectors. These higher-end dust collection tools are popular with professional woodworkers. They feature a conical chamber where the air swirls to separate out heavier chips and shavings that fall into a collection compartment. The finer dust continues through, past the impeller and into a filter bag.

Dust collection tips

• Don't sweep, if you can avoid it. Sweeping with a broom kicks up more dust and debris into the air. Use a shop vacuum instead.

• The key rule: trap dust and shavings at their source. Once dust is in the air, you've already got a problem.

• Mount an ambient air cleaner to your ceiling if you create a lot of fine dust. A cheaper version of this tool is simply a box fan with a pleated filter attached, installed in a window so it blows dusty air out of the shop.

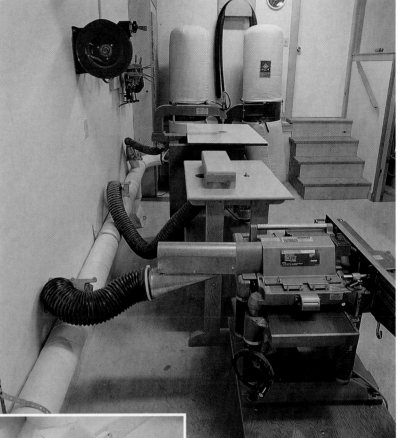

A fairly sophisticated dust collection system is one of the highlights of this Handyman Club Member's shop. In addition to a separate, dedicated hose for each tool, a floor vent (left photo) is tied into the system. Sweepings are simply swept up to the vent, then drawn in when the collection system is turned on.

Air volume requirements for stationary tools	
Tool	**CFM Volume**
Band saw	300 CFM*
Belt-disc sander	300 CFM
Drill press	300 CFM
Jointer	350 CFM
Lathe	500 CFM
Planer	400 CFM
Radial arm saw	350 CFM
Scroll saw	300 CFM
Table saw	350 CFM
* Cubic Feet per Minute	

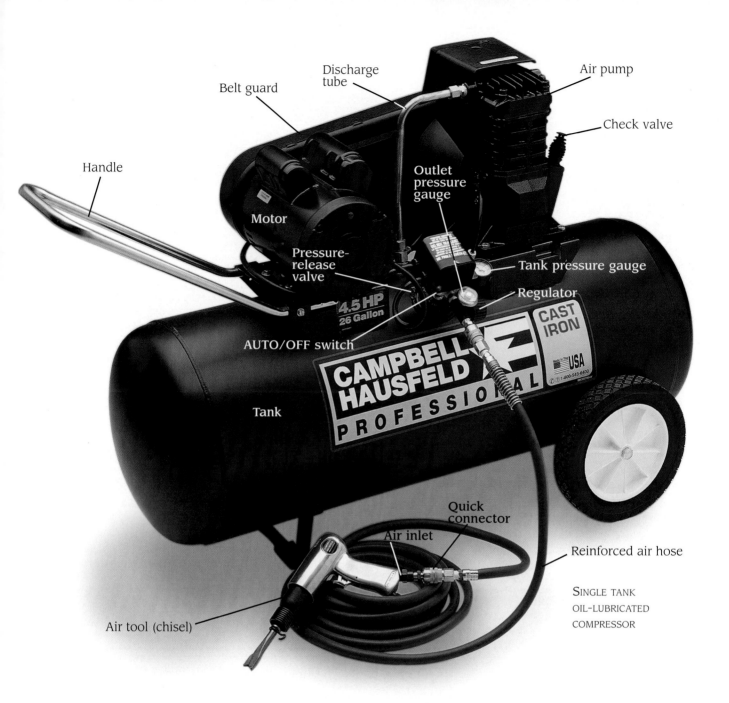

Handle

Belt guard

Discharge tube

Air pump

Check valve

Motor

Outlet pressure gauge

Pressure-release valve

Tank pressure gauge

4.5 HP
26 Gallon

AUTO/OFF switch

Regulator

CAST IRON

CAMPBELL HAUSFELD
PROFESSIONAL

Made in The USA
1-800-543-6400

Tank

Quick connector

Air inlet

Reinforced air hose

SINGLE TANK
OIL-LUBRICATED
COMPRESSOR

Air tool (chisel)

Air Compressors & Air Tools

Air tools can spoil you. They make some jobs so easy that you'll never go back to the old way of doing things. For instance, once you use an air-driven finish nailer to attach trim moldings, you'll chuckle every time you see someone toiling away with a hammer and nailset. If you've got a roofing project on your chore list, you'll definitely want to look into a pneumatic roofing nailer. The list of air tools made today is long, and sometimes surprising. Did you know you can buy an air-powered caulk gun? But for the most part, these tools are simply compressed-air

driven versions of many of the electric power tools discussed elsewhere in this book.

The heart of the pneumatic tool set-up is the air compressor. Although you can use gas-powered compressors with most air tools, electric compressors are by far the favorite for shop use. Like most tools, air compressors come in a wide selection of size, style and power.

Air tools range all the way from simple $10 air nozzles, up to complex, precision engineered tools that rival the top-of-the-line tools among their electrical counterparts (both in power and in price). Fans of air tools usually enjoy them for two basic reasons: they're quick and powerful, and they're generally much easier on the ears for ongoing use, (provided you're not working right next to the compressor).

Air Compressors & Air Tools Fact Sheet		
Application	**Compressor**	**Air Tools**
Light use	Tank-less compressor or single-purpose power washers, tire inflators etc.	Power-washing nozzle, tire nozzles, inflator needles.
Moderate use	1- to 2-hp oil-less compressor with twin 2- to 5-gallon tanks, single 10- to 12-gallon tank, or single 3- to 5-gallon "pancake" tank.	Nailers and staplers, random-orbit sander, grinders, power washer tool, sandblaster, paint sprayers.
Heavy use	3- to 5-hp, 20 to 30 gallon oil-less or oil-lubricated compressor, or 40-to 60-gallon vertical tank compressor.	Grinders, chisel/hammers, large-capacity nailers, metal nibblers and cutting tools.

OIL-LESS TWIN TANK AIR COMPRESSOR

Air compressor types

There are two basic types of air compressors: *tank-type,* with the tank serving as a reservoir to maintain the air pressure, and *tank-less* models. For providing power to air tools, you'll want a compressor with a tank. While the tank-less models cost less, and often claim to be usable with pneumatic tools, they seldom have enough capacity to drive common pneumatic tools.

Tank types. There are many different types of compressors with tanks ranging from 2-gallon twin-tank models *(See photo, left)* up to large vertical tanks that hold 60 gallons or more of air. A good choice for home shop use is a 20-to 30-gallon single tank compressor *(See photo, previous page).* But if you plan to move the compressor around outdoors frequently, a machine with less tank capacity should be able to run most of your air tools, while retaining its portability. Many roofers, for example, use a pancake-style compressor, with a disc-shaped tank (usually around 3 gallons) beneath the compressor unit. Twin-tank models are also popular, especially if you're planning to use the compressor continuously. On these models, a tank/pump control monitors the air pressure in each tank, filling one while the other is in use, then switching to the full tank for constant air pressure.

Horsepower. The size of the motor has a direct impact on how much air pressure is created by the compressor. The maximum air output affects which tools you can and cannot use with an air compressor. Smaller, portable compressors and lower-end 12-to 15-gallon tank compressors usually have 1- to-2 hp

TIP:

Invisible rust. Avoid buying used air compressors: the cast-iron tanks, even when well maintained, will eventually rust. But because the rust forms on the inside of the tank, there's no reliable way to assess the tank condition.

Oil-lubricated air compressors are like cars. Make sure you use the right type of oil (check your owner's manual or look for labels on the tank), and make sure the right amount of oil is in the tool at all times by checking the dip stick regularly. Change the oil every three months.

The regulator adjusts the amount of air flowing out through the air hose. An outlet pressure gauge next to the regulator gives precise readings of air volume.

TIP:

Keep it in the closet. Air compressors can be very loud and, after long exposure, can even damage your hearing. Always wear ear protection when using the compressor. Another way to minimize the noise is simply to house the compressor in an out-of-the-way closet or corner. Just make sure the area has some ventilation and fresh air supply.

motors that can drive many, but not all, air tools. A compressor with a 3 hp or larger motor will run just about any air tool you can hook up to it.

Lubrication. Air compressors require good, steady pump lubrication to keep the moving parts running at peak efficiency. Most home-shop air compressors made today are low-maintenance *oil-less* models with a self-contained lubrication system that doesn't require replenishment. The only real drawback to oil-less air compressors is that they tend to be loud when running.

Oil-lubricated air compressors are usually on the large side. Unlike oil-less compressors, these require periodic changing and replenishment of the oil *(See photo, above)*. Typically, oil-lubricated compressors run cooler and quieter than oil-less models. Check the dip stick regularly to make sure the oil level is okay.

Air compressor basics

Air compressors draw air in under power, forcing the air into a holding tank

where it stays under pressure until it's released through a hose and past an air tool, powering the tool. A regulator next to an outlet port on the tank is opened to release an air stream *(See photo above)*. The wider you open the regulator, the greater the force of the escaping air. Most air tools are rated to perform best under a specific amount of air pressure *(See chart, page 152)*, so you'll find an outlet pressure gauge next to the regulator to tell you exactly how much air pressure will flow through the hose.

While air pressure is a very beneficial power source in many ways, harnessing it does create some maintenance issues you won't encounter when using electric power. The main enemy of air power (and of compressor tanks, especially) is moisture. As air compresses, the moisture condenses inside the tank and can even travel through the air hose and cause problems for your air tool.

To combat the moisture problem, air compressors have a *drain plug* on the underside of the tank. Unplug the air

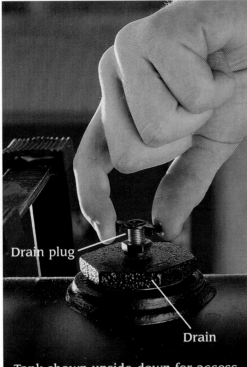

Drain plug

Drain

Tank shown upside-down for access

Unscrew the drain plug and drain the air compressor tank of water. Drain the tank at least once a day when using the compressor, and also drain it periodically even when the compressor is not in use.

compressor, then loosen the plug and drain out any condensation at least once a day when the compressor is in use (*See photo above*). If the drain plug is at all stubborn, you may find it easier to turn the compressor upside-down for plug removal (but make sure you return it to normal position, with the drain on the underside, and allow enough time for all the water to drain out). Relieve the tank pressure down to 10 PSI before unplugging the drain.

You can also purchase an in-line water filtration system (some compressors are equipped with them) to catch any moisture that makes its way out of the tank and through the air hose (*See photo, right*). These accessories are especially useful when using the compressor in areas of high humidity, like basements.

An *air filtration system* is standard issue on all air compressors. These usually function much like a breather filter on a carburetor. A high-density air filter fits into a slotted filter housing, and air is drawn through the filter into the air

pump. Inspect the air filter element every week or so, and replace it if it begins to plug up.

Air compressors are equipped with an *ASME safety valve* that automatically releases pressure from the tank if it builds too high. Usually located next to the air outlet port, the safety valve should have a metal ring that you can pull to make sure the valve is functioning properly. Test the valve every week or so. Note: The tank pressure is usually pre-set by the manufacturer.

Another valve, the *check valve*, is posted at the inlet port. The main passage to the tank, this valve is supplied by a metal tube from the air pump. It's a one-way valve, so it allows air to flow in, but not to escape.

Using an air compressor

The air compressor doesn't have a conventional ON/OFF switch or trigger, like other power tools. Instead, most models have an OFF/AUTO switch, with AUTO being the "ON" position. Some handymen who make daily use of their air compressor leave it in the AUTO position indefinitely. In this setting, a sensor in the tank detects if the tank pressure drops below a specific pressure

In-line water filtration devices are fitted with couplings into the air line as a last line of defense to keep moisture away from your air tools. Empty the moisture container as water collects, and change the water filters regularly.

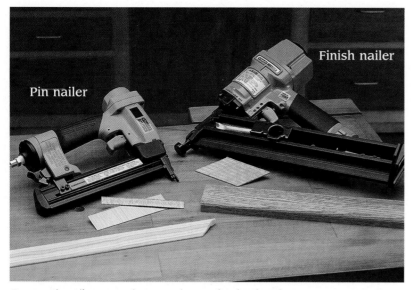

Pin nailer

Finish nailer

Pneumatic stapler

Pneumatic nailers come in many sizes and styles, but the two most common are probably the pin nailer *(left) and* finish nailer *(right). The smaller pin nailer (also called a brad nailer) is a good tool for installing trim and joining lighter woods. The finish nailer accepts larger nails, and can be used for casework and general wood joining. Most pneumatic nailers are loaded with nail cartridges. Because the cartridges differ by brand, try to stick to using nails made by the same company that made your nailer.*

The pneumatic stapler is an ideal tool for fastening thin sheet goods to a frame. The crown style staples flatten out on impact for excellent holding strength, with the head of the staple recessed.

point, and the air pump kicks on automatically to restore the pressure to the level set on the tank pressure gauge. That's why you often hear air compressors kicking into life in the middle of the night.

But if you don't use your air compressor regularly, switch it to OFF and unplug it after every use. It may take a few minutes for the tank to rebuild pressure when you need it, but you'll save on your electric bill, and save wear and tear on your air pump.

To run your compressor, plug it in and set the switch to AUTO. When the tank pressure is correct, the pump will stop running. Attach an air hose and air tool to the air outlet. Open the regulator and adjust it until the outlet pressure gauge shows the correct pressure for the tool you're using (90 PSI is the most common operating pressure).

Air Tool Power Requirements (typical)			
Tool	**Volume**	**Compressor**	**Pressure**
Nailers/staplers	2 to 9 CFM*	½-to 1-hp	70 to 120 PSI**
Impact hammer	3 to 4 CFM	1 hp	90 to 100 PSI
Impact wrench	4 to 8 CFM	1 hp	90 to 100 PSI
R.O./finish sander	4 CFM	2 hp	90 to 100 PSI
Sprayer	2 to 8 CFM	¾-to 3-hp	90 to 120 PSI
Die grinder	5 to 6 CFM	1 hp	90 to 100 PSI
Sandblaster	4 to 5 CFM	1 hp	40 to 60 PSI
Drill	3 to 4 CFM	1 hp	90 to 100 PSI
Straight-line sander	8 CFM	2 hp	90 to 100 PSI
* Cubic Feet per Minute		** Pounds per square inch	

The palm nailer is one of the handiest air nailers. The shaft contains a recessed drive plunger that can hammer-in conventional nails in spots too tight for swinging your 16 oz. claw hammer.

Air Tools

Practically every electric power tool has an air-driven equivalent. Drilling, nailing, stapling, sanding, driving, grinding, sawing, routing and shaping, metal cutting, chiseling, riveting, ratcheting, sandblasting, caulking, polishing, spray painting... if it's something handymen do,

there's a good chance you can find an air tool that will make it easier.

By far the most common uses for air tools are driving nails (of all varieties) and grinding. Used mostly for auto body work and other forms of metalworking, air-powered grinders and die-cutters are the lifeblood of the serious metalworker.

Because each air tool requires a specified amount of air pressure and volume to function, always check the *CFM* and *PSI* rating before purchasing a new air tool to make sure your compressor can handle it. Look closely at the ratings—they sometimes differ for occasional use and ongoing use.

Attaching air tools. Hooking up an air tool is simple. You simply slip the air inlet valve at the end of the tool into the hose coupling, pull back on the quick connector, press the tool in until it's seated, and release the connector. But before you attach the tool, there are two steps you need to be aware of.

Teflon tape. Teflon tape, sold at any hardware store, should be wrapped around all threaded couplings to ensure an air-tight bond. You'll need to use it between the tool and the inlet valve, and on all threaded joints where hose couplings are attached (*See photo, below left*).

Lubrication. Most air tools should be

TIP:

Watch out for oil. After lubricating an air tool (*See photo, below right*), wrap the tool in an old towel and run it for 10 seconds or so to clear excess oil from the inlet valve. If you don't cover the tool, the excess oil will spray at a high volume, causing at least a mess, and at worst personal injury.

Wrap teflon tape around the threaded parts of all threaded joints between the air tank and the tool. This includes hose couplings and air inlet valves.

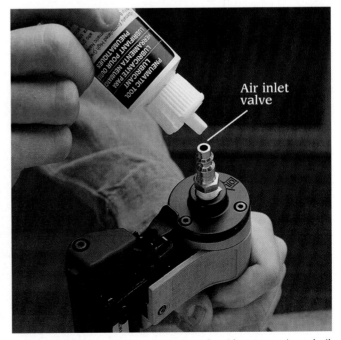

Lubricate the inlet valve on most air tools with pneumatic tool oil before every use. Some tools require more lubrication than others—check your owner's manual.

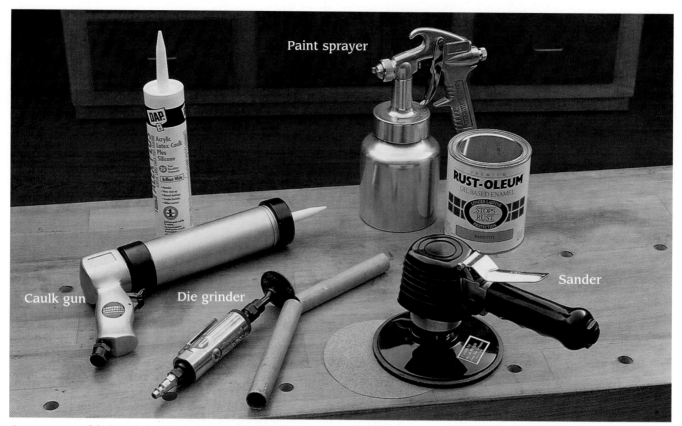

Some more useful air tools include: a caulk gun for large-scale caulking jobs; a die grinder for grinding and smoothing metal and for making clean cuts in some metals; a sander, used mostly in metal working and paint removal; and a paint sprayer for applying finishing materials.

The air chisel/hammer is designed to break up concrete and mortar, and to loosen or cut through rusted nuts and bolts. The coiled spring retainer around the chuck area of the tool extends to help hold the chisel/hammer in place.

lubricated with pneumatic tool lubricant before every use (See photo, previous page, right). Place a drop in the inlet valve before connecting it to the hose coupling. But check the owner's manual whenever you purchase a new air tool. A few may not require lubrication, and others need to be lubricated in additional spots or require a larger amount of lubricant. All air tools that require lubrication should also be lubricated prior to storage.

Be sure to clean your air tools thoroughly after every use. Store the tools in their carrying case, if they came with one, along with any bits or accessories you use with the tool. And it's also a big time saver if you jot down the lubrication instructions in a visible spot on the case.

Using air tools may seem a little intimidating at first, but they're very similar to electric tools once you get the hang of it. In fact, in some ways they're better. With a pneumatic nailer, for example, you can drive nails with only one hand, allowing you to hold the workpiece in position with your free hand. And though a pneumatic caulk gun may seem extravagant, the even pressure from the plunger creates a smooth, symmetrical bead that's hard to match.

Air tool types. Here is a list and brief description of some of the most useful air tools.

• *Nailers:* a *2½" finish nailer* (longest nail capacity) is probably the most versatile, since it can nail casework, moldings, paneling, and even floor underlayment or roof sheathing; a *pin nailer* (brad nailer) is good for attaching more delicate moldings; a *roofing nailer* will make short work of a burdensome task; other nailers include *angle nailers, stick nailers* (2" to 4" nail capacity); *timber nailers,* and *framing nailers* for driving common round-head nails into framing members.

• *Staplers:* Crown staplers in various styles and sizes handle staples from ¼" to ½" wide, and up to 2" long. Can be used for everything from attaching cabinet backs to shingling.

• *Die grinders* are designed for grinding, polishing and deburring metal when fitted with a grinding wheel. Can also be used to cut conduit and light metals cleanly when fitted with a cutting wheel.

• *Angle grinders* for fast smoothing of rough cuts in metal.

• *Sanders:* Many varieties, including *random-orbit* for a smooth finish, *dual-action* for aggressive sanding, *vacuum sanders* for efficient dust removal, and *triangle (detail) sanders* for precise sanding in hard-to-reach spots.

• *Cutoff tools* cut steel pipe, fiberglass, or tubing (very useful for working on your exhaust system).

• *Drills:* ⅜" and ½" VSR (variable speed reversible) for general drilling jobs. Hammer drills for masonry drilling.

• *Impact wrenches* for removing rusted nuts (especially lug nuts on tire rims).

• *Air ratchets* for fast, smooth tightening and untightening of bolts.

• *Polishers* for buffing paint, wood, metal and plastics—a natural for detailing your car.

• *Caulk guns* deliver smooth even caulking bead without fatiguing forearms.

• *Chisel/hammers* break up masonry, remove mortar for tuckpointing, loosen or break nuts and bolts.

• *Paint sprayers* for fast, smooth delivery of finishing material (some limits may apply to material types).

• *Sandblasters* for fast paint removal, cleaning brick, polishing hard surfaces. Also used for etching glass.

A sandblaster and sandblasting supplies are used to remove paint, clean brick and other hard surfaces, and for etching and polishing. Requires blast media of fine glass beads (reusable).

Give your garden hose a little boost with an air-powered power washer, used commonly to wash cars, siding, and pavement.. The model shown above can discharge 3.4 gallons per minute at a velocity of 365 mph. It also has an inlet port for connecting detergents and other chemicals.

• *Power washers* are another favorite of the auto enthusiast, but can also be used to pressure-clean siding or to begin the paint removal process when painting your home. Also used to wash down driveways and sidewalks.

Air inlet

Air cap/nozzle

Material
control
knob

3-stage
turbine

Handle

ON/OFF
switch

Trigger

HVLP PAINT SYSTEM
High Volume Low Pressure
Classic Finish™
HV3000
6 PSI · 65 CFM

Air outlet
port

Air intake
filter

Canister

Hose
connector

Air hose

HVLP
(HIGH VOLUME, LOW PRESSURE)
SPRAYER

COMPRESSOR-DRIVEN
SPRAY GUN

RUST-OLEUM

The compressor-powered spray gun is fast and affordable, but creates more overspray than the HVLP sprayer.

Paint Sprayers

You can always apply finish or paint to a project with a brush, pad or cloth, but the new generation of spraying equipment offers accuracy, speed, consistency and efficient use of materials, at a reasonable cost. If your mental image of spraying equipment is the guy in the bodyshop with the big spray gun, and a husky air compressor spritzing out a high pressure blast of air, then the new generation of *HVLP* (high volume, low pressure) spraying equipment will take you by surprise.

Paint sprayer types. The three main types of paint sprayers on the market today are *electric airless sprayers, compressor-powered spray guns*, and *HVLP systems*.

Electric airless sprayers are popular with do-it-yourselfers, mostly because they're stand-alone tools with relatively low price tags. They don't handle latex paint or other heavier materials well, and they tend to be very loud. But for applying thin-bodied materials (like

deck sealer) they're not a bad tool.

Compressor-powered spray guns are used extensively in auto body work, and most people who use air tools will purchase a spray gun attachment because they're inexpensive. But they're also relatively messy and inefficient, typically only delivering about 25% of the material being sprayed.

HVLP systems, however, deliver 80% to 90% of the paint or finish, at low pressure, for a softer, easier-to-control spray. That means you use less of that expensive paint or stain, and have much less of a mess (the overspray) to deal with. HVLP spray systems don't use compressed air, relying instead on a steady supply of air at about 3-to 6-PSI from a special turbine. You get tight control of the spray pattern, adjusting it from a narrow pinpoint pattern, to as wide as 12". HVLP systems can be used with acrylics, stains, lacquers, oil

Air compressor-powered paint sprayers produce a heavy cloud of material under high-pressure.

The HVLP sprayer delivers a fine mist at low pressure, reducing overspray and creating a smooth finish.

and latex paints, enamels and varnishes. They're compact and portable. For the typical home workshop, you'll probably want a single-stage turbine with a 7-amp or higher motor. Professional models typically have two-stage or three-stage turbines with 9-amp or larger motors. HVLP spray guns are connected to the turbine with an air hose. Excess air usually escapes from bleed holes in the gun when it's not being used.

Using paint sprayers. Practice is what makes the difference in spray painting. You need to learn what combination of distance, spray pattern and speed (movement of the gun) gets the results you want. Also, be sure to read the sprayer manufacturer's instructions for filling the canister and using the tool—these techniques vary greatly among tool types and manufacturers. Your work area

should be clean, dust free, and the proper humidity and temperature for the material being sprayed.

Make sure the material you're spraying is the proper *viscosity*. Fill the *viscosity cup* that comes with the sprayer with the finishing material you're using, and clock the time it takes to empty through the hole in the bottom (*See photo, left*). Compare the time to the manufacturer's recommendations for that material, and thin according to the instructions on the can if necessary.

Cleaning paint sprayers. Pour any leftover finish back into the container, then pour a small amount of the appropriate solvent into the canister. Spray the solvent into an empty can until the solvent comes out clean. Disassemble the gun assembly and clean the individual parts in solvent (*See photo, below right*).

SAFETY TIP:

Ventilation is critical when spraying paint and other finishes. Equip your finishing room with an air cleaner/ventilation system, and equip spray booths with a filtered exhaust hood. Wear a respirator when spraying.

Use a viscosity cup to time the flow rate of the finishing material, thinning as needed to match the specific flow rate for your paint sprayer.

After each use, disassemble the spray gun nozzle and assembly, and clean the individual parts using the solvent recommended for the finishing material used: usually mineral spirits (oil-base), water (latex), or lacquer thinner.

Index